A STORY OF LOVE

AT DREAMS' END

MARY TIFFIN

Amanda
Believe→*
Blessings
Mary T
11/21/17

Published by Firefly Scribbles, LLC, Lewisburg, PA

Library of Congress Cataloging-in-Publication Data

Library of Congress Control Number: 2017902859

ISBN: 9780998739007

First Edition

Publication date: March 29, 2017

Printed in the United States of America

www.MaryTiffin.com

Dedication

To David, to Daddy... the sweetness of that word.
Let us focus on the sweetness of what we had together,
rather than what might have been.

"*I have found the paradox, that if you love until it hurts,*
there can be no more hurt, only more love."

~ Mother Teresa

"This book effectively chronicles a woman's courageous search to do the right thing by her husband and for her sons."

~ Warren Pete Musser, The Musser Group

"At Dreams' End is a personal story that deals with loss but is really about love and hope. Tiffin takes us on a journey that is heartbreaking, at times funny but, more importantly, always inspiring."

~ Beth Rigazio, Screenwriter, "Raising Helen"

"At the heart of Mary and David's story is hope, simple and overpowering. It's a hope that they've passed on to others through these stories. This book is a testament of faith, and a reminder to all of us to find light in dark places."

~ R. Craig Coppola, CRE, CCIM, SIOR | Principal, Lee & Associates, AZ and author of The Fantastic Life *and other books*

"For those of you who have experienced the pain of a loved one battling a serious illness, Mary Tiffin's book exemplifies courage, hope, and the power of love. *At Dream's End* makes you appreciate your family and friends each and every day. This honest and powerful story will touch your soul and stay with you for a long time to come."

~ Mary Jo Monusky, Executive Director, Arts in Reach, Portsmouth, NH

"At Dreams' End is a story of love, family and faith. This is an emotional roller-coaster that takes you on an up-and-down, twist-and-turn journey to the true meaning of devotion."

~ Donald Webb, Account Executive, Code Elevator, Philadelphia, PA

"What a truly amazing love story told with compassion, humility, humor and sadness. I felt a part of it from beginning to end. It is a canvas from which I felt not only Mary's thoughts but the thoughts of those who loved her and David. It was awe-inspiring to read of such hope and love, and feel so connected to Mary, David, Christopher, Michael, Stephen, Mary's friends and family. If you are going through a tough time, read this book for renewal in your love of God, the power of prayer and the strength gained from loved ones. Thank you Mary for writing this and sharing your most intimate thoughts throughout your journey."

~ Catherine Hale, Co-owner, Hope Road Honey

"*At Dreams' End* is about life, real life. Reading it, I felt a sense of time and space, love and hope, gaining the full affirmation that from the darkness of life, light ultimately shines through. Thank you for opening your heart and sharing your story. It's simply beautiful."

~ Kathy Heasley, Founder and President, HEASLEY&PARTNERS

"*At Dreams' End* is a remarkably honest and touching story about love, loss and resilience. Unforgettable and utterly absorbing, Mary Tiffin's words will have you crying and laughing to the very last page."

~ Christina Russo, Educator, New York City Public Schools

"*At Dreams' End* touched me to my core. I had planned to read a few chapters at a time and found myself reading it in its entirety in one sitting. A loving, true-to-life story that explains the journey a family goes through when a loved one is terminally ill. A beautiful description of enduring faith and how God works his plan. A life that was supposed to be with her beloved, turned into a life *because* of her beloved."

~ Karen Newcomb, Speech Language Pathologist,
Midd West School District

"The title of this book says so much, *At Dreams' End*. We all dream and pray and want all the wonderful things life can give us. Mary reminds us what we ultimately find out if our eyes are opened: that we don't pull all the strings. But if our love is strong, nothing in life can ever really take that away. I love the very real way this was written, taking us step-by-step through her journey, and I will reread this lovely story that warms my heart and reminds me to live in love."

~ Deborah Potter, Retired Educator,
Arlington Central School District, Lagrange, New York

"This is a remarkable story full of love and faith; a story that's on your mind for days after you turn the last page. It's a reminder that God listens, and He works through the most unlikely of heroes to inspire and to galvanize. *At Dreams' End* is the story of how a woman with an unshakable faith, coupled with a clear vision of love and a dose of good humor, unleashes the potential of a community that BELIEVES. Wonderful!"

~ Nancy Marr, President & Owner, Marr Development Companies

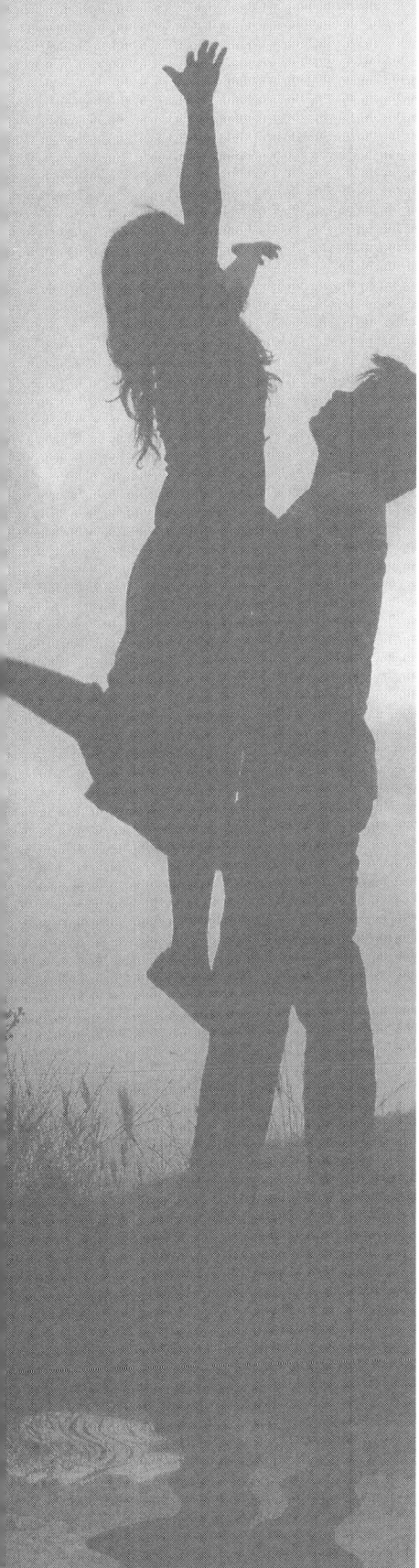

PART II

PART III

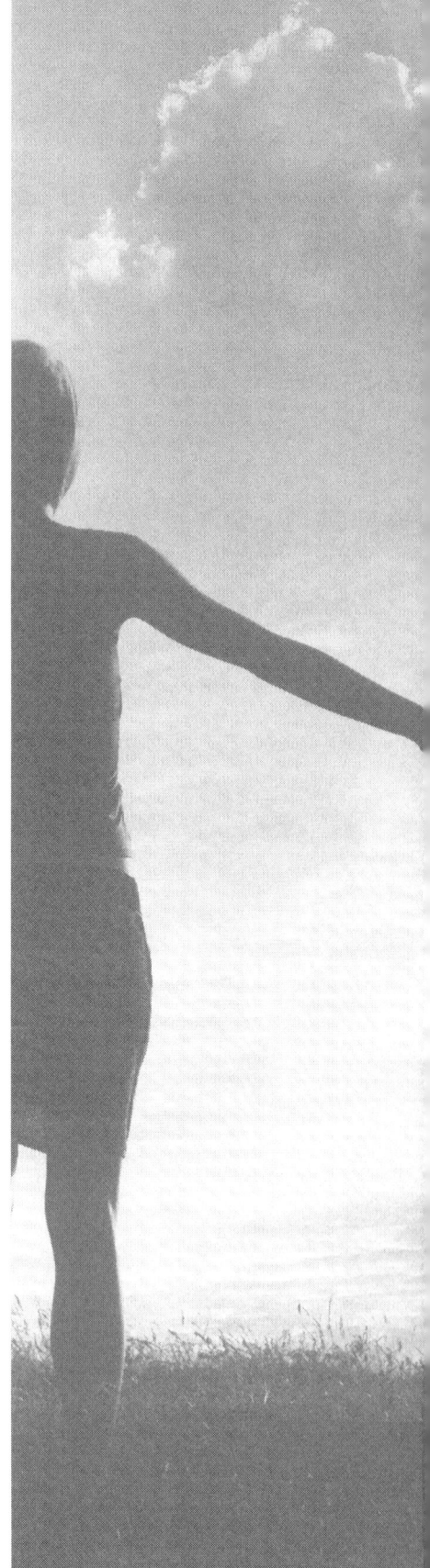

Author's Note

"To speak the name of the dead is to make them live again, and restores the breath of life to him who has vanished."

~Inscription on the tomb of Tutankhamun

This book would not have been possible without the loving prayers and support from the thousands of emails received August of 2002 through May 2003. Some of you may recognize your words but not your name. Know that all the names have been changed to protect anonymity and that much of the original wording, minus a few typos edits is exactly how I received it. Thank you again for all the love you sent me in these and the hundreds of other notes of concern and prayer that helped David, our family and me in the most difficult of times. And thank you for proving the power of prayer...9:00 pm.

With love,

Mary

Foreword

No one goes through life without tragedy. As the Dean/CEO of Johns Hopkins Medicine for 16 years, I saw people daily whose lives had been turned upside down by illness. People never expect it to happen to them, until it happens.

This book, written by Mary Tiffin, tells the story of such a tragedy. I first met Mary when her husband became ill in 2002 and have stayed in touch with her ever since. Her faith and strength have been an inspiration to me and many others.

The book begins sharing a bit about herself, her marriage in 1993 and how her and her husband, David's, lives evolved once they had children. Then in 2002, David experienced back pain and severe fatigue. He became acutely ill, was admitted to the hospital and then to the ICU. Mary tells us her thoughts at this time and then the diagnosis: acute lymphocytic leukemia.

Subsequently Mary and David decide that the only treatment for a cure is a bone marrow transplant. Mary researched the best hospital for the procedure and the two decide that Johns Hopkins Hospital is where they should to go. Hopkins was one of the early pioneers in bone marrow transplant and had significant experience including a dedicated unit for these patients.

In late 2002, Mary and David travel to Hopkins for treatment. Mary outlines in vivid detail the ups and downs of treatment. Emails between her and her friends, family and loved ones paint a very graphic picture of the uncertainty at that time.

But this story is not about illness. This story is about people, the people who cared for David medically, those who were his friends and many who became friends throughout the world. So many of the people who cared for David were wonderful, connecting with him and Mary as people first. Some others went about their task of caring as though it was a job. All kinds of people make up the world, and we encounter them all. Lessons, both good and bad, are everywhere.

Mary's book is no exception. It is full of good lessons. I took away several from Mary's struggle. First, her religious belief was so strong that it allowed her to remain whole and keep her family safe. What an example to set. Second, the many friends that were back at home were great support to her, as were her and David's parents. The importance of community spoke loudly. Small towns have real value and that fact shines in this book. Third, I marveled at Mary's willingness to be open and share. Fearlessly she reached out to people for support. Even Cardinal Keeler of Baltimore called from Rome to let her know David was in his prayers.

Probably the most important lesson from Mary's life is that most of us need religious support and support from friends during such difficult times. As I reflected on the power in this one truth became clear. We all are those friends to someone, to many people actually, in our lives. Mary shows the impact we can have in others' lives by showing us the impact friends, new and old had in her's and David's. Miraculous impact in some instances. This book is a true reminder that when tragedy strikes someone in our lives, it's up to us to reach out, and to be there. Our lives are busy, but none of us is so busy to not spare the time to help. Thank you, Mary, for showing us the impact we all have on others.

~ *Edward Miller, MD*
Dean & CEO, Emeritus
Johns Hopkins Medicine

Prologue

We are all products of our upbringing and our ancestors' stories. Through them, their lives, their struggles and triumphs, we become equipped, or not, to handle what life throws our way. Lucky are we who learn from childhood how to not only enjoy the successes, but also cope with the inevitable curve balls of life. In my time so far, I have experienced both in large doses. Successful careers, the joy of motherhood and now, a growing company sparked from the most unlikely of beginnings.

My earliest memories were of my parents. I remember my mother was all personality, unrelenting energy and drive; my father, on the other hand, was more reflective, slower, and the consummate perfectionist. Of his many good qualities, what I recall most notably was that my father was very resourceful. He was a 'Mr. Fix It.' Dad could look at and fix most anything, mechanical or electric. That skill I believe, was born out of his own life experiences.

Dad was born in New York City in 1923, right in time for the Great Depression. He would often tell stories of his childhood. He described an America, vastly different from mine of late 60's and early 1970's. Dad's childhood tales were often of people, countless people, who couldn't find work, banks that went under, taking the life's savings of many, and an America in financial ruin. He described a population without hope. A stark contrast to my America with my safe and protected home, full of the typical middle class abundance. But more importantly my America, was a place when a kid could be a kid without fear, without worry.

My America was in technicolor, it was alive and vibrant. Dad's America seemed like a grainy Black and White reel, it was of dark and despairing. As a child, it was hard to grasp the contrast between the two places. We were in the same country, but in different 'worlds.' Maybe because Dad's stories were still so real and vivid, their echoes remained, their impact lasting.

I learned about hardship, real hardship, from the safe perch of my childhood home by dad's accounts. My father always described himself and his family as being more fortunate than others. His father owned a business that survived the times, his mother had a trade and could help the family. Dad was also surrounded by a large, loving, and supportive family. Those were his luxuries during that era.

So naturally when one member of the family suffered, they all suffered. "Love begins by taking care of the closest ones—the ones at home," said Mother Teresa. This was the case when my dad's favorite and much-loved younger cousin, Evelyn, was in a car accident. The accident was physically and emotionally devastating for everyone.

He also shared the story of how his widowed Aunt 'Lala' Ray and his Mother, 'Nonni' took care of Evelyn's injuries every day after her very long hospital stay. My Lala and Nonni became Evelyn's nurses and rehab team. They helped my Dad's 'crippled' cousin for the rest of her life, some 35 years after her accident.

My father would relive his childhood trauma, when for years, he would share the story of her accident and suffering. The fact that my Lala and Nonni took care of their daughter/niece without complaint, against all the odds and without any of the social and government systems, set the example for me of what family members do for each other. Evelyn survived thanks to the love and care she received, and enjoyed a relatively normal life despite the limitations.

These women were heroes. My Lala and Nonni lived hope and resilience. They had hope that Evelyn might survive and maybe even walk again. They were resilient enough to keep pushing and not give up. I never had the opportunity to tell my Dad, but I was and continue to be so grateful to my father for his stories of the Depression. They have been a foundation of strength and of perseverance, thanks to them.

Years later when speaking with my dad, siblings, and cousins, I am not sure if I could ascertain where my Dad and his family were on the socio-economic scale. It was never clear. What was clear, though, was my Dad's feelings about that time, the feeling that during the most difficult period in our world's recent history, that they were fortunate, and although times were tough, they were together, and they still had moments of joy and happiness even in this bleakest period.

That lesson still resonates with me. I apply hope and resilience to every aspect of my life. David and I lived hope in his illness. I live it with my sons. And I apply it to my business. But I didn't always. Good times have a blinding effect. David and I were caught up in the thought that because we were Americans, living in this wonderful and blessed country, that we would be immune from the heartache that my father and his family suffered. David and I planned and dreamed, threw all caution to the wind, had our lives mapped out. We were caught up in the prosperity of our modern-day American lives. We were living our dreams. We felt inoculated against the struggles of my Dad's America. I was certain that my America was not my Dad's America. Dad did the heavy lifting; he took one for his team.

My dad's stories and our own lives have taught us; life has no guarantees. Life's tragedy knows no time, it knows no country, it neither knows, nor cares of personal circumstance. It can be arbitrary, random and equally devastating. I've been grateful for Dad's first-hand accounts of the Great Depression. After David died, I'd reflect on the struggles of my relatives and how they did what needed to be done. The struggles of those who have gone before have helped pave the way for managing my own struggles.

I often wondered what lessons our children will take away from their own childhoods and all us ancestors. What strengths have we imparted? Their experience is vastly different from my own. They have grown up without a father. David will always be Daddy to them. He didn't live long enough for them to grow up and change that name to Dad or Pop. There is such sweetness in that. And yes, some sadness, too. The beauty is that David can remain the dream of what a boy and a young man need the most, and that's a role model. To a little boy, an idol.

When I think about from where I have come, I feel some relief. It's been a long and at times solitary journey. I've heard it said that I've done the heavy lifting for our family. I disagree. I witnessed the very hard work that David did at Johns Hopkins in the Bone Marrow Unit. The work I'm doing here pales in comparison to his fight and the courage that he demonstrated in the fight for his life. David continues to be my inspiration. His life is another chapter in our generation's history. And we won't know for decades exactly how the lessons, whatever they are, will impact the lives of our children. But they certainly will.

What you are about to read could not have happened the way it did without the lessons from my family, without the history of love and inspiration that was and is my family. I know I would neither be living the life I'm living today, nor the mission of creating light from the darkness in all I do, had it not been for my ancestors' inspiring lives. They lived in the darkest of times and managed to find the light again. When darkness fell upon David's and my dream, I knew that if this was to be our dream's end, that we would have to seek the light again.

Mary

Prologue

PART I

From the Mouths of Babes

For years, when I needed to talk or was bugged about something, I called Johannah first. She is my cousin and has always been my go-to person in times of need. That is, except for that period I spent with my most beloved. Johannah was my bff, my idol, four years older than me, as smart, cool, pretty, fashionable, more so than anyone I knew. She was always there for me, no matter what challenge I found myself in, for as long as I remember, more like a sister than a cousin. Although several decades had passed and many states separated us, when my story began, we were still as close as we were when we were little kids...

I pulled Johannah's name up in my contacts and pressed "call."

"Oh, helloo, my daaahlingg! How are you and your babies today?" I received her reply to my hello.

"Good, Jo, got somethin' for you... So, little Michael came home yesterday after school to tell me that one of his friends from school, a boy named Nick—his father died," I told Johannah in my weekly call.

"Ugh," Johannah replied, having heard so much sadness.

"But I said to him, 'Michael, how can that be? Mr. Juarez is fine; you must be mistaken.' And he said, 'No, Mom, it's on Facebook and my friends are commenting on Instagram. They are saying they are sorry about Mr. Juarez.' And, my God, Jo, he was right! A forty-two-year-old man went into the hospital and died from an infection—two days before Christmas."

"Oh, that is horrible. Poor family," Johannah offered.

"Yes, leaving his wife and two kids, right before Christmas. Just too terrible."

"Oh, my God," my cousin responded.

"I just hate that this stuff happens. It's so horrible. I really don't know them that well, but it breaks my heart for them. To think of the pain they're suffering ... This family will always associate the Holiday as a time of their greatest sadness. I pray for their peace."

"Oh, I'm sorry," Johannah said.

"Horrendous. But here's what's interesting: when I was talking to Michael about how he could help his friend, he said that he thought that Nick had it worse than he had it. That statement surprised me. I asked Michael what he meant. And he said he thought it would be harder to get over your dad dying when you are fourteen, than having a dad who died when you're two. And added that he barely remembered anything about his dad, and that he'd gotten used to it.

This stopped me. The thought of my kids in that kind of pain kills me. It was bad enough to live through the loss of a husband and a father, but to be reminded of my children's pain was so much worse.

"God, honey, it's awful. I'm so sorry," my cousin replied.

"And then Michael said, 'Don't get me wrong, Mom, both are *bad*! Mine is just a little better, I think.' I told him that was a good way to look at it. But in my mind, I was thinking either way is bad; losing a parent is just wrong. Wrong, so wrong."

"Yeah, I know. It's totally wrong," Johanne echoed.

"After almost twelve years, I still find it hard to believe that David is not with us. In a million years, I would have never dreamt that it would be this way. It just stinks, there's no other word for it; it just stinks, it really, REALLY stinks." But it is what it is..it's our life.

The Boy Before the Man

For ages twelve and under, the unoffical Olympic obstacles course trials were held in the basement of Jim and Margaret Tiffin's house at 724 Colgate Lane in the Nottingham Green neighborhood of Newark, Delaware.

The neighborhood, across the street from the Newark Country Club, was within walking distance of the University of Delaware. Nottingham Green was home for hundreds of school-age children, many of whom spent their summers at the Swim Club or Barksdale Park. The Tiffin's street alone, had seventy kids. On one side of the Tiffin's street were the McCalls and their six kids. And on the other side: the O'Briens, with all ten of their children, and then down the street were the Sullivans, the Brewsters, the Babcocks, and the Leightens—a playing paradise for the kids on the block. With all these kids around, it was always easy to pull together games of baseball, football, or basketball. It was a place where the dads worked during the day and the moms stayed at home with the kids. There, the Tiffins developed fast and strong friendships. Jim and Marge were pleased with their choice in neighborhoods; they felt it was the perfect place to raise their tow-headed children.

David, their second child, was a lanky boy. He was of average height for an eleven-year-old but was dwarfed by his older brother, Patrick, with his much stronger build and presence. David's friends noted that his eyes had a "secret-agent" quality—on some days they were blue, and on others, green. But every day they had a sparkle, which belied his calm and quiet personality to reveal a hint of his true mischievousness. A smattering of freckles crossed his cheeks and nose to complete his all-American-boy look.

David never met a ball he didn't like—baseball, basketball, football, skee-ball. If it was round and it fit in his hand, David was attracted to it like a magnet. The boys of Nottingham Green were often involved in a pick-up game of some sort. If David wasn't playing a sport, he enjoyed watching them.

The winter of 1968 found the Tiffin Family and most of Nottingham Green tuned into ABC to watch the Winter Olympics in Grenoble, France. He delighted in watching Jean-Claude Killy win the downhill races, while his mom, Marge, and sister Melissa cheered on Peggy Fleming to win the Gold in Figure Skating.

Every day at school, David and his friends shared the excitement of the Olympics. David was so inspired that he decided to build his own training ground in his parents' basement.

"Jimmy says this isn't an Olympic event and that we're stupid to practice this way," ten-year-old Roger Brewster said as he finished his first lap around the basement, now out of breath.

"Aw, big brothers don't know everything. You don't know, they might just add this event if enough kids practice. So, you timin' me?" twelve-year-old David asked at the "starter's line."

David and some friends created the course from old pillows, boxes and repositioned furniture. It was the perfect course for David and his friend Roger to do their winter training. After several practice runs, the boys had designed the perfect course, with equal lengths of crawls, sprints, jumps, and a dive to the finish line.

"Hold on," Roger said, pressing the buttons on the Casio watch.

"Ok, on your mark, get set ..., GO!" Roger yelled. David sped off to the first station.

"You know, Roger, I think this course is keeping us in shape for basketball," David said as he crossed the finish line.

Basketball was David's sport, and, if he could have, he and Roger would have been playing ball in the basement, but the ceilings were too low. So this obstacle course was the next best thing.

"Yeah, I think I'm getting stronger already," Roger said as he did milk-jug curls at station number two. Roger lived three houses down, and the boys had been friends for as long as either could remember.

"If you keep training like this, Roger, you'll be a starter on the Nottingham Green twelve-and-under team," David said. "C'mon, Rog, your turn. On your mark, get set . . ."

"David? David?" his mother was calling from the top of the stairs.

"Yeah, Mom?"

"Are you straightening up the basement? You remember I told you that you needed to do that today." It was Saturday morning, and his mother had sent him to the basement to straighten up his stuff. David had used the opportunity to invite his friend over for some more work on their timed trials.

"Oooh, okay, Mom. Can we do a few more laps first?

"DA-vid ...," his mother responded.

"Okay, Mom."

"Another lap?" Roger mouthed to David.

David nodded and quietly said to his friend, "Your turn. On your mark, get set, go."

After twenty minutes, David's mother, Marge, could hear them running, laughing, and jumping. She decided to go down and check on the boys' progress.

"David," Marge said. David was diving to the finish line, made of several of his mother's scarves tied together between two of the basement support beams. Roger held his right arm up, with his left hand holding David's Casio, timing the run.

"One minute, twenty-four seconds. THAT'S A RECORD, DAVE!" Roger was jumping up and down.

"David, are you boys cleaning up your stuff?" his mother asked, looking at the assorted piles of stuff. "Boys, the record breaking must wait for a few days. We're having company. I need this stuff picked up now."

"Aw, Mom," David said.

"Now, David."

David started kicking the boxes toward the corner. Roger started to pick up and pile the pillows back on the couch as Marge headed back upstairs.

The boys finished picking up the room and began to head up the stairs.

"Rog, that was fun ..I'm gonna keep working on our course 'cuz I want to try and be an Olympian someday."

"Dave, that would be really cool, I'm not sure what sport you'll do, but I'm glad you're my friend, 'cuz I know you're gonna be famous someday."

Fixed Up... Again

"They're right, it really does happen when you least expect it."

"Okay, so how tall is he?" I asked, thinking, *"OH, NO! Here we go again. Not another one."* This was Maureen's third attempt at fixing me up. My mind raced trying to come up with an excuse to avoid another fix-up.

What was it with people anyway? Why the incessant need to fix people up?

Did I look that desperate? I quickly ran to the mirror, pushed my bangs back. Yup, just as I suspected, no stamped expiration date. I leaned closer into the mirror, examined my face—at twenty-eight, no signs of a beard/mustache, or unsightly warts... So why the BIG rush?

Perhaps my friends and family were a little more objective or knew more than me. Maybe they knew that these things snuck up on you. Or was it that my parents wanted to get me, their remaining and blindly single daughter, married before I entered Old Maidenhood? I sighed.

"Maybe Old Maidenhood is working for me. I'd rather be an Old Maid than hang out . . ."

"Mare, are you listening?"

"Oh, yeah, your friend... How tall is this guy?"

"Tall."

"How tall?"

"*Very* tall."

"How tall is 'very tall,' Mo? Fill me in. Details: Over five-foot-eight? Under five-foot-eleven? Over six-foot?"

"Yes, I think so . . ."

"Which one?"

"I don't know. I just think you will like him."

"Ayie, ayie, ayie, ayie . . ." With Mo at five-foot-one and me at five-foot-eight, we had differing perspectives on what was considered tall.

I sighed. *"Here we go again."* Maureen Gilligan was prone to exaggeration. "That's BLARNEY," I'd often blurt as she'd tell some outlandish tales. We'd been friends for more than eight years. When I was a college student in Virginia. I would come home from Mary Baldwin on holidays and join Mo (as I called her), our friends and the rest of the Saturday night crowd at the local dance club, the Sunbury Social Club.

Maureen chose to enter the workforce over college. She now took great pride in her position as a receptionist at a very busy doctor's office. She was perfect for the job—efficient, happy, and very chatty. The patients always loved to see her welcoming face.

Now at twenty-eight, Maureen Gilligan was still very much the pixie-esque fix-up fairy of her younger days. She had a quick smile, bubbly personality, and petite frame flitting around trying to create happiness for others.

"Oh, you're going to love this guy. He's wonderful. Cute, so nice, so sweet."

"Why is he available, if he is so sweet and cute?"

"Because he was waiting for you.....I think he recently broke up with a long-standing girlfriend."

As she was talking about the great qualities of this guy, I kept wondering why she didn't reserve this Mr. Wonderful for herself.

Mo's first attempts at fix-ups had involved family members who fell pretty short of making a "love connection."

"Okay, Mo, this is the last time. No more fix-ups after this. Three strikes and we are both out."

Besides, at that time, I wasn't really in the mood to date anyone. I had returned to my parents' house for a much-needed quiet vacation. From the minute I'd graduated from Mary Baldwin six years earlier, I had worked non-stop on my career. It was time for a break. I'd moved with my career a couple of times up the East Coast, finally landing in Manhattan to work in the fashion industry.

Not only did I need a break from work, but I also needed a break from dating. Not just from dating, but from dating New York City men. I was growing tired of the "Masters of the Universe" type guys I met in the City, which yielded for me a lot of disappointing, dead-end relationships. I needed a break from all of it.

So, going home would be the perfect place. It was, after all, so anti-New York City. I needed a place to chill to get a small respite from the insanity. I knew a perfect place to go: the little town of Lewisburg.

Lewisburg is a little town in Union County, Pennsylvania, thirty miles southeast of Williamsport, the Little League capital of the world, and sixty miles north of Harrisburg, the state capital. The population of the area was approximately 20,000 at the 2010 census. Located in central Pennsylvania, it is home to Bucknell University and Lewisburg Federal Penitentiary.

Lewisburg was our own Mayberry RFD: a picturesque, quaint little community complete with smiling, happy neighbors, flowers blooming, birds chirping, and crickets doing that cricket thing at night. Lewisburg was tranquil, relaxed, and cordial. It was the opposite of Fashion Avenue of the City that was fast-paced and energetic. I loved New York City; its rhythm was in my soul, elbows were in my ribs, and its size was enveloping. In New York City, I felt I had found my niche, my forever home. I had planned to never, ever, leave.

Fixed Up... Again

New York is Where
I'd Rather Stay...

It all started with a television show.

While it is true that some people's lives are changed by an event, maybe a great book, or a particularly compelling documentary; my life's course was permanently altered by a sitcom: "Green Acres."

For many years my parents, native New Yorkers, longed for a simpler, quieter life for their family. They talked about wanting to leave New York and move to the country like Oliver Wendell Douglas and his wife, Lisa, on the show, "Green Acres." They talked about it a lot when the show appeared on TV. I didn't really worry about it too much; it was sitcom, not PBS. Our entire family was born-and-bred New Yorkers. People just don't leave New York, unless, of course, they are in the witness protection program. Besides, west to us was New Jersey.

On a spring afternoon in 1972, I overheard my parents talking at the kitchen table. Dad proclaimed, "That's it, Jeanie! We're moving to the country."

This news was like an earthquake in our apartment; it was seismic. On that day, I swear, I felt the earth's plates shift. I remember it vividly. I was sitting in our living room in the middle of our red leather couch, still in my St. Phillip Neri's school uniform, totally immersed in my *Weekly Reader*, when I swear I felt the pages of that classic educational newspaper shake.

Shake, shake, shake. *"Oh no, that can't be good,"* I thought. Rumble, rumble, rumble.

"That move sounds serious. Could there really be something to this?" I wondered. I got off the couch and walked toward the kitchen to eavesdrop on my parents' conversation. I heard them defining a plan. *"Surely that silly talk of 'Goodbye city life, Green Acres we are there?' Can't be a reality. The country—who needs the country? We have everything we need here in the city. The country? The country? Sounds like it was more likely to fall into a continental drift,"* I told myself.

I thought I had a fairly accurate view of the country. Besides "Green Acres," I watched "The Andy Griffith Show." I knew all about the country. I knew that their aunts looked like Bea, all the kids wore pants that were too short, and no one wore shoes. It was like an entire world of Huckleberry Finns. From the looks of Opie, Pa, and Aunt Bea, no one used an iron. Did they dry clean in the country? I never saw a dry cleaner in Hooterville or Mayberry.

How could we, how *would* we, survive?

Earlier in the month, I had overheard my parents talking to my aunts and uncles about our Uncle Georgie, the youngest of my mother's siblings. They were talking about how strange he had been acting since he reported seeing a flying saucer hovering over the Crestwood exit of the Bronx River Parkway. *Uncle Georgie was acting strange, my parents were acting strange—could this somehow be related?*

What on earth possessed my parents to think of packing up their kids and dog and traveling west? Was it my parents' yearly trips to the Cimarron Dude Ranch they spoke so glowingly about? Was it those black cowboy boots hidden in the back of my mom's closet? Were my parents worried about an alien encounter, or, worse, an abduction off the Crestwood exit of the Bronx River Parkway?

Like many large families in the early 70's, we all got together for dinner at least once a week. My aunts, uncles, and cousins would spend a day or night gathered with our grandparents. These weekly feasts were so large that they rivaled most families' Thanksgiving dinners.

I was always fascinated by the adults' conversations. Their stories were often very colorful and expressive, thanks to the help of some very animated uncles. To me, our family dinners were the best form of entertainment. Who needed a TV or the movies? The time around the table was much more fun and far more interesting. Looking back, this time together was truly the best part of my young life, and I appreciated it even as a child. It was at one of these most wonderful and happy events, that parents dropped the bomb: they announced excitedly and nervously to my grandparents and the rest of the family that they would be fulfilling their dream to move to the country. We were moving to Pennsylvania!

My grandmother scrunched up her face and looked like she did not understand. She stuck her right pointer finger near her ear to adjust her hearing aid. My aunts and uncles thought it was a joke.

"It's not a joke, I assure you," my dad said. "It's our dream." He had this kind of dreamy, sort of starry-eyed look, like he was on drugs or something.

"Right, Jeanie?" he gave a nod to my mom, looking for backup.

"We want to move to the country. A home in the country would be a dream come true." She, also, had that same 'high-on-fresh-air' look.

It was not, however, a dream that was shared by my entire family. They didn't need fresh air, they had all that New York had to offer, who needed fresh air, too?

My grandfather had come to America from Greece as a young man. He had already made the *big trip*; he couldn't imagine moving beyond here. I guess he hadn't given much thought to a life that existed outside of the metropolitan New York City area.

"Pennsylvania?" our relatives bewildered.

"Who lives in Pennsylavaaania?" my grandfather asked in his thick Greek accent, then answered his own question, "The Amish do, that is who."

"You are not Amish. What will you do in Pennsylvania?" my grandfather asked. "Do the Amish use dry cleaners? I don't think they use buttons. So they will have no use for dry cleaners!" my grandfather, a dry cleaner, proclaimed.

Even Uncle Alien Georgie, whom you'd think would be intrigued by travel to faraway places, seemed less than thrilled. I called my mom's youngest brother Georgie, 'Uncle Alien' after his UFO report.

"Why Pennsylvania? Jersey is closer if you want to get out of New York," Uncle Alien piped up.

But my parents would not be deflated and kept saying that it was "not that far"—a mere three hours from our family home in Westchester County. But from the shock and disbelief of our relatives' reaction, I felt like we were going to the moon.

My parents, buoyed by their new country dream, responded that we were going to love it in the country. We'd get a big house and maybe some horses. My aunts and uncles understood my parents' dream to create a new life in the country, but seemed surprised that they would *act* on this dream. This whole move to the country thing was really starting to snowball, or hay bale; now the entire family was involved.

So on Tuesday, May 23, 1972, I knew it was time to make my stand.

"I'm *not* going!" I told my parents. "I'll stay here. I don't want to move."

"It's an adventure!" my mother said about our move. "You'll love it, Mary Mathilde. The country's the best place to live," she said as she walked away. She always walked away when I dug in.

"I will stay here and live with Grandmother and Grandfather. I am *not* going to Pennsylvania."

My parents chuckled a little as they left me—I didn't take that as a good sign, you know, them walking away as I was digging in. Still, I knew I had to hold my ground.

I saw how my stand worked out when, on a June day in 1972, I found myself squished between my sisters, Lynette and Laura, traveling to the town of Godknowswhere, Pennsylvania.

We're Pennsylvaaaanians!

Nearly four hours after we began our trip, Dad brought the car to a stop and turned off the engine. It was night. Pitch black. The darkness was pierced only by the bright stars in the sky and the perfect full moon.

"We're here," Dad exhaled and said with relief as he smiled and grabbed my mother's hand. "Kids, this is Lewisburg."

"Yes, we're here," Mom reinforced, surprisingly giddy for having just gotten off the wagon train.

"We are where?" I thought, too tired to speak. I looked out the window of our 1968 Dodge Polara and saw nothing. I was stuck in the middle of the backseat. On one side was my older sister, Lynette, sleeping and sleep-shoving me over toward my younger sister, Laura, who was using me as a pillow. With the shoving and pillow propping, throw in one tolerant and sweet but restless German Shepherd at your feet, you don't get a lot of sleeping time on trips like this. Or at least, I hadn't.

I pushed Laura off my right shoulder and leaned forward. She slid back behind me in the space and continued to sleep, this time on Lynette. *"Oh great, I just lost the space I'd carved out,"* I thought to myself. My older sister moved toward Laura, totally squeezing me to the front edge of the seat.

"Oh, for Pete's sake . . ." I pushed Lynette's leg. "Lynnie, get up. We're here."

"What? Huh?" she said, rubbing the sleep out of her eyes.

"Sheesh, how is it everyone is enjoying this sleep? Hurry up already. This will take forever; I gotta get outta here. I have been cramped too long."

My dad was the first one to get out of the car. One small step for Dad, one giant leap for our family-kind. Then Mom went next, followed by my brother, Billy. The front seat of the Polara was clear. I was trying to get out of the car, trying to disentangle myself like a fish in a net, flopping, flipping, and stretching to get out. Slowly but surely, my sisters woke, got out, and stretched. One at a time— yawn and big stretch. Yawn, stretch—another one out. *"Dear God, they are slow. I'm so glad the car's not on fire."*

We looked around. It was dark. There were houses; no skyscrapers, no apartment buildings, no office buildings; there was space and there was sky, lots and lots of sky. Everywhere you looked, a totally unobstructed view of the heavens. It was the opposite if claustrophobia—I felt overwhelmed by the abundance of space, an "airstrophobia." And it was quiet. It was that kind of quiet that was loud—so quiet that you could hear yourself breathe.

I'd never seen or experienced a place like this before. But I guess my parents had, because it did not seem to bother them. They seemed thrilled.

"Smell it!" my dad said.

"Smell what?" I thought in the deafening quietness. I was in a total sensory over - or rather, underload.

"The air! Smell the air. Doesn't it smell great?"

I took a big whiff. I thought, *"It smells like… like… like… air. A little thick, a little hot, but it was like… like… like … AIR."* Maybe I had to give it a couple of more breaths.

We all stood fixed beside the car, arms akimbo, noses pointing up in the air like displaced metropolitan bloodhounds. My mom, my dad, and us kids—just breathing. The only car rider that didn't look like a totem pole was our German Shepherd, Trouble. She was not remotely interested in the quality of the air. She had other things on her mind; being trapped on the floorboard for the whole trip led Trouble's nose in a different direction. She ran to the nearest tree.

My dad said in awe, "This is the main boulevard, it's the main street. It is called Market Street."

"Ohhhhhh," we, his chorus of kids, sleepily answered.

We were on Market Street and we seemed to be the only ones awake at ten p.m. No one else was on the street, no lights. From a twelve-year-old's vantage point, it looked like we were in a ghost town.

I sought cover behind my still ebulliently breathing dad.

That first morning in Pennsylvania was not what I had anticipated. It was confusing. For starters, we were not living in a dilapidated farm house like the house on "Green Acres." We had a nice house. I didn't see a single tractor drive through town; there were only cars and trucks. Everyone was shod; they all wore footwear: sneakers, shoes, sandals, that sort of thing—no patent leather of course, but no horse shoes either.

Lewisburg was a little town and people lived in houses that were close to each other. No apartment buildings or skyscrapers, but houses. And since folks lived in houses, you got to see the sky, a lot of sky—the town was very sunny.

The neighborhood was nice and there were a lot of kids with whom to play. My parents were delighted with their new town. I remember Dad smiling and whistling a lot in those days. Mom seemed happy, too. She spent a lot of time outside, loving that fresh air. Sometimes I would see her outside in our backyard examining the grass, almost studying it. A few weeks after we settled into our new home, I saw Mom outside with some shears and a pot from the stove, and she was cutting weeds out of the yard. My mother was cutting the dandelions and putting them into the pot. She was so excited that she called my grandmother to tell her that she was going to cook dandelion greens. I'd never seen my mother pick anything out of the ground in New York and eat it. I remember thinking something was definitely wrong with my parents: all of a sudden, Dad can't stop whistling, Mom is eating stuff from the ground, my uncle Georgie sees aliens. The adults in my family had totally run amuck. Good God, what's next?

Lewisburg was our first stop in the country, but my parents sprouted true Pennsylvania roots when they built our house in the tiny hamlet of Winfield. Still not a "Green Acres" farmhouse, our home was a traditional two-story, four-bedroom, two-bath house, minus the barn and the cows, horses, and chickens. Coming from Manhattan, my parents still considered it country living.

My father loved his basement workshop where he had all his tools and supplies carefully and neatly—very neatly—hung and labeled. I admit, I enjoyed watching my Dad work. He was a right blend of artist and engineer. He was particularly skilled at envisioning something and then making the vision a reality.

My dad was one of those dads who could fix anything, and I was that kid who was always watching. When I say my dad was an artist of sorts, it's because I could describe something, sketch it out and my father could build it. He could take concepts, make drawings, find the appropriate materials and create them into real things. I had so much fun at taking ideas and making them come to life.

There was nothing that my father could not create; to him, everything was workable. I provided him with countless sketches that he would bring to life in the workshop. It wasn't until I was about sixteen that my Dad started getting weary of my creations, or maybe he was just getting weary. My parents did have a house full of teenagers at that point. Come to think of it, when we were teenagers, Dad spent an awful lot of time in his workshop.

My parents were happy as clams with the new life they were creating for their family. Although the summers were so wonderful, the winters brought heavy snows—storms like we'd never experienced before. For our New York relatives, this meant that traveling to our house for the holidays was out of the question.

Route 80 through the Pocono Mountains became very treacherous. So, no one came to see us in the winter.

Our wonderful, large and entertaining family holidays of days past were now just Bill, Jean, and us kids. Not nearly as much fun as they were when the entire family was around. I was even beginning to miss Uncle Alien.

The days turned into weeks, weeks into months, and months into years. We, according to my grandfather, had become 'Pennsylvaaaaanians'. We'd grown accustomed to the cold winters with deep blowing snows, we dropped our New York accents, picked up a Pennsylvania Dutch inflection, planted roots longer than Mom's dandelions, and created a happy life in Pennsylvania. But always in the back of my mind was my return to New York to continue where I had left off. Before I knew it, I was graduating from the high school, and I had my opportunity to depart my country life and rejoin the city dwellers.

Return to New York I would—just not so quickly.

A Visit to My PA Home

I walked into the house and found my mother at her usual spot doing a crossword puzzle at the kitchen table.

"Mom, it's so nice to run here, no one tries to run you over," I'd just returned from a run on the gentle winding streets and lanes of my childhood town.

"People actually TRY to run you over when you run in New York?" My mother asked alarmed. And then to my father in the next room, "Did you hear that, Bill? People are trying to hit your daughter as she runs in the city. Oh, dear Jesus, Mary Mathilde!"

"I'm sure they're not aiming for her, plus she's fast, so she'd dart out of the way," My dad responded with his typical humor, in his barely-alarmed way.

"Mo-ther, that is not what I meant...What I meant is that here, people give you room on the road, and they wave to let you know that they see you. Makes running easier when you feel like you're NOT going to get killed. No bob-and-weave action needed here."

I had a lifelong love of running. It's always been a gift to me. I found it to be the perfect exercise. You need very little gear, almost no prep, and the benefits outweighed any kind of kinks that I felt in the first two miles. I started running daily in college and just kept running. Running became my therapy, it became a meditation of sorts for me. I enjoyed running wherever I landed in a city with my work or vacation, and I kept my running shoes close. Running around Winfield was different than running in other areas I'd lived. The enjoyment started pretty much the minute I hit the street here, because it was just a safer place to run.

Ring......ring.....my phone was ringing.

"Mom, hang on... I've got to get that."

I could hear the phone ringing in my room and I was waiting for a girlfriend's call to confirm our weekend plans back in the city. I'd returned from New York City for an extended vacation after yet another creepy experience in this month's sample of the "Jerk of the Month Club," my unfortunate dating pool. I was tired of going out with the same old types of men, with the same old lines and the same old mega size egos.

I was home for a few weeks visiting family, and, happy as I was to be with them, I was still itching to go back to the place I loved so much—New York, the town that really understood me, even if I did not understand its men.

Ring... Ring... Ring...

"Hello."

"Hello," said an unfamiliar voice.

"Damn telemarketer," I thought.

'Hello, is this Mary?" Impatiently, I heard the voice again.

"Damn, they know my name. Crafty little buggers." I was mulling over exactly how hard I should slam down my phone when the person on the other end of the phone started what I knew would be a relentless spiel... "This is Mary." Bracing for the next line, I was wondering if I should have just hung up before affirming it was me.

"Well, hello, Mary. This is David Tiffin, Maureen's friend."

"Former friend," I thought. *"Who is she giving my number to now? Who is this guy?"* Remembering the string of not-so-greats she had subjected me to before... "Oh, hello." Not so effectively hiding my disdain.

"Did I catch you at a bad time?"

"Yes. I was kind of... I was kind of running out." Still seething about my number being out there and wondering where else it was—bathroom walls, dive bars, bus stations, park benches? *"AAAAUUUUUGGGH!"*

"I work with Maureen, and she mentioned that you were new in town..." It was off-putting.

"Well, I'm not really that new. I'm new/old."—correcting him.

"Oh, really? What is new/old?" he asked.

"Um, listen, I'm really busy. What did you say your name was?" Feeling confident that I'd perfected my snarkiness.

"David. David Tiffin," he said, totally oblivious to my snark.

"Well, David Tiffin, I am only back here for a short period."

I was rushing to get off the phone, and he was relaxed. He asked me a question or two, and somewhere during the first three minutes of the conversation, I realized that he was really putting off my off-putting feelings. I'm not exactly sure how, but somehow this Mr. Oblivious got me to chat with him for about thirty minutes. This David Tiffin kept asking questions—not like an interrogation, but a natural, easy conversation. *"This is different,"* I thought. *"A man who can actually carry on a conversation, how novel."*

And even more amazing was that after forty-five minutes, I surprised myself when I agreed to meet him at a local restaurant the following night. At twenty-nine, I figured why delay the disappointment? Let's get this over with as soon as possible. Why waste the time and effort of several days wondering if this man, too, would be a card-carrying member of the JOMC (Jerk of the Month Club)?

It Had to be Fate

We were both dreamers, romantics in every sense of the word, and we would marvel at that fact that although our lives had traveled in many different directions, that somehow, some way, we still found each other at the right time and in the right place: Front Street in Northumberland, Pennsylvania.

We were also opposite in many ways, David was sports, all sports, every sport. If he wasn't playing it, he was watching it. He was the ultimate fan. I, on the other hand, was bookish, played the violin, loved all things art and music. David could read music about as well as I could draft a fantasy football team. Yes, we were opposite, but in the area of our values and dreams for the future, we were the same. How we met often baffled me. It had to be fate.

I was gathering my jacket and my bag.

"You going somewhere?" my dad asked.

"Yeah, Dad, I'm going to Front Street to meet this guy, a friend of Maureen's. If he's a goof, I'll be back in a half hour. If he's nice, I'll be out a little longer." Dad, who was always amused by the unexpected, laughed. I wanted him to laugh and not worry about his middle daughter and where I was heading. I was, after all, twenty-nine years old, not a sweet child of sixteen, but I was still his daughter.

"Have fun, honey," Dad called as I headed out the front door of our house.

I arrived at the restaurant and grabbed a seat at the table off the bar. I looked around and saw no one meeting this guy's description. A couple of guys here, a few women there, but no one who appeared to be looking for someone. Then a few more guys entered. Two of the three took seats at the bar, and the third—and perhaps least attractive—was headed my way. He was around thirty-five, right age; about five-foot-eleven, wrong height; looked about seven months pregnant; and was follicly challenged. I prayed, *"Please, dear God, don't let this be the guy."* And thought, *"He certainly would not be the first man to lie about his height."*

"Hi, Denise. Hey, Vickie," he said to the table beside me.

"Hi, George," they responded in unison.

"Phew, so close," I thought. Then, *"What am I doing here?"* Followed by, *"Okay, I've waited long enough. And that last one was a little too close for comfort."* I decided to grab my pocketbook and bag, and go home. *"I'm not hanging out for another George—or Jorge or Giorgio, for that matter. I'm getting out while the coast is still clear."*

I was grabbing my stuff and about to stand up when I heard, "Well, hello, Mary" from above me.

I looked up and started to giggle. For as cool as I try to be, whenever I see a cute man, I start to giggle. I really hate that about me. I giggle when I am surprised or nervous. My giggle often makes me angry because it messes with my finely crafted NYC persona.

"Were you leaving?" he asked.

He was tall and cute-ish/handsome. He was tan and tall, really tall, and had a really sweet, dimpled smile. He was wearing a white shirt, and tan and pink plaid shorts. I couldn't help but notice that he had really nice arms and legs, even thought he could benefit from Garanimals.

Still giggling. "No, I was just going to grab a different seat," I lied.

"Oh, good. I would hate to have missed you," the man responded.

"Cheeseball line," I thought to myself.

"You must be David Tiffin?" I said, ignoring his comment.

"Shh, don't say that too loud, people might find out," he teased, and chuckled.

And as if on cue, Denise and Vickie from George's table said, "Hi, DAAA-VID"

"Well, hello, ladies. Hi, George."

"Hey, Dave."

David said, "I like your idea of that table over there," pointing to the table against the wall, further from George and his backup singers. "I'd like to join you, if I may?"

"Sure," I said. *"Stop giggling, Mary. You're not sixteen. So uncool,"* I told myself.

We moved to a table closer to the wall and made ourselves comfortable.

"Good move. It's only a matter of time before George and the girls get rambunctious," David said.

"Did he just say 'rambunctious'? Who uses the word 'rambunctious'? Again, what am I doing here?" I asked myself.

"So you know them well, do you?" I asked.

"I'm the UPS man for this area. So I've gotten to know everyone around here," David replied.

Everyone who entered Front Street seemed to know or at least acknowledge David. The Front Street Station was a popular bar and restaurant in the area.

"You're pretty popular," I said, noting all the hellos and waves.

"I've been here for a while. Northumberland is a good town and the people are really nice. So what brought you back to Lewisburg, Mary?"

We talked and talked, as you do on first dates. My overall impression was that he was different from the guys I was accustomed to. As he had on our telephone call, he seemed engaged in the conversation, was a very good listener, and seemed nice enough. I actually thought he was "too nice." It was my experience that when I met guys who were this nice, they were generally hiding something, and that something was yucky.

This David Tiffin was an interesting combination of confidence and sweetness that was very interesting and very easy to be around. So when he talked about maybe getting together again, I thought, *Why not? He's handsome, seems nice, is easy to talk to, but I wonder what the yucky is?*

It Wasn't Until...

Truth be told marriage was not a top priority for me, especially considering my run of the JOMC members. I was firmly focused on my career and loving my role as 'Auntie' to many nieces and nephews. My siblings had demonstrated that they were indeed quite fertile and were reproducing like rabbits. With every turn there was the announcement of a new baby and the joy of a Christening.

Being an Aunt to many is a great arrangement, I could always feel like a parent without bearing the ultimate responsibility. I would just borrow a 'little darling', whenever my sibs needed a break, which seemed like often. I had the fun without the fuss, my nieces and nephews always saved their worst behaviors for their parents, while I enjoyed the pure bliss of Auntie-hood. The 'borrow the babe deal' was a win/win for everyone.

While no cause for alarm for me, my mother may have had other concerns. As I was thoroughly enjoying my career and single life, my mother thought I should be thinking about a family, as in my own. She related a conversation she had with our Parish Priest (she spoke to the Priest. Is this the stuff you bring into the confessional? Bless me Father, for I have sinned, I think I'm raising an Old Maid!) She had a conversation about my independence and general lack of husband and family prospects. "You know Mary Mathilde," Father Lawler said, "you may not get married."

"*What!*" I thought...

Might not get married? What about her years of admonitions to not EVEN THINK of marriage until we were at least 26, when our education was complete and we were mature?'

Did my mother forget her own advice? Jeez, I was nothing, if not obedient! And let's face it, Mom and Dad were no spring chickens on their wedding day."

It wasn't that I didn't think about marriage and a family, I just didn't want to marry 'Any Guy' or worse the 'Next Guy'. Til' death do you part seemed like a very long time if you didn't choose carefully. I was much more methodical in my dating and actually, I dated a lot. I had perfected my 'weeding out' process. My sister called it snobbish, I preferred 'selective.' Even though there were so many nice men along the way, maybe it was my immaturity or general boredom, but I rarely took the time to get to know them further. So the number of men who actually made it to date three and onto actual boyfriend status, well, that was a much different story.

The men that became my 'official' boyfriends were extraordinary in one way or another. I always thought of them as superlatives and gifted in at least one area. These great guys were either extremely smart, successful, athletic, or handsome. There was something about each of them that stood out. But as exceptional as these wonderful and generally hunky men were; boyfriend doesn't always cross the great divide of Holy Matrimony.

It wasn't until I met the sweet, unassuming and superlative in every way David Tiffin, that I actually wanted to get married.

A Little Aftermath Drama

Ring... Ring... Ring...

"Hello."

"Hey, Mare. G'mornin'. You awake?"

"Well, yeah, now I am, thank you. Dang, what time is it, girl?"

"It's ten thirty, time for you to be up. I've been up for hours. I tried to let you sleep, but I couldn't wait any longer. So how did it go?"—Maureen's voice, oozing with enthusiasm. Maureen would interrogate you like she was interviewing for the CIA.

"He was very nice."

"How late were you out? I called till about twelve."

Oh, God, my room was next to my parents' room, and a ringing phone at midnight meant one thing—certain maiming, accident, or death. "I'm sure my parents appreciated that one. They probably pictured me in a body cast or dead with my guts strewn all over the highway—so unsightly. Thanks."

"Sorry, but I had to hear—you know me. It was everything I could do to stop me from heading to Front Street to spy on you. You're lucky I had to work."

"Okay."

"So, what did you think?"

"He was very nice, as I said." Talking to Mo with my eyes closed, hoping I could give her the minimum, then return to my very best friends—my pillow and sleep.

"Did you think he was cute?"

"I thought he was..." My pillow was calling, *"Mary, come back."*

"Oh, my God, it's like pulling teeth here. You are trying to blow me off; I can hear it. But you owe me!"

Oh, God, she pulled the old Catholic guilt card, the oldest trick in the book.

"Okay, you finally got your tape measure right. He's tall. He told me he's six-foot-three and, like, a half, so that was nice. He had gorgeous legs and really nice arms. That UPS thing is really working for him," I said, hoping that was enough—still not sure if I wanted to commit to waking up.

"He's really into exercise," Mo added.

Dang it, it wasn't. She wants more. *"She really should work for the FBI,"* I thought.

"Yeah, I see that. But he is not, like, freakishly big, like the Incredible Hulk, so that's nice."

"What did you think of his face? His looks?"

"Oh, Mo, you and your details," I thought. "He's cute."

"That's it?"

"Well, the dimples are cute, really nice, interesting eyes, a really strong jaw line, and he was super confident. I would say he was really handsome, but because he seemed so nice, he seemed more regular, so I would say he was really cute, very comfortable in his skin. I didn't get a lot of weird hang-up vibes."

"It's because you have been jaded by those New York City A-holes. You're not accustomed to decent men."

"That may be the case, but he seemed sweet and, you know, genuine, but I've been wrong before." Thinking back to the slew of losers I'd dated.

"He *is* sweet! I have known him for six years, and he's a doll! And listen, every woman in that place falls in love with him. Hell, the entire town of Northumberland is in love with him."

"That's nice. I can see he has appeal. He's charming." Thinking, *"Darn you, Maureen, this is my Beauty-Rest time."*

"Are you two going out again?"

"I don't know. We might."

"Well, I did talk to David this morning," Maureen revealed.

All of a sudden, I decided it was time to wake up! I sprang up to a sitting position, opened my eyes, and thought, *"Good morning, America!"* Maureen had my interest.

"Oh, yeah?" I said coyly, trying to not sound too interested.

"Do you want to know what he said?" Maureen asked, with a smile in her voice.

I thought, *"Like you're not going to tell me!"* Mo has not kept a secret in her entire life, ever. She was certainly not the person to rob a bank with.

"I don't know. If you feel like it."

"Well, are you sitting down?"

I looked around my bed, fluffed my sheets, adjusted my pillows to create a bedrest. "Huh, well, now I am." Thinking, *"Just get on with it."*

"David thinks you are beautiful. He actually said, 'She's gorgeous.' And he also said that you appeared to be very, um… what was the word he used? … Let me see… FIT. He said, 'Thanks, Maureen, we had a great time. She was gorgeous, really fit, and funny, too. I had a great time!'"

"Are you telling me the truth, or is that more *blarney*?"

"It's the truth!"

"Mo, swear on your mom."

"I swear on my mom and all things holy."

The swearing on the "mom and holy things" was the sign that the no exaggeration rule was invoked; it was a straight-talk-only conversation. She passed the truth initiation.

"Obviously, then, it's clear this man has great vision and extraordinarily good taste as well! No, really, he *does* sound like my kind of guy: tall, cute, and blind! What a combination," I said, and we both giggled.

"So, how late were you out?"

"We closed Front Street. I think I got home around one forty-five."

"Will you guys go out again? I think he is planning on asking you again, Mare."

"He said something about the movies." In our meeting, we had discussed our mutual love of going to the movies.

"So, you'll go if he asks you?" Mo prompted.

"Sure, why not? I could do that, or babysit my nieces and nephews, pair socks, or deep condition my hair--you tell me which seems more exciting. But I swear to God, if you tell him that, this will end our friendship. I'll never tell you another single thing ever, ever again. Do you hear me, Maureen?"

"I'm not going to say a word, cross my heart," Maureen said, and I pictured the gesture that she would make immediately before she would run out and tell the next person she saw.

What Mo didn't know is that David and I had already talked about going to a movie. So I was not going to be surprised if he called.

Somewhere around noon my phone rang again.

"Mare, where are you?" It was my girlfriend Kim, one of my best friends in the City.

"Yeah, oh crap! Kimmy…."

"I was calling all night. What happened? I thought you were coming?"

"Oh, crap!" I said again.

"Bill, Frank, and I were waiting for you to arrive in Hoboken. I thought you were in an accident in the Poconos. I was afraid to call your parents."

"Oh my God, honey, I am so sorry. I thought I called you."

I also thought, *"My parents must have been freaking out!!! Phone ringing all night, first Maureen, now Kim. I'm surprised that they didn't get the National Guard after me."*

"So, I'm guessing that you're not coming? You're home."

"Kimmy . . ."

"Mare, you didn't call." Kimmy was not angry, but confused.

"What's going on? The last time we spoke, you said you'd be here by seven, we'd grab dinner in the City, and then come back to Onieals. Bill was so excited to see you. Mare, he *really* likes you—he told his brother."

Like many young professionals, Kim worked in Manhattan but took the PATH train into the City each morning from her much more affordable and spacious apartment in Hoboken. She'd been dating Frank Fasciano, a very confident twenty-nine-year-old attorney, since she moved to the neighborhood about a year ago. They met at Onieals, a popular bar in town, and it became a favorite place to meet after work.

I'd been returning to New York City every weekend to hang with my friends. I didn't want to interrupt the social mojo I had so carefully crafted. Bill Fasciano was now part of my social life. Kim and Frank had fixed me up with Bill. Bill was Frank's brother, and we had gone on a couple of really good double dates. He, like Frank, was an attorney with a real estate company in the City. At thirty-one,

Bill was beginning to feel comfortable in his career and was starting to focus his ambitions on a family and a future. The truth was, Bill was handsome, smart, successful, had great manners, and was well-traveled. Frank had told Kim that he thought Bill and I made a great couple.

"You should have seen him last night—every time the door opened, he kept looking to see if it was you. Somewhere around midnight, he figured you were blowing us off, and got pissed."

Bill was fun, but he was also really serious. I knew he was really interested in finding the right girl and forming a serious relationship. I'm pretty sure he would have made someone a good partner and I'm sure he would have made a great dad. But I just wasn't sure if he was 'the guy' for me.

"I'm sorry, Kimmy. I spaced out."

"Well, are you coming tonight? We can make dinner at my apartment and rent a movie. I heard there are some new ones at Blockbuster."

"Kimmy, would you mind if I stayed in P-A this weekend?" I asked Kimmy, not believing those words were coming out of my mouth.

"Are you okay? I mean, do you feel sick, or something?" Kim sounded even more confused.

"No, I'm okay. I just feel like staying here," I said, wondering, *"What is wrong with me?"*

"Wow, you want to stay in P-A? But what about Bill? Mare, I think he was really hurt."

"I'll call him today. I'll make it up to him," I said, but was not sure how much I really wanted to commit to making up to him.

"Okay."

"Kimmy, I'm sorry. I don't know where my head was. Did you guys have fun?"

"Yeah, it was fun, but it would've been more fun if you were there."

"Next weekend for sure, Kim. I'll tell Bill that, too."

"That sounds great. So, let me tell you who we ran into at Onieals . . ."

Kim and I talked for another fifteen minutes. We had become instant friends when she walked into the accessory showroom of the company where I worked eight years earlier. She was a beautiful, blue-eyed blonde and always had a steady boyfriend. The friendship had the feel of a lifetime relationship. In our time together, we spent more time laughing and acting like first-graders. In our roles as part of the New York fashion scene, we were able to go to all of the fun bars and restaurants, with car service always ready to pick us up. We never had to worry about taxis because we had access to limos. We knew we were so lucky.

Kim was a great girl and a better friend. She was the type of girl you could really trust, so I hated letting her down. What was wrong with me? *"I love New York. I want to be in New York, not Pennsylvania. Maybe I am coming down with something?"*

Ring … Ring … Ring …

"Now, what is wrong with that phone?" I thought. "Hello."

"Hello. Is this Mary Santucci?"

"Oh, hello, David Tiffin." Repeating his first and last name as one word, as he did with mine.

"Well, hello, Mary Santucci. How are you this fine day?"

"Hokey, but kind of cute," I thought.

"I'm good, David Tiffin."

"Well, I'm looking at the papers, and there's a coupla movies playing at the Fox. But there is one that I thought you might like—it's called "Mr. Destiny," with Jim Belushi and Linda Hamilton, and I was wondering if you'd like to see it with me?"

"Um."

"Okay, is tonight too soon to ask?"

"Huh?"

"I was wondering if you'd like to see the movie tonight?"

"Oh, this man has totally breached the coolness code of ethics. He is asking me out way too soon to maintain any coolness façade. He has jumped the second-date rule by five days. Someone oughta tell this poor guy he is way outta line." "Um. Let me see… Sure, what time?" *"Hell with the coolness; maybe they don't have that codebook out here."*

"How about I pick you up around six thirty?"

"Great, that sounds good. I'll see you then."

"Thanks, Mary Santucci."

"Sure, David Tiffin." *"Did he just say 'Thanks'?"*

Within the first few months of meeting David, I found myself spending more and more time with him and having less of a desire to return to New York. And before I knew it, an unsuspectingly sweet, kind, and gentle relationship grew with this man. I stopped looking for what could be wrong with him as a reason for why he was available, and enjoyed the unusual gift that he *was*. Much to my parent's amazement and delight, I decided to find a job, remain in Pennsylvania, and fall head over heels for this David Tiffin.

After nearly two years of dating, we married on April 24, 1993, and it was the happiest time of our lives.

Dreams Do Come True

The early days of our married life were everything we'd hoped they'd be. Months after we returned from our honeymoon we moved into the home that we built. We worked hard, traveled far, and continued to dream and build on our dreams.

We'd both come from entrepreneurial families, so it was natural for us to want to eventually start our own business. I was creative, David enjoyed and was very strong in finance. As we would discuss our future business, we always knew that I would create, just like my dad, and David would handle that 'other stuff.'

But our biggest hopes and dreams revolved around starting our family. We were married almost 3 years when our family grew by one, but our joy grew exponentially.

With each of our three sons' arrivals, seeing them for the first time was like nothing we'd ever experienced. With Christopher's arrival in April of 1996, I remembered feeling instantaneous and absolute love at first sight. Like so many new parents, David and I were in awe of the miraculous gift of a child.

David thought it was so wondrous, in fact, that before the doctor even left the delivery room after Christopher was born, David was quickly calculating when we could have baby number two. I, of course, thought it was great, but would have liked to have caught my breath, or at least, had the chance to stand up, before we started planning again.

And I certainly had an opportunity to do that. Michael did not join us as quickly as we planned. Our efforts to give Christopher a sibling were met with several years of sadness and frustration with multiple miscarriages and very difficult fertility treatments. The monthly disappointments combined with my break from my daily stress reliever (my runs) led to a difficult time for our little family. But when he did make his debut, we were so thrilled and delighted with his arrival, that we were downright obnoxious in our happiness. David and I were at our supreme and ultimate happiest as our family was growing. So, it came as no surprise around Michael's first birthday that we found out we would be rounding out the Tiffin Trifecta! Tiffin tot number three was on the way. We loved our lives; we felt so lucky, so blessed. But we also had our feet anchored to the earth and sometimes it was uncomfortable.

Bloated. I am fat. My breathing is labored. *"Why did I do this to myself? Pregnancy does not have to look like this. Just because I'm sharing space with another human life, it doesn't give me license to eat everything in sight. Really, now, I need to know when to step away from the Drakes cakes. Those Ring Dings and Devil Dogs are no friends to me. I really need to get back to running as soon as this little darling makes a debut."*

"I feel like a beached whale. And it wouldn't be such a bad feeling if I didn't look so much like one. Dang, I should have paid more attention in my first trimester—well, and that second one, too. Who am I trying to kid—the whole thing," I said, scratching my perpetually itchy baby tummy as I was cleaning up the kitchen after dinner. We'd put Christopher & Michael to bed and I had a few dishes to put away before I could relax for the night.

David was laughing. "Don't worry, you'll lose it. You've done it before. Why don't you sit down and I'll finish here?"

"Thanks, honey. I should've known when to drop the fork and step away from the table. This weight is too much."

I waddled to the family room and lay down on the couch.

"Phew, not long now." I could see my reflection in the dark screen of the TV. Oh boy, this was not a good look. Just not a pretty sight. I quickly pressed the on button on the TV remote.

While I was pregnant with Christopher I had a little morning sickness, no weird cravings, the correct amount of weight gain, a quick delivery, and a rapid weight loss after. Chris was a Big Gulp- sized baby when he was born; at nine pounds and 3 ounces. He dwarfed all of the other newborns in the nursery at our local hospital. Christopher was born looking very serious and intent. I mean really, he was literally blazing trails for his siblings to come.

My pregnancy with Michael was different, since we'd suffered the multiple miscarriages, we were so nervous that we wouldn't be able to bring him to full term. To be safe, for the first time in my life, I became a couch potato. I temporarily gave up running and was very careful about my movements. I didn't want to do anything to jeopardize this little one. As a result, I gained a little more weight, maybe an extra ten pounds. Never being much of a sitter, I did develop a new appreciation for relaxing. Michael was born looking so relaxed and comfortable. He was also a pretty baby, a lot of people would mistake him for a girl when they saw him as an infant.

But our third baby—whoa! Katie, bar the kitchen door! It seemed like I gained ten pounds on the night of conception, and then continued my love affair with the fork and knife the entire way through to this point for a 45 pound weight gain, feeling really uncomfortable in my final month.

David came in and gave me a glass of water. "Remember what Dr. Redtran said—you need to drink lots of water."

"Ummm, thanks."

David sat down at the opposite edge of the couch and grabbed my feet and held them into his lap. He gave the greatest foot rubs. "So, how'd your appointment go today?"

I had just started my weekly obstetric visits to prepare for the birth of this baby, as we were inching near our due date.

"Well, I was there for a while. They did blood work—I am severely anemic— and when they did my blood pressure, they found out that my blood pressure was really, really low. Dr. Redtran said she couldn't believe that I was even standing up."

"Oh, yeah?" He was listening and watching TV at the same time.

"David, I'm glad this is our last baby." I kicked him to get his attention.

"I can hear everything you're saying!"

"I think I am getting too old for this and I don't think I could do this again."

With baby number three, I seemed to be constantly exhausted, sick with every bug that floated by, and my migraines had been relentless. I wasn't enjoying this pregnancy, plus I was worried most of the time. "The doctor said she couldn't explain the anemia, but it would help to explain why I was so tired. She asked if I was taking my prenatals, which, of course, I have been. David, I have a bad feeling."

David stopped rubbing and looked at me. "You do?"

"Yeah, I feel like . . ." I started to cry. "I feel like this delivery is going to be [crying] very, very hard."

"Honey, is this about the weight gain?" David knew that I wasn't really happy about the extra weight I was carrying.

"No. I mean, I probably have less energy from it, but this is different."

"How do you mean?"

"With Christopher, I was worried about the unknown and being able to do it. With Mikey, I worried about the known, and it was a different worry. But with this baby, I feel like . . ." *"Don't say the words; you can't say the words; don't tempt fate."*

"What?" David looked perplexed—I'd been fine two minutes earlier, and now I was crying.

"I can see you're really bugged. Is it because you're not sleeping?" David asked.

"No, I don't think so, but who knows? I just have this odd feeling," I said.

"Okay, what kind of strange feeling?" Over the years, David had learned to trust my heebee jeebee feelings—not that they always panned out, but there was often some wisdom from listening to them.

"Can't say it; don't want to make him worry." Crying; I was just looking like another crazy, estrogen-driven, pregnant woman.

"What, honey?"

"I feel like I'm not going to survive the delivery. And I feel like I have leukemia or something." My cries turning to sobs.

"C'mere, honey. You'll be fine; we'll all be fine." He was hugging my vastness.

"No, I mean it. I'm really scared… I feel like something is very, very, wrong."

"Everything'll be fine, you'll see. You've just been under more pressure with this baby," David said.

"I've just had this bad feeling for a while, and I have to say this… [sobbing now]… Please find someone decent to raise our sons—a really good woman, like Megan Troutman. [lump in my throat] She would love my children like her own. Please don't date anyone who seems nice, but is really creepy and selfish."

"Honeybaby, you'll be fine. We'll be fine," David tried to reassure me.

"But there's something wrong with my blood, I just know it."

"It's okay. Everything is okay."

"And I've decided to get an epidural this time."

"Okay, if that will make you feel better." David was clearly uncomfortable, but as much as I hated making him uncomfortable, I felt that I needed to plan our family's future.

"I think an epidural will probably be a good experience," David added.

"Yeah, I heard you don't feel anything." And if I was going to DIE—*that's what it was, I felt like I was going to die in childbirth, wouldn't that just be the ultimate joy/devastation*—I was going to do everything I could to enjoy seeing my new baby and not feel myself go.

I decided to stop talking about it when I realized how upset I made David. He was so big and strong, but he was equally so sensitive when it came to his family. I could see that I was causing him stress. I had made my point, had offered my thoughts on my replacement, now I would just shut up.

"So, let's talk about names," David offered to be more positive. He was the king at changing the subject. "What are we going to name this little one?"

Delivery Number 3

"C'mon, Mary, just one more push." *"What the heck were we thinking? Two is the perfect number. I am too old to go through this. Dear Jesus, what is wrong with me? Better question: What is wrong with that epidural?"* I asked myself.

"Honeybabyloversweetie, you can do this," David coaxed.

"Uhhh." I thought, *"This is it; three time's the charm. I am so done with labor; three children will have to be enough."* This was already taking more time than I'd anticipated.

"C'mon, honey," David gently encouraged.

I was tired. *"Mary, this is it; you can do it."*

"We're almost there," David followed.

Yes, I was tired—not like a twenty-four-hour labor story, but tired for a Mary kind of labor. Truly, I didn't have reason to complain. Christopher's labor and delivery had lasted an entire four hours from start to finish. Michael's was an hour and a half. And since I felt that I was getting more accomplished at this birth thing and halving my time, it was my estimation that Tiffin baby number three should have arrived forty-five minutes after we started. But this baby was into serious overtime, having outlasted my mini epidural of two hours earlier.

"Mary, Mary, everything you got, do it," instructed my nurse midwife.

"Yowww!" I said, giving it my all.

"Here we go, Mary, David. It's a… it's a… it's a little *boy*!"

In that second, I said goodbye to my dreams of mother/daughter shopping trips, manicure/pedicure bonding time, and any idea that one of my children would be attending my alma mater, a college for women—all dashed in one last push. *"Goodbye, girly future!"*

"I'm sorry, honey," David whispered, as if he were reading my mind. "We can try again."

A pang of guilt struck me as sharp as any labor pain that I just experienced. *"What the heck was wrong with me?"*

"No, no, David; he is beautiful," was all I could say with my combination of exhaustion, exhilaration, and embarrassment that David would think that I would be anything but overjoyed with this little bundle of happiness.

And he was *beautiful!*

And when Stephen arrived, he was very different. Christopher was such a cute little boy, Michael was a pretty baby boy, and Stephen—the fairest of them all—appeared to be laughing. His stick-straight-stand-up hair and his sprite little face just made you smile. He had the infant kind of face that was a quick giggle.

"Three sons. Okay, I am the mother of three sons." The theme song from "My Three Sons" played in my head. *Dooo dooo dooo doooo... Boy, those sitcoms of those seventies really did imprint on me.*

"What am I going to do with them? I'm a girly girl. Heck, I went to a college for women, worked in the fashion business, had an allergy to snakes, snails, and puppy dog tails. What could I do for a son? Or three?" I felt unprepared and ill-equipped. With each of their deliveries, I thought, *"Here you go, David, here is one for you.....and another one, and ANOTHER ONE."* I knew David would teach them how to be good men. I felt confident they would learn from their dad how to be decent human beings, the most important lesson of all.

Those thoughts of spending Saturday morning with mani/pedis with a mini Mary disappeared when I looked at our tiniest addition, and realigned my thoughts to spending Saturdays at the soccer fields or Boy Scout events. *"Three boys. I can handle three boys. I have David,"* I told myself.

Three boys. That wasn't so hard; things could be worse. I could have three boys and a house full of dogs—now, *that* would be hard.

This Time Seemed Different

By the time we brought Stephen home, David and I felt that we had become old pros at this parenting thing. But I could not help noticing something different and worrisome about David—he seemed he be really tired, unusually tired. At forty-four, David was always in very good physical shape. Although his favorite was basketball, the man never found a sport that he did not enjoy playing. Stories of his youth often involved his excelling at or leading his teams to local or district championships. He was a natural and gifted athlete; exercise was woven into David's fabric. And now as an adult, it was very natural for him to go to the gym five to six days a week, and if he wasn't at the gym, he was biking, swimming, skiing, or playing baseball. Exercise was always so important, but for some reason, his exercise routine really seemed to be hard work this time. I noticed he'd lost weight. And for the first time in our marriage, he looked so strained.

I told myself it was the new burden of this growing family. David was a tremendous planner. He would work late into the evening working on our finances to plan for the boys' education and our retirement. Perhaps our newest addition was increasing his "provider stress." It really wasn't something I, too, felt; I always felt that the future would take care of itself. But David was much more proactive about our future. I tried to allay his fears by working really hard at my career, and I felt that we were in a really comfortable place. But David still worried, and maybe, just maybe, this worry contributed to his weight loss.

In our nine-plus years of marriage, I had found my husband to be very easygoing and easy to get along with. But it was a marriage like all marriages that was surrounded by the pressures of a two-career home with, now, three little boys.

In general, it was hard to shake him. He often spoke glowingly of the lessons he'd learned from his father and grandfather Caine. David loved and respected both and saw them as great role models. From these men and others he admired, he learned to be a man of great character, and held strong beliefs and convictions. I had lucked out when I found David Tiffin. So whatever was bugging David, was *really* bugging him, and, by extension, was bugging me.

He started complaining about back pain around the time of Stephen's birth, but this was not unusual. David had a lot of aches and pains, but he was still able to play with the boys, have fun, and do stuff around the house. Aches and pains, like exercise, were a part of my husband. I chalked it up to his years in sports.

On a Tuesday in June 2002, however, he was in so much pain he went to his physician, who treated him for muscle strain and sent him on his way. The prescription that David was given did nothing to alleviate the pain, but he continued to work and play through it as our house was still so fresh with new-baby happiness.

We were planning Stephen's christening in July when David decided to try the chiropractor affiliated with his UPS Center to help with his nagging back pain. He thought he might need an "adjustment." David used chiropractors from time to time. When David came home from this adjustment, he was feeling much worse. But he continued to see the chiropractor and had several additional adjustments, one that nearly immobilized him.

We were standing in the kitchen. David had both arms on the island and he was leaning on the island, clearly in pain. I started to rub his back.

"Where does it hurt?" I asked.

"Right there," he said, pointing to the area above his hips. "God, it really hurts."

"Does this feel any better?" I was rubbing as hard as I could.

"Ummm." Noncommittal from David.

"David, you lost your butt!" I said, shocked. His shorts were hanging off of him, and it was at that moment that I noticed how much weight he had lost.

"Oh." Then he added, "Heat seems to help the pain a little."

"Okay, you've got to see a real doctor, David. This guy is a quack and I don't agree with his hocus pocus, cracking your back, not taking X-rays. That is all wrong. What if he hurts you? What if there is something wrong with your back and he is just aggravating it with his back cracking?"

We'd been so busy with the joy of Stephen's arrival, trying to find some new kind of balance as our family expanded, that I didn't have the time to see what was in front of me. And now, I was hit by a wave of anxiety washing over me, increasing my heart rate and making my skin flush. My husband was losing weight and not feeling well. It hit me.

"No, it's nothing," I told myself and pushed it away. For as much as I adored my husband, I'd become immune to his complaints about body pain. He was equal parts beat up athlete and hypochondriac, so I learned to not be too alarmed. *"This is just David."*

"Honey, I am just going to lie down for a little while."

"Okay, David," I said, turning to fold yet another load of laundry—trying to cram in as many chores as I could while our newest angel slept.

"This pain seems different," I told myself. *"He is not a daytime napper."* The doubt crept in again.

"Mommy, Mommy! Stephen needs you!" Christopher announced as he ran into the room, grabbing my arm to tug me into the family room. "Come on, Mommy."

"Ok, baby, I'm coming." But turning first toward my husband, I said, "We're going to have a full house tomorrow, David. And I don't want you heading back to that guy, he is just making you worse. I need you to be okay. Tell UPS you need a medical doctor, a real doctor, okay?"

"Sure. Rest first."

As I was walking into the family room, I thought God couldn't let anything be wrong with my husband. He knows that I would be lost without him. We had just had our third son, for Pete's sake. God wouldn't do that; it doesn't work that way. "God *has been way too good to me in my life to let something awful like that happen. Our lives are perfect. Nope, David is fine.*"

"I'm coming, my angel boy," I announced to my crying infant. "Momma's coming."

No Bowling Today

Christopher was crying. He was sitting on the steps with his face in his hands. My six-year-old love of my life, our biggest boy, yet still such a little boy, sat weeping softly. I sat down on the steps beside him. Michael was playing quietly by himself and the baby was sleeping. It was so unusual for me to have a few seconds when I felt like I was not spinning plates.

"Ah, what's wrong, honey?"—scooping him up into my lap, looking eye to eye with our darling Christopher.

"Daddy doesn't want to go bowling," Chris said. The two were best buddies. In David's eyes, the sun rose and set on Christopher, and Christopher adored his daddy in return. I would often joke with David that the only time Christopher would acknowledge my existence was when he was hungry. David and Christopher had had an instant connection and it continued. Our Christopher was truly a Daddy's boy.

On that day, David had promised to take Christopher and some of his friends bowling. He'd wanted to spend some fun time with Chris, as he'd been so busy with all the other activities surrounding the arrival of his new brother. When the two were together, it was hard to tell who was having more fun, Christopher or David. They both relished their special time together. So it made sense that Chris was so upset that Daddy did not want to go, and it also didn't make sense that David didn't take his son bowling.

"Ah, Chris hang on, let me talk to Daddy."

I put Chris down and walked through the kitchen and the family room and out into the garage.

"David," I called.

David had a routine. Every summer Saturday, he would get up and have breakfast, then head to the garage, where he would assemble, tune, and gas up his arsenal of yard tools. All lined up in order of use. David took tremendous pride in our yard, so the Saturday morning routine became a ritual—all of the tools ready to create the perfect yard. Naturally, David was in the garage.

"David?"

"Hmm," I thought, *"the garage doors are down. That's funny."* The garage doors were never down on a Saturday. David would have had to open them to get to the shed to take out the lawn mower and the weed whacker, and the trimmer, the edger, the blower, and all of those of things that he uses.

"David?" No answer.

Christopher was walking behind me.

"Mommy, Daddy's not in the garage," he said.

"Yes, I see. But how do you know that, honey?"

"Daddy is upstairs."

"Upstairs?"

"Upstairs, Mommy."

"What do you mean, upstairs?"

"Daddy's in the back room."

"Huh?"

"Daddy's in the guess bedroom." We had adopted Christopher's sweet mispronunciation of a few years earlier of our guest bedroom. We thought it appropriate that Christopher called it the "guess room" because it became our general drop-off spot for extra items that could not find a home in any other room. The "guess room" held extra framed pictures, small pieces of furniture, extra lamps, re-gift-ready gifts, old comforters, cases of diapers and wipes, and bonus packs of paper towels and toilet paper. It changed weekly, and often you would have to guess what you would find in there. Now, I would guess my husband was in there as well.

"Huh?" I thought as I bounded up the steps, walking past Michael, so grateful that he was amusing himself with his blocks and books. I opened the guest room door to find my husband had carved out a spot and was asleep on the brass four-poster bed.

"David?" I roused him.

"Hmm," he responded.

I grabbed his right shoulder and shook it. "David"—this time even louder.

Nothing.

"David! What are you doing?"—this even louder, and I shook him some more.

"Huh?"

"Honey, what are you doing? It's Saturday—you are supposed to be Lawnmower Man!"

He groaned.

"David!"

"What!"

His response caught me off guard. David was calm; he was not prone to being emotional. I was the emotional one. It wasn't like him to respond this way.

"What's going on?" I asked more quietly.

"I'm sleeping," was his reply.

"David, you promised Christopher that you would take him, Jack, and Clay bowling today."

"Yeah, Daddy," echoed Chris. I had just realized that Christopher had followed me up the stairs and was standing behind me.

"Ah, buddy, I can't. Daddy is so tired. Maybe another day."

"David, c'mon, time to wake up." I pulled his arm. I thought to myself, *"You're tired? Try being a source of food for another human being around the clock while chasing two other little boys."* If he was tired, I was the walking dead! *"I'll show you tired."* I was starting to get miffed. Christopher needed this time with his dad.

"Chris, why don't you go and play with Mikey, and Mommy will be with you in a few seconds."

I closed the guest room door behind him. Even though we'd been so happily busy these past couple of months, that niggling feeling of dread had never left me. It always hung in the peripheral. No matter the joy, the sense of foreboding hung over me like a dark cloud, threatening our every moment. Now the cloud was starting to produce rain. Again, with David in the room, the fear came out; something was definitely up. But rather than acknowledge it, I pushed it away, anxious to return to my happy place. But I had to nag my husband up and out the door for me to get to my happy place.

"David, it's Chrissy's day. You promised him."

"I... I... can't."

"What do you mean, you can't?"

"I just can't, I'm so tired. I just want to sleep. I need to sleep."

"Sleep? You need to sleep?" I was miffed, and started to go over my list of thirteen or more things that I did that morning on four hours' sleep.

"Yes, sleep." And he turned over and went back to sleep. I knew when I'd been defeated and this was it.

Leaving the guest bedroom, as I pulled the door shut behind me I didn't know if I was more frustrated or worried, but I made a mental note to call my doctor for an appointment for David.

Christopher ran down the hallway when he saw me emerge.

"So, Mommy, is Daddy going to take me?" he asked, head tilted with his hands clasped together, prayer-like. He always did this when he wanted something badly, and it was usually followed by a "please."

I crouched down to Chris's level. "Not today, honey. We'll play at home today. Maybe next week. Daddy is just super, super tired."

"But, Mommy, you're awake. It's daytime."

"Yes, but Daddy needs his rest. He really works so hard for us."

"He can sleep when we sleep at night, and I want to go bowling!"

"Not today. Maybe next week."

"Please, Mom"—again in his sincere beg pose.

"No. You, Michael, Stephen, and I can play at home."

"No! It's just not the same!" Chris stomped his foot and ran into his room. I could hear him crying in his room.

"Mommy, Mommy!" I could hear Michael's sweet voice downstairs. I went to the stairs and looked down.

"Baby. Baby," he said, pointing to the bassinete. Michael was watching his little brother cry. "*Oh, jeeze,*" I thought, "*how long has this been going on? But more importantly, how did you get downstairs, Michael?*

"Christopher, you are right. Things are not at all the same."

PART II

My Husband Can't be Sick

"He's yellow. David's yellow," I whispered into the phone. "Mom, I need you and Dad to get over here. I am taking David to the ER."

"What do you mean, he's yellow?" my mother asked.

"I mean like a banana, a taxi cab, a rain coat. What do you mean, what is yellow? Yellow is yellow. His skin is yellow! Jeeze, Mom. Jaundice yellow. He was feeling tired all day yesterday and couldn't get out of bed a lot, so this morning when I woke up I saw yellow. I called Dr. Brown, told him about what he had been experiencing, and he said get him to the ER right away. So can you and Dad come down and…?"

"Your father and I will be right down."

My parents lived nearby, so it took under ten minutes for them to get to our house. But when they arrived, they found David in the family room all ready to go. My mother shot me a look of alarm when she saw David's color.

"Hello, David," my mother said softly.

"Oh, David, do you feel pain?" my father asked, also clearly alarmed by my husband's color.

From the moment my parents had met David, they, like me, thought he was too good to be true. I often wondered who was happier on our wedding day—me, that I married David, or my parents, that he joined the family.

"Hi, Mimi. Hi, Pop," David said quietly.

"Oh, David, it's probably gall stones. Have you ever had a gall stone? It looks like gall stones," reassured my dad.

"No, I never had gall stones."

"Well, I'm sure it is something like that," my dad added, trying to sound confident.

"Well, you go and we'll take care of the boys. Just keep us posted, okay?" my mother added, directing me out the door.

"Yeah, sure, I'll call as soon as we find out," I said, helping David into the van on the passenger's side.

Our local hospital, Evangelical Community Hospital, was only seven miles away. The last trip we had made to this hospital was filled with happy anticipation—we were going to deliver baby boy, Stephen. We had been so excited just three months before. On this drive, however, our emotions were fear and uncertainty. What a difference a few months can make. We said little to each other besides what I learned from our Family Medical Encyclopedia.

"You know, honey, I think that my dad was right, that gall bladder issues would certainly explain this back pain, exhaustion, and probably that funny color of your skin. And you know, when we go to the ER, there is a pretty good chance that we will have to wait because there are probably much more serious cases that ours."

"Oh, okay," he replied, too sick to say more.

As we pulled into the ER, I was deflated. For a Sunday morning, the ER was packed. As I looked at the crowd in the waiting area, I thought there was no telling when we would be seen. I was worried for David. As I scanned the waiting room, I tried to determine how serious the other patients were. There was a combination of elderly and very young, with some in between, and quickly sizing up their presentations, I thought we were in for a long wait. After we registered, David took a seat, bent over, and placed his head in his hands. I looked at him and thought, *"Oh, dear God, please have them call us soon."* And it was as if God answered at that very moment, because the triage nurse called David and said that he would be seen immediately.

"Oh honey, how lucky for us!" I said, feeling incredibly unlucky, realizing that we had moved way up on the scale of serious illnesses.

The next few hours happened both so fast, but also in slow motion. The emergency room doctor started asking questions about David's symptoms: when had they begun; did it ever get better, and if so, what made him feel better; any changes in eating or sleeping patterns; when had he turned yellow; where was he receiving care; if he had lost weight and how much? In the middle of the questions, David fell asleep and became very difficult to rouse. The doctor ordered blood work, and when those results came back, he ordered more.

After about an hour, that doctor, accompanied by another ER doctor, came into David's bay and told me that my husband was very sick. It was surreal. When they spoke, I saw their mouths moving but I caught only some words.

"What?!"

"He has no blood in his body."

"We are still doing tests."

"He will need blood transfusions. We have ordered the units."

The words were bouncing off me. By now, two other doctors entered the ER bay and were assessing, evaluating, and comparing notes on David.

"There is also a problem with his kidneys. Kidneys are failing. We have to get his kidneys working," said one.

It was more than I could take in. "What?" I asked.

"His liver is failing—organ toxicity, total organ failure. Could be a very serious virus. We need to get David stabilized in the ICU," said the other.

"What? David in an ICU? No, he barely uses Band-Aids."

"David needs *more* blood," the first ER doctor announced as he returned to the bay ninety minutes later.

"What? Where did the other blood go? Is he bleeding internally?"

"It may be cancer," I heard another assert.

"Whaaaat? How?"

David was receiving transfusions while he slept. They were ordering more blood. David's body seemed to be empty. Couldn't he get a disease from a transfusion? By then, he had received several.

The doctor's words made me dizzy. With each new consultation, the lump in my throat would move to a pit in my stomach where it would roll around and around.

I had just had my third son, a son. Another boy. *"My husband can't be sick. God wouldn't let that happen,"* I said to myself. *"No, God wouldn't allow this to happen. No, God wouldn't allow this to happen,"* I kept telling myself. I couldn't really wrap my mind around what was going on. I called my parents to report in, to tell them they were still testing and to tell them what I knew. I also asked them to call my in-laws, David's parents, Marge and Jim, "Goo Goo" and "Pa," to let them know what had been happening.

Surely this would pass quickly. I prayed that this would be over soon. I had confidence that God would not let anything happen to this sweet man. Life doesn't happen that way.

I was praying quietly when an ER doctor returned to David's ER bay, and I remembered my Dad's diagnosis and asked the doctor, "What about his gall bladder?"

"It's not his gall bladder, Mary. We think it may be something else, but we are checking." He paused. "David has pancytopenia. That is the name for a reduction in the number of red and white blood cells, as well as platelets. It could have been caused by any one of a number of conditions, from simple drug-induced bone marrow reaction to another blood illness. Has David ingested any excessive amounts of medicines lately?"

"David, drugs?" I thought. *"No way."* "No, no drugs."

"Painkillers, anything?" the doctor prompted.

"Oh, wait. David has been taking a lot of Advil for his back pain. A lot of Advil."

"How much Advil?"

"Like eight pills a day." I had told David that I thought he was taking too much, and now look what happened!

I was, by then, talking not only to the emergency room physicians and a friend who was a pathologist, Dr. Bill Diets, but a new physician had entered the room. His name was Dr. Patel, and he was a hematologist. Dr. Patel was also joined by our obstetrician, Dr. Redtran, to offer support.

"No, that should not cause this."

"Then what would it be?"

The two other physicians allowed Dr. Patel to answer the question.

"Mrs. Tiffin, we believe that your husband's condition is not the result of taking too much Advil. We are highly suspicious that something else might be going on and we need to rule that out."

"What would that be?" I asked, feeling like I was going to be sick.

"We need to rule out leukemia."

"Leukemia? No way," I said to myself. Then aloud, "What about a virus?" I grasped at something I kind of understood.

"The severity of pancytopenia and the underlying pathology determine the management of the condition and prognosis. Thus, identification of the correct cause will help in implementing the appropriate course of treatment or therapy. I'd like to have your permission to perform a bone marrow biopsy. That will provide us with the most conclusive answer," Dr. Patel offered.

"What the heck is going on here? Someone wake me up, please!"

"Okay, please do what you need to do to make David better," I said. The world was spinning and my insides were trembling. But I had to stay the course for my sleeping David; I was his voice. "Will you do that now?" I asked Dr. Patel.

"Yes, I would like to. It shouldn't take more than a half hour; forty minutes."

"Okay. May I ask if there is a phone anywhere I could use to call my parents?"

"Sure, Mary. Dr. Patel, I will show her," Dr. Redtran said, and guided me out of David's room to a consultation room a few doors down. "Mary, if there is anything that you, David, or the boys need, just let me know. I am so sorry."

"Thank you, Dr. Redtran, thank you."

She hugged me and left.

I picked up the phone and dialed our house.

Ring once.

Ring twice.

Ring three… "Hellloooo, Tiffin residence, Christopher speaking," he said with a giggle.

"Hi, sweetie."

"Hi, Mommy. How's Daddy? Did he get a band aid? Can you put him on the phone?"

"Oh, Chrissy, Daddy is still really tired. He is sleeping right now here, too. So he can't really talk. Can I talk to Grandma?"

"Sure, hold on… Grandmaaaaaaaaaa … And away from the phone, I heard him say, "It's Mommy."

"Hi, honey. So what is happening?" my mother asked.

"They are ruling out leukemia," I said, bursting into tears.

"Leukemia? No, how can that be?" my mother asked. "No, that can't be right. David can't have leukemia."

To hear my mother say David and leukemia together in the same sentence was more than my stomach could handle. It started to roil uneasily. This time I could not stop myself—I got sick in the trashcan by the door. And no longer were just my insides shaking, but now my whole body was shaking as I sobbed, because deep down I knew the doctor was right.

There Must be Some Mistake

The bone marrow biopsy did not seem to bother David. He was sleeping soundly when I returned after my call to my parents. The plan was to support him with blood products and fluids and to continue to monitor his systems while we waited for the biopsy results. When I knew that he was safe and sound for the night, I returned to our van and started the engine and closed the door.

"What just happened?" I said to myself, trying to reconstruct and make sense of the day. *"David sick? No way. Can't be; he's the picture of health. It would be impossible for him to have leukemia."* I rationalized by mentally listing all of our anti-cancer attributes: we eat organically, never smoked, drink in moderation, exercise daily. No, there must be some kind of mix-up, a mistake in the lab.

"I'll ask the doctors. People make mistakes every day, we're all human. Perhaps they mixed-up the slides in the lab. I would understand. These things must happen every day, I'm sure." I envisioned a lab with hundreds of slides all around and a doctor picking up the wrong one, thinking it was David's. *"Yes, yes, I am sure that is what happened—a mix up. David couldn't have cancer. Someone else less fit, not David,"* I told myself.

The funny thing about intuition, even the most deliberate defense mechanism can't push it away. The wave of panic returned with the feeling that our perfectly wonderful home life, my children's foundation, seemed to be slipping away, careening out of control. I barely got the van door open when I got sick. Twelve hours that seemed like twelve years after I had left in the morning, I returned to our house.

My parents and sister greeted me, but after listening in disbelief to my report of the day, my father went to sit by himself in the living room. My father handled things quietly. If David did have cancer, this would be round two for my parents— ten years earlier, my brother Billy's wife, Jill, had died of cervical cancer, leaving Billy to raise their three boys alone. For my parents, the similarities for their family were frightening.

While my dad was quiet, my mother was "take charge." And Mom's take charge generally involved food- and house-related activities. She'd cooked for everyone and done several loads of laundry while we were gone. We were now sitting around our kitchen island. "You need to eat, Mary Mathilde." Mom always called my first and middle name when she meant business.

"I can't eat, Mom; I'll throw up."

"You must eat. You have to keep your energy up. Besides, you are nursing your baby," Mom reminded me.

"Oh, my God, I totally forgot about nursing while I was there. How was my baby? I had a few bottles in the refrigerator that I pumped." I had been getting ready to return to work, so I had been pumping to anticipate my absence.

"You're going to need to pump some more," my sister Laura said. What Laura didn't want to say was, *We might have enough for the next day or two, but we are going to need more if this goes longer.*

"I have an idea," my mother said, almost sensing what lay ahead for us. "You have given Stephen Alexander a good start. Why don't we use what we have, and introduce formula and see how he does? He is such a good little boy. He gave us no trouble at all. And that Christopher, oh, he is a darling big brother, helping us find where everything is. And that Michael—what an angel. The boys were all angels!" my mother said as she prepared for me a big pile of whatever she'd made.

My dad poked his head into the kitchen to add, "Yes, you have sweet babies."

With a nod toward my father, my mother said, "Your dad helped me get them ready for bed."

"Christopher was trying to stay up, but he fell asleep on the couch waiting. I carried him up about a half hour ago," Dad added.

"Thanks, Pop."

My mother put a plate of food in front of me.

"Mom, I'm sorry, but I just can't eat this."

"You have to."

"I'll throw up."

"Just try," she encouraged.

My mother was a very good cook and she loved to cook for her family. Cooking, for her has always been a form of therapy, a coping mechanism. So I tried. But her cooking was not working for me that day. After the second bite, I realized the food was not going down but up, and ran to our powder room.

"I told you I can't eat, Mom. It's not going down. I'm sorry, but thank you. I'm going to go upstairs and kiss my babies' goodnight."

I could hear my mom cleaning up the kitchen as I entered Stephen's room first. Looking into his crib, I saw that even in sleep, the tiniest of our Tiffins was smiling. This boy will surely bring such joy to this family. I made the sign of the cross over him, kissed my fingertips and placed them on his head. "Goodnight, little prince. Momma and Daddy love you." I made sure his monitor was on and quietly shut the door.

I went into Michael's room next. He was hugging his stuffed animal, Mr. Horsey, close to his chest. He fit so perfectly into his Lightning McQueen toddler bed, he looked so safe and secure. Everyone said that when Michael was born, he was the image of me. Michael might look like me, but he definitely had his dad's sweetness and spirit. And as he slept, he exuded this calm and beautiful spirit. If Christopher was a daddy's boy, Michael was a momma's boy.

I checked on Christopher last. The nightlight in his room cast a soft light on our biggest baby boy's face. I sat at the foot of his new big-boy bed and said a silent prayer for my boys that their daddy would be okay. Always a light sleeper, he stirred. I bent down to kiss him and he woke.

"Hi, Mommy," he said, and turned over.

"I love you, Chrissy. Good night."

"Night," he murmured.

I exhaled as I closed Chris's door. My boys were safe and sound. Peacefully and blessedly oblivious to the panic of today. Tomorrow will be a new day. Maybe it would be a better one for David, too. Sleeping children, such a calming sight.

I joined my family—my mother, father, and sister Laura—who were now sitting in my living room.

"You're exhausted," my mother said.

"Yes, and Stephen will be up in a few hours," I replied. He was only three months old. "I am supposed to return to work tomorrow." My family leave had officially ended the previous Friday, and I was scheduled to return to work the next morning, bright and early.

Laura said, "I called Don and told him what was going on. He said not to worry about tomorrow."

"That's a help. Thank you."

"Mary, your father and I are thinking it's a good idea for you not to be alone tonight, so Laura said she would spend the night," Mom said.

"I don't think that is necessary. I'm just going to take a quick shower and go to sleep."

"But what if the hospital calls and you're needed there?" Laura asked. My sister had been an operating room nurse for more than fifteen years, so she'd given David's situation some thought.

"Okay, Lude. Did you bring your PJs or do you need a pair?"

"Joel brought some over. I'm all set."

"We'll let you get some sleep, honey, and don't worry—just pray," my mother said.

"God better not let anything happen to him, or I'll be so pissed at *Him*!" I declared.

"Oh, don't you dare talk that way, Mary Mathilde!" my mother admonished. And added, "Just pray."

"Hmm… G'night, Mom. G'night, Dad."

Before falling asleep, I called the ICU to check on my husband. The nurses said that he'd been given another unit of blood and was sleeping soundly.

Now that all my men were asleep, maybe I, too, would find sleep—and wake to find this entire situation was just a really awful nightmare.

So This is Really Happening

I was awoken at seven thirty by our nanny, Heidi. From the moment we'd met her, Heidi Raymond, we knew we'd stumbled onto someone great. My mother had found her six years earlier when I needed to return to work. Like the Heidi from the Swiss novel, she was blonde and young and cute. She was also very responsible and so playful. The boys adored her, and she was as much a part of our family as any of the boys' aunts and uncles. David and I would often remark that we really didn't know where our family would be without her. Heidi was a gift.

"Did someone forget she had to go to work today?" Heidi asked with a giggle. Heidi had been with our family since shortly after Christopher's birth, and, although it didn't appear in her job description, alarm clock is a role that Heidi performed occasionally and seemed to get a lot of humor out of.

"Oh, Heid, thanks a lot." *"Whew, life is back to normal. Heidi is here."* I was relieved. *"All that stuff from yesterday was a bad dream."*

"Did you have a problem with baby boy last night?" she asked.

"What do you mean, Heidi Ho?" I asked as I sat up in my bed, thankfully rubbing my eyes and that nightmare out of my head.

"I noticed that Aunt Lulu [another of my sister's nicknames] is here." The guess bedroom door was open and she'd seen Laura still sleeping.

My relief was short-lived, and that knot in the pit of my stomach returned. I lay back down. "Crap," I muttered.

"Everything okay?" Heidi asked.

"Heid?"

"Yeah?"

"Sit down. I have something to tell you." And I told Heidi the events of the day before.

"That can't be, just can't be. Like you said, I'm sure there is some kind of mix-up," Heidi responded.

"I don't understand either. But I need to get to the hospital. I'll wake up Laura and talk to Christopher. If you can handle the rest, Heidi?"

"Don't worry, Mary, everything will be okay. Again, there must be some mistake."

"Yeah, I'm sure, but I better get there."

I woke Laura and told her that I had to get to the hospital. She got up quickly and joined me.

When we entered the ICU that David had been transferred to, Dr. Patel and the intensive care physicians were already with him. They said he had had a quiet night, but they had some pressing concerns—for one, his kidneys were not recovering.

"Okay," I thought. *"So, this is really happening,"* I told myself as my mouth went dry and the lump in my throat got bigger.

The mention of the word "kidney" always caused me alarm. About a year after we'd moved to Pennsylvania in the 1970s, my mother had become very, very sick. She was in bed for many weeks before she was admitted to this hospital, where she teetered on the edge of life for several months. No one knew the cause of my mother's illness, until she underwent exploratory surgery and it was determined that Mom had a necrotic kidney. After the removal of her kidney, her health improved, but had it not been for that surgery, we probably would have lost my mother. From that point on, I understood and respected the role a healthy kidney played in our healthy bodies. In my mind, kidney problems equated near death.

All the doctors and nurses were working quickly and talking quietly as I watched my husband fall into a deeper and deeper sleep. *"David is so strong, whatever it is, he will shake it,"* I kept trying to tell myself. *"My husband is so amazing."*

I sat in the room, so hopeful that this was some really nasty virus. *"Hospitals and doctors make mistakes all the time. Look at all those lawyers on the commercials just salivating for mistakes just like this,"* I reassured myself.

My sister went home to check on her kids, and I was with my sleeping husband when a nurse popped her head into the room.

"Mary, you have a call at the nurse's station," she said. "You can take it over here."

"Hello."

"Hello, Mary." When I heard my father-in-law's voice, I started to cry.

"Hello, Pa," I said. "I'm so sorry. I don't... don't ... know what is happening."

"I spoke to your parents last night and this morning. Goo Goo and I are on our way down to be with you, David, and the boys. Is there anything you need?" Pa asked.

"Just for David to be okay. That is all I need, Pa."

"That is what we want. Everyone here is so very concerned and wants to help."

"Thanks, Pa," I said, and hung up and returned to the chair beside my sleeping husband.

Talking to my father-in-law made it seem more frightening. Saying the words made it more real. I decided it would be better if I would not talk for a little while, until I learned something more. I didn't think I could handle any more talking.

I must have fallen asleep, because I remember dreaming. I dreamt about a sunny day, about David and me playing outside with the boys at the marina. It was a simple, but a happy dream.

Dr. Patel came in and gently woke me. He was accompanied by Dr. Redtran, Dr. Brown, and a nurse I had not met. "Mrs. Tiffin, I really did not want to wake you up, but I think that we need to have a conversation."

Dream over. I was awake.

"We got the results back. I'm very sorry to tell you this, but your husband, David, has a disease called Acute Lymphocytic Leukemia, and it is very important that we start treating him immediately. He was prescribed prednisone yesterday when he was admitted, and that will help, but he needs to start on a rigorous chemotherapy regime."

The room was starting to spin and my stomach was starting to turn, but I couldn't move. I felt frozen. Just as I feared. I had watched my sister-in-law, Jill, die. We had three sons, just like Billy and Jill. *Have David and I repeated their curse of threes? No, not my David.*

"Mary," Dr. Redtran said, "I know this is the bad news." She directed my focus back into the room.

"Yes, this is bad news, very bad news. Is it possible that there could be a mistake?" I was still clinging to the hope that someone, anyone, could have messed up.

"I understand that this is very difficult to hear," Dr. Patel said. "Especially after everything you all have been through."

The loss of Jill, our infertility, and new baby Stephen were no secret in the small medical community. "But to answer your question, it is possible; but in David's case, not probable." Then he went on, "And a more immediate issue for us . . ."

"Wait," I thought, *"There is something more immediate than starting immediate chemotherapy? What? Where was my simple, happy, sunny life? What happened to our little dream life? Let me go back to sleep, please."*

"David's kidneys are failing. We think he might need dialysis." *Wait, what the hell? Dialysis. I wish that they would just stop talking so I can go back to sleep...* Although this was not what he intended, Dr. Patel's words were like big slaps in the face over and over again. Because he was a gentle man and I sensed that he was trying to be as compassionate as possible, I did my best to rebound from his slaps and remain upright. But remaining upright took every ounce of my energy. I just wanted to lay down beside David. But I couldn't. I had no other choice; David was counting on me.

Pulling it together, I asked, "At what point will it be determined that he needs dialysis?" *"Stay in the game, Mary,"* I told myself.

"We are going to call in Dr. Bruin, our nephrologist, to evaluate. But if it is decided that he does need dialysis, we won't be able to do it here. He will need to go to a tertiary care hospital," Dr. Redtran said.

"I don't know what that is, a tertiary care . . ."

"That's Geisinger. And our recommendation is to get him transferred today," Dr. Redtran added.

"That way, they can direct his chemotherapy and watch his kidneys," Dr. Patel said.

"But I love and trust this hospital. I love Evan." Having delivered our boys in this hospital, David and I felt safe here. I was afraid to leave our comfort zone.

"For this, you need Geisinger," Dr. Redtran assured me. "We'll still be here if you need us, Mary."

"It's too much?" I asked, meaning David's problems were too big.

"David needs Geisinger," Dr. Patel echoed.

"Okay, let's do what we need to do then." And they scheduled the transfer.

I called my parents, in-laws, and Heidi, and told them all what was happening. "We are being transferred to Geisinger"—saying the words but not really believing they were coming from me.

Shell-Shocked... Just Shell-Shocked

When he was admitted to the Bush Pavilion, eighth floor (BP8) of Geisinger Medical Center, my handsome, sleeping David looked perfectly tranquil from the neck up, but the entire length of his long arms was bruised from the repeated attempts to draw blood for the tests and insert IVs for treatments. Black, blue, purple, red, and yellow blotches covered the span of my husband's strong arms. I was relieved he did not have to see this.

I sat in the room shell-shocked. It seemed like it had been a month since we'd gone to the emergency room, but it was only Tuesday. A mere two days provided ten years of wear. How had our lives changed so dramatically so quickly? What did we do wrong to deserve this? How could this be happening?

My parents and David's parents sat with him during the day, and I took advantage of their presence to run home and see our boys. Because David was so susceptible to infection, all visitors were required to wear gloves, gowns, and masks. Our parents sat in a circle around David's bed, looking like a group of older doctors perched just waiting to operate. Always friendly with each other, they seemed at a loss for words now, going for long periods of time in silence. But when they spoke it was about the boys, and they spoke hopefully about David getting his treatment and getting back to normal. Then my dad decided to let Pa and Goo Goo know what he and my mother were talking about to help out.

"Jim and Marge, Jean and I feel this is a terrible thing that has happened to our families. We are so sorry about it. We feel just terrible."

Goo Goo started to cry quietly and Pa leaned over to comfort her.

"We really love David," my mother chimed in.

My mother-in-law could only nod in acknowledgment.

"And Jean and I talked about this, and we can work out a schedule to do all that they need to do help the kids and Heidi with the boys and get David better," my dad said.

"And Bill has volunteered to take David to his chemo appointments," my mother added.

"Thank you," my father-in-law said. My mother-in-law wept quietly.

My parents got up from their chairs and went over to hug my in-laws. They hugged and cried. After a little while, my mother said, "Don't worry, it's going to be okay. David will be fine. We just need to pray."

"Yes, he'll be okay. He has to be okay," my mother-in-law was able to say.

After a few days on BP8, David finally woke up. I was so grateful. I desperately needed to be able to talk to my best friend again. David looked at his black-and-blue arms and asked, "Was I in an accident?" He had no awareness of what had happened.

I did my best to explain some of what was happening, and let the doctors explain the rest. David, so true to form, was worried about me and the boys.

Within a day or two, Geisinger was able to stabilize him and begin treatment, but that was just the very beginning. Receiving a cancer diagnosis is like arriving in a foreign country without a map or tour guide. You recognize certain things, but it is a very different world. Doctors speak to you in English, but, although you recognize your language, you question your intelligence, your ability to comprehend, and your ability to communicate back. I was running on adrenaline, caffeine, and the need to protect and get the best possible care for my husband. Nothing else mattered at that moment. I had one goal in life, only one goal, and it was to make David Tiffin well.

But I was still trying to wrap my mind around this leukemia diagnosis, and I was still fighting with why it did not make any sense. And where was God in all of this? I felt angry and abandoned.

It wasn't until after our priest, Father Nessel, came to see us that I could deal with this. In my mind, I kept asking God, *"Why David? He is the sweetest, most kind man there is."*

And almost as if Father Nessel was reading my mind, he said, "Many people ask the question, 'Why me?'"

"Actually, Father," David said, "why not me?" David's question stilled me. David had a way of doing this, stopping me in my tracks. I was thinking in one direction and my husband was thinking in another. And he added, "I'd much rather it be me than a little child. I'd hate to see a little child go through this."

"Well, David, that is very gracious of you. But we don't know why these things happen. They are the things of life," Father Nessel said.

"The things of life," I said it almost as a question. I tried to let it settle in.

"Yes, the things of life. We rely on our faith to carry us through these difficult times."

"The things of life," I repeated, and looked at David. Realizing that I was squeezing his hand, I relaxed it a little, and smiled hopefully.

"I think we are going to be just fine, honey," I said to David as I kissed him on the forehead after Father Nessel left. "All of a sudden, I feel much better. Don't you?"

"I feel okay," David said, lying.

We lied to each other a lot in those days, but it was only about the situation and how we felt about where we were. We never really shared how scared out of our minds we were. I would not let on how I felt absolutely terrified every minute of every day. I was jumpy. And he would not share his fears with me, either.

In our years of marriage, we learned, like so many couples, that the other's mood or feeling often significantly impacted our own. Now more than ever, I saw it as my job to eliminate any worries or fears for this man, my husband. I wanted his only consideration to be achieving wellness. David would only be surrounded by positives and good news.

Acute Lymphocytic Leukemia, or ALL as it is called in the oncology world, is a blood cancer that has a very good cure rate in children. When it appears in adults, however, the disease is much angrier and much more virulent. We were told by David's physicians at Geisinger that with his particular type of ALL, the prognosis was bleak.

Like many who receive a devastating diagnosis, we spent the first couple of weeks in a state of disbelief and bewilderment. But we were soon able to gather ourselves and commit to fighting the disease. We felt confident that no matter the odds, we would beat this foe. After all, statistically speaking, *someone* has to survive.

David had the elements to be in the survivor group. He was healthy before leukemia, that is, and we had a great support system and a very strong faith. In essence, David Tiffin was just not a candidate for cancer, but was a model for survival.

Life with a blood cancer is handled in fifteen-minute increments. You learn that your life can change when the clinician enters your hospital room. In the past, you relished your hopes, plans, and dreams for the future; now you fear the future if you can allow yourself the luxury of thinking about it at all. A blood cancer makes you an emotional fire-fighting professional, putting out fires for not only your sick loved one, but all those surrounding him as well.

With a serious cancer diagnosis, you learn to live in the here and now. You relish the present. You learn to squeeze the happiness out of the moment. Happiness seems to be amplified because you recognize how fleeting it can be, and you fiercely guard against threats to those happy moments. You learn to hold your breath when a doctor enters the room; because you worry about the news he will deliver.

David felt comfortable at Geisinger. He liked his care team. They were a group of dedicated and friendly oncology physicians and clinicians who responded quickly to David's ever-changing leukemia related challenges. He said he actually didn't mind getting chemo because the nurses made it fun. We were immediately buoyed when he entered remission with his first round of chemo.

In November 2002, David and I were at a scheduled clinic chemo appointment. We were feeling more optimistic than we had been in weeks. We had developed a rhythm and were finally able to take some deeper breaths. We were neither totally relaxed nor hyper vigilant. We'd adopted a this-sucks-but-we-can-handle-it attitude. We even made a couple of "kick cancer's butt" jokes.

At this scheduled appointment, we learned that our remission joy was short-lived; the disease had returned with a vengeance in the middle of his treatment. David's falling out of remission early in treatment indicated that the disease was really aggressive, and our options were limited. That is when the physicians told us that David's only chance of living, our only chance of survival, would be a bone marrow transplant.

Dr. Ted LeChae, David's oncologist, and Sue Parnell, his nurse navigator, entered the room holding some paperwork and brochures.

"Hello, Dr. LeChae, Susan," my husband greeted them—so cordial, I thought.

"Hello, David, Mary."

"So, what do you have for me?" said David, nodding toward the papers.

"Well, I have your labs and some additional information."

"Okay, on what?" The hospital had to get tired of our million questions—all we did was ask questions.

"David, I understand that John James, your physician assistant, told you the results of your latest bone marrow biopsy. We found cells in your marrow—this is an indication that you are no longer in remission. I am here to confirm that and talk about our next steps for this unfortunate position we find ourselves in."

"*Oh, okay,*" I said to myself, holding my breath and squeezing David's hand. I noticed my heart starting to beat faster.

Dr. LeChae continued, "I am afraid that with you coming out of remission so early in your treatment, we have to re-evaluate what we are doing and look for a more aggressive method of treatment. I have consulted with the team here and I have put your case out for consultation with colleagues around the country. I am waiting for their thoughts."

"Damn it, damn it, damn it, damn it. Just when things are looking up . . ." Aloud, I asked, "So what do you mean by more aggressive treatment?"

"Well, since David is out of remission, he no longer qualifies for the study and he will be off the protocol," Dr. LeChae responded.

"Does that mean you can't treat my husband?" I asked, wondering, *"What is this man talking about?"*

"No, it just means that he won't be administered those drugs in that sequence on the study," was Dr. LeChae's answer.

"What? Please excuse me if I appear dense. I think it is imperative that I understand what you are saying. Are you saying that because he is no longer in remission, you are essentially stopping treatment? Is that what I am hearing?" I asked.

"Absolutely not; we are just not following the protocol. David will not be in the study. But we will still treat him. Of course," Dr. LeChae said.

"Well, why didn't you say that first? And who the hell cares about your damn study? I care about David," I thought to myself, but chose to say instead, "Oh good. I was hoping that I was misunderstanding. So, you will treat him with different drugs?"

"Yes, we are looking at different therapies. The gold standard, if you will, however, for these types of situations, appears to remain an Allogeneic stem cell transplant bone marrow transplant."

"Oh, my God, did he just say what I thought he said?" David shot me a quick look. *"Did you hear what I just heard?"* he was projecting onto me. Our new feelings of hope were so fleeting. Yes, we both heard it—Dr. LeChae had said, "bone marrow transplant." Up until then, the doctors had discussed bone marrow transplant as a last-step measure. We never thought we would be facing this option a mere two months after his diagnosis. The doctor and his nurse were saying a few more things and gave us David's labs, as if that mattered right then.

"More time; we need more time," I begged God. Once again, I had that feeling of the wind being knocked out of me. I felt like we were drowning and we couldn't get up for air. Blind-sided yet again by a disease that could throw so many curves at us.

Two months earlier discussing a bone marrow transplant seemed so distant, but now it was right in front of us. The talk of finding a donor, administering lethal doses of chemotherapy and radiation, and being rescued by the donor marrow, made the room spin. But the only spin that I could afford at that moment was to turn this into some kind of better news for David. I had to flip it and look for any hint of good news to hang onto.

I saw Dr. LeChae's mouth moving and I looked back at David. He looked stunned. *"I have to end this now,"* I thought.

"Dr. LeChae, Susan, thank you for your time. And for this information. I think we have entered overload and we need to process what you just said. I'll let you know when we have questions, by fax or I'll call. Thank you, thank you very much."

Dr. LeChae and Sue left the room.

"That's bad news," David said as he lay back on the exam table trying hard to fight back the tears.

"It was not what I expected, either," I told him. *"Gotta bounce back up, find a positive spin, protect David's thoughts, find the good...find the good...."* I told myself.

"Okay, transplant—we didn't want to do it. But the good news is that we have an option in bone marrow. I feel lucky about that. All of your cancerous marrow will be eradicated and we will start fresh. I think that sounds good. And did you hear Sue? Because of your ethnic background, the Bone Marrow Registry will most likely find a match. I think those are two things working in our favor."

David did not answer. I saw something in his eyes that I had never seen before—resignation. The previous week, he had pointed to an article in the newspaper about a man who went to Philadelphia for a bone marrow transplant and died during the process. My husband was without words. I hugged him.

"You are the love of my life," I told him. "I won't let anything happen to you in transplant. I promise."

"I love you, Mary."

"We'll get through this, David. I know we will." I was trying to shoo away the resignation. "Let's see what's in this stuff that Dr. LeChae gave us." It was time we got to work.

One of the papers Dr. LeChae provided was a list of hospitals that performed these specialized and delicate procedures, and it was our responsibility to elect one of those hospitals. Many were within a 300-mile radius.

"So, honey, it looks like we need to make a few road trips. Let's look at this list and try and determine our next steps." I spent the next few hours and days reviewing Dr. LeChae's list and comparing those hospitals with other national institutions that had high success rates with Allogeneic Bone Marrow Transplants. We toured several, but there were a few standouts.

After interviewing several hospitals and researching as much as I could about David's type of transplant, we chose the Johns Hopkins Hospital in Baltimore, Maryland. The bone marrow transplant (BMT) program at Johns Hopkins is internationally known and it was a Johns Hopkins researcher, George Santos, who, more than forty years before, had established regimens that would lead to bone marrow transplantation—the process of taking marrow from a healthy donor and injecting it into a patient. Since that time, BMT has become an accepted curative therapy for a broad range of diseases, including malignant diseases involving the bone marrow such as leukemias and lymphomas. More than 5,000 bone marrow transplants have been performed at Johns Hopkins, and it does around 300 transplants each year. For David's type of aggressive Acute Leukemia, we needed an experienced BMT center. After meeting and interviewing the team at Johns Hopkins, we knew there was no other place for us.

During the previous few months, our community had come together in a way only a small town could. Many people felt connected to us through friendship, our places of work, or the boys. We'd been the recipient of gifts of blessed generosity and support. The community wanted to help. They offered gifts of child care, transportation, and financial aid, but I wanted something special from our community. I wanted as many prayers as we could get. When people asked what they could do for us, I would ask them to pray for my husband. I needed David to be well. I knew that the medical staff would do everything in their power, I knew that my boys would be at home safe with Heidi and my parents, but I knew David needed prayers. Strength to fight, strength to overcome, and strength to be healthy.

I wanted to keep our community of supporters posted on the newest developments, so rather than calling everyone to inform them of the news, I chose to send an email.

From: Mary Tiffin
Sent: Wednesday, November 27, 2002 10:21 AM
To: BVT Friends
Subject: David's Transplant Schedule

Hi all,

I just got off the phone with Johns Hopkins, and I wanted to let you know what our schedule will be for David's bone marrow transplant.

Monday and Tuesday, 12/2 & 12/3: Pre-transplant testing.

Wednesday, 12/11: Consent form signing.

Thursday, 12/12: Admission.

Friday, 12/20: Transplant.

David will be inpatient for a month. Then he will be receiving daily therapy and treatment as an outpatient for four additional months at Hopkins.

I ask that you please pray for David's full recovery and that God will allow us to enjoy our wonderful lives with our children.

Have a wonderful Thanksgiving. I am truly thankful for all of you.

Mary

To which we got some thoughtful responses:

From: Ken Sanger
Sent: Wednesday, November 27, 2002 10:33 AM
To: Mary M. Tiffin
Subject: Re: David's Transplant Schedule

Mary,

Our family will be thinking of you through this trying period. If you need help driving to the hospital, or if we can take care of the boys, we will be happy to help as much as we can. Please call and let me know.

Ken

From: Kim Edwards
Sent: Wednesday, November 27, 2002 10:44 AM
To: Mary M. Tiffin
Subject: Re: David's Transplant Schedule

Stay strong, Mary!!! Please contact me if I can do anything for you!!

God bless all of you! Our prayers are with you.

Love,

Kim

From: Ernie Klemper
Sent: Wednesday, November 27, 2002 11:12 AM
To: Mary M. Tiffin
Subject: Re: David's Transplant Schedule

Hi, Mary.

Thanks for sharing this information. I think of and pray for David, you, and your family every day. I have faith that everything will work out for you. I know that this must be so hard, but I hope you will find a little comfort knowing that we are all concerned and keep you in our thoughts and prayers constantly. I've been keeping in touch with your office rather than bothering you, but if you ever want to talk or have anything I can help with, please just say the word. Your family is a very special one, and I hope that the transplant has positive results and everything starts to turn around for David and your family.

Your good friend,

Ernie

P.S. toodlelooooo!

From: Saddles40
Sent: Wednesday, November 27, 2002 1:54 PM
To: Mary M. Tiffin
Subject: Re: David's Transplant Schedule

Hi, Mary.

Peter here.

This is good news. It is an answer to all of our prayers. I often think about you and David, and it is always happy thoughts. David is a fine man, friend. He also has a strength of character that will carry him through these treatments. Driving home last night, I thought about the time we were coming to your mother's house for Thanksgiving and turned around because it was snowing so hard. It was snowing like hell.

Take care and give kisses to all those stinky heads. Your cousin,

PJ

From: Saddles40
Sent: Wednesday, November 27, 2002 1:54 PM
To: Mary M. Tiffin
Subject: Re: David's Transplant Schedule

Dear Mary,

I want you to know that you, David, and your beautiful sons have been and will remain in our prayers. Not a morning or evening goes by without all of us praying for you. I am forever thinking of you. Nicholas' speech therapist came over the other day to visit (he is done with speech) to give us the best news. One is that her husband, who had a bone marrow transplant a little less than a year ago, is almost fully recovered. He had many rough times and discouraging news, but he is now fantastic. The other news is that they are expecting twins in May. The news that she is pregnant made Ed improve almost miraculously. Karen is also praying for David.

I tried to call you a couple of times but never got you. I am sorry for not trying again, but that does not mean I am not thinking of you. I love you guys and I will light a candle for you at Sunday's mass.

Give kisses to all.

Happy Thanksgiving,

Pattie, Peter, Matthew, Kristiana and Nicholas

From: Karen and Tom
Sent: Wednesday, November 27, 2002 10:12 PM
To: Mary M. Tiffin
Subject: Re: David's Transplant Schedule

Hi, Mary!

Happy Thanksgiving to you and your family!

I was happy to hear things are moving along for David's transplant and that his sister was a suitable match after all. I think of you all the time, and we all pray for David all the time. We just moved Brian to the guest room, which is more spacious for him, and in the process of switching his things over, he discovered big wooden rosaries that he never knew he had. Before naps, he always asks if we can pray for Mr. Tiffin! Your husband has quite a following!

Well, I will sign off now. I hope you all have a Happy Thanksgiving and that God answers all our prayers.

Love,

Karen

From: Maynard, Ed
Sent: Sunday, December 1, 2002 9:21 PM
To: Mary M. Tiffin
Subject: Re: David's Transplant Schedule

Mary,

On behalf of myself, Connie, Isabella, my parents Tom and Ellen, we are all praying in unison for David. My very best wishes. Let me know anything I can do to help.

God be with you.

Ed

In the weeks before we took off for Hopkins, I had started working on a different project. I knew the odds were stacked up against us. My husband was very ill. I knew that David's disease would require a miracle. I had faith in our physicians at Hopkins. I was also confident that David and I would remain positive throughout this entire experience and would do whatever it took to achieve wellness and to maintain our family.

And I had absolute faith that "with God, all things were possible." As far as I knew, God was still in the business of miracles. Gathering my closest family and friends, I asked them to ask all of *their* friends to pray regularly and often for David in their places of worship. What started out as three local churches with the first request quickly spread to fifteen churches throughout the Susquehanna Valley. Yes, we needed those prayers to join our medical care.

Trying to be Thankful

We were all sitting at the table. It was Thanksgiving. My mom; my dad; my brother, Billy; my sister Laura; her husband, Joel; their kids; David; me; and our babies. We had decided to have Thanksgiving at home, so David would not have to leave the house. We had just finished eating and were resting.

"Dinner was delicious, honey," my dad said.

"Yes, everything was wonderful," my mother echoed.

"I really like the sweet potato fluff," Laura chimed.

"My favorite was the stuffing," Christopher added.

Everyone was trying so hard to be happy and grateful, but David's diagnosis hung over us like a dark and heavy cloud. His Leukemia and the upcoming transplant was scaring all of us. We were quiet. And David, normally a great host, was noticeably quiet.

Uncomfortable with the silence, my mother asked, "Does anyone want dessert?"

"No, Mom, I think I'll wait. I'm pretty full," my brother-in-law, Joel, responded.

"I can't," my sister Laura said.

"Is there any ice cream?" Laura and Joel's daughter, Olivia, asked.

I was thinking about all that we had to do before we went to Johns Hopkins, and then it hit me—Christmas card pictures! We wouldn't be here for Christmas, but I still wanted to send our Christmas cards.

"Our Christmas cards—we haven't taken our pictures."

David looked at me as if to say, "You're kidding, right?"

"I want to send out cards this year, and, instead of it just being the boys, I want our family of five to be in the picture. Billy, can you take the picture?" My brother was the family photographer.

"Sure," Billy said.

David said, "Wait, honey, don't you have enough to do without worrying about Christmas cards? I'm sure no one expects us to send cards this year."

"I'd like to send a card of our family. I want to remind people to pray for us," I said.

"Okay," David said.

Getting up from the table, I asked Billy and Joel, "Can you help me move the furniture in the living room?"

"Break's over. Let's get to work," Joel said.

"Sure," Billy said, getting up and heading to the spot in front of the fireplace where we take pictures every year.

"Laura and Liv, can you find something cute to put on the boys? David, you get dressed, and I'll find the camera."

Within minutes, Laura had the boys dressed, the chairs were positioned, the camera was ready, everyone was ready for our pictures, when David came down the stairs.

"Got a little problem," he said.

We all froze. All eyes were on David. What was he going to say?

"What is it, David?" I asked.

He lifted his shirt and pointed to his unbuttoned dress slacks. "Seems as if I may have gained a coupla' pounds." He laughed. "There is no way I can button them!" He chuckled.

"Okay, you're a fatty!!" We were all laughing—David, Dad, Mom, Laura, Joel, Billy, me, and the kids. It felt good. The humor that had always been such a big part of our relationship had been conspicuously missing these past couple of months, so it felt good to laugh again.

"Ah, honey, don't worry. Sit in that chair. Do what we women do—we'll cover you with children. No one will notice your pants are too tight."

"Okay, Tiffins, say 'cheese,'" Billy said. Christmas 2002 was recorded. It became one of our first family pictures of the five of us.

This is Really Happening…

"You're so much neater than me," I commented on how Linda was carefully folding all of the clothes I had thrown in a pile to pack for our trip. "I would have just thrown them into the suitcases and dealt with it when I got there," I added.

"This will be easier on you when you unpack. You won't need to pull out an iron in addition to everything else you will be managing." Linda Brown was one of my dearest friends. We'd met through business and had been friends, at this point, for more than twelve years. Linda was the kind of friend you could always count on. She was thoughtful, sweet, even-tempered, and loyal. Her calm nature always created a peaceful environment. She was also very organized. And on this day, I needed all of Linda's skills to get ready for the trip to Baltimore. Linda was always ready to lend a helping hand, and she had come over to help me pack.

"Okay, let's see. It looks like you have all of the household supplies." Linda checked the list. "Laundry detergent, dishwashing soap, Lysol spray and wipes, toilet paper, paper towels, and napkins… are we missing anything?"

"Windex! Here's the Windex!" I said, passing her the bottle.

"Oh, you and your Windex," Linda smiled.

I had a thing for Windex—it cleaned everything. Maybe it was the Greek in me, but I used Windex on everything: glass, wood, doors, countertops, kids. Didn't matter the surface, everything shined with Windex. It was my "go to" cleaner.

"Okay, now do we have everything?" Linda asked.

"I don't think so." Several churches had put together "moving boxes"—household items for David and me, as we were moving into an apartment for the duration of David's care.

"We can't forget this"—pointing to two large boxes of with tissues, stationery, small pillows, books, throw blankets, cookies, and spaghetti sauce.

"That was so kind. Did you say that was Heidi's church?" Linda asked, about the box of thoughtful items.

"Yes. It was so kind. We were so touched," I said.

"Well then, let's move this to the door, so that we can have everything in one place," Linda said as she lifted the box and brought it to the front door.

"And this one." I pushed a box toward the front door.

"Okay, what's that?" Linda asked.

"It's a box of our complementary and alternative healing tools. There are funny movies for laughter therapy, David's favorite music, pictures of the boys, and relaxation music. I read about the different aids that other patients bring to transplant."

"Okay, now personal items: deodorant, shampoo, conditioner, skin care, and your stuff. Right, Mary?" Linda asked.

"Right. And we can't forget this box of food," I said, pointing to the box of microwave popcorn, crackers, cereal, chips, and pretzels.

Because David had heard that patients often lose weight in transplant, he was working hard at putting weight on. He'd been enjoying his snacks, so to forget this box would be a big no-no.

"Oh no, you can't forget that!" Linda giggled, aware of David's new love of snack food. Sizing up the pile for Baltimore, Linda said, "Well, this should keep you for a while. Maybe not the entire four months, but it will get you over the initial period, and then we can replenish what you need."

"Linda, I really do appreciate you helping me with this," I said.

"Oh, honey, I'm here for you. Both Terry and I are. We really don't want you both to have to worry about anything when you are down there. And if there is anything that you need, I want you to call us right away, okay?"

"Okay."

"Baltimore's not that far away," she added.

We sat down and took a break.

"Okay, so that article that *The Daily Item* ran was great. And a lot of people have been asking me about you and David. You're both here now. Have you given any thought as to how you will be able to continue to communicate with this support group that has developed? This community loves you both and they want to know."

"And I need them to keep praying for David." Taking a minute to think, I said, "Maybe I'll just continue with those emails that I started? You know, sometimes I just don't feel like talking about it. It's better for me to write, anyway. Maybe the people that I send emails to can share the emails with other people. Do you think that will work?" I asked Linda.

"Kind of like David and Mary point people. I think that sounds like a great idea."

"So I'll start with the emails that I have."

Then back to our packing.

"Except for the frozen meals your mom prepared, I think you are all packed and ready to go," Linda said, appraising our work.

Looking at out bags and the boxes, the knot in the pit of my stomach came back. *"This is really happening,"* I thought. *"This is really happening."*

This is Really Happening...

A Wish for Love and Prayers

With the family photo we'd taken at Thanksgiving, I had extra Christmas photo cards printed to send to churches as a reminder to pray for David. I thought it would help connect the prayers to a person. I was organizing a lot of our prayer connections in the days immediately prior to transplant.

David had prepared himself, as well. A friend and leukemia survivor, Dave Burnside, spent time with David to help him prepare for the transplant. David had bulked up, increasing his weight from 210 to 240 pounds.

"I'm enjoying eating, and they say you lose it in transplant. Gotta be ready," he'd say.

We were packed. We were as ready as we could be. I tried so hard to ignore the knot in the pit of my stomach, thinking David's had to be bigger. The night before our trip, I sent an email to my co-workers who had been so supportive of us since David became ill.

From: Mary Tiffin
Sent: Tuesday, December 10, 2002 11:54 PM
To: BVT Distribution List
Subject: Thank you

To all of our friends at BVT,

I wanted to take a few moments before David and I leave for Baltimore to let you know how I feel. You all have been so wonderful and kind in your actions and prayers. We have been so touched by you all. Thank you.

I feel so incredibly lucky to be working with such a great group of kind, caring, and compassionate people. Your friendship, alone, has been a gift.

Have a beautiful Christmas and a healthy New Year.

Mary

From: Hanna Bulger
Sent: Wednesday, December 11, 2002 8:51 AM
To: Mary M. Tiffin
Subject: Re: Thank you

Best of luck to all of you as well! I hope you have a safe trip and successful results. Thank you for the lovely Christmas photo card, and look at you all in the newspaper this morning ☺. What a beautiful family portrait!

Merry, merry.

We'll all be thinking of you!

Hanna J

From: Bernie Miller
Sent: Wednesday, December 11, 2002 10:50 AM
To: Mary M. Tiffin
Subject: Thinking of you

Dear Tiffins,

I have been thinking about you guys off and on all day. I hope things are going well for you. You are in my prayers and highest thoughts. We found a wonderful surprise in the morning edition of *The Daily Item*. It was the *most wonderful* photograph and story about your family! We are proud to call you our friends, and we know that this story will have a happy ending.

Blessings and love to all,

Debbie and Bill

PART III

To Baltimore for a Cure

David and I packed our car and left our little boys in the care of our nanny, Heidi, and my parents, and headed to Johns Hopkins on December 11. We left in the middle of the worst ice storm that Baltimore had seen in years. The normally two-hour trip took more than four hours. In a way, the unrelenting pelting of the ice provided a chorus from the clouds as we navigated our way through the treacherous trip. Little did we know how portentous this drive would be for the rest of our journey.

"It's nice! And look, we have a great view," I exclaimed as I opened the door to our fifteenth-floor apartment on Charles Street. There were windows around the entire apartment, and we had a great view of the north and east side of the city.

"Oh, look, David, there's the Basilica"—noting the Baltimore Basilica a few blocks over on Cathedral Street. "It's beautiful. I think that is a good sign that we can see it from our apartment, don't you?"

"Sure, honey." David was less enthusiastic.

"And look, there is the hospital. Can you see Johns Hopkins?"—pointing to the east. "According to the social worker at the hospital, it is less than five miles. So we can be there in a flash." I was looking from window to window. "I like our apartment. Don't you?" Our new home away from home would be a two-bedroom, two-bathroom, furnished apartment on the fifteenth floor of the Charles Towers building.

"It's nice. It's comfortable," he said, testing the couch for the most comfortable spot.

"Honey, you take it easy. I'll start to make ourselves at home, and I'll put some of this stuff away."

"That sounds good. I'll just check this out." David was examining the TV remote, scrolling through the channels. "TV's not bad." The pace of our lives never allowed much tube time, but with David's illness, he could watch Fox News and ESPN whenever he wanted.

I heard David from what would be our new bedroom: "And they have a TV in this bedroom and the guest room as well. So we won't fight over what to watch."

After I unpacked and put away the food that was in the boxes, I sat down beside David.

"The rest can wait till later," I said, figuring I'd have a lot of time to get organized.

"Good. I'm glad when you sit down; you should try it more often." Over the years, David had complained that I was always doing something. He said I never sat down. So I sat with my husband.

"Listen, since the weather has improved, why don't we go to the Inner Harbor and have a nice dinner before I am stuck with hospital food for who knows how long?" David suggested.

"Oh, that is a great idea! Like a date! Honey, we could have a date!" I jumped up, never feeling too comfortable with the concept of relaxing. And now, with my general nervousness about the next few days, there was no way I could remain seated for too long.

"I'll be ready in five minutes," I added, so happy that David felt strong enough and safe enough to go out.

We headed a few blocks to the Inner Harbor, which was lifeless. The bad weather must have kept everyone away. Many of the restaurants were closed for the evening due to the storm. Not to be deterred in our quest for a nice night, we searched for a decent place to dine. The only place open was a steak house. A good number of other stranded and hungry diners had found the place as well, and there were about eight to ten people at the bar.

"Look, David, we stumbled onto a happening spot."

"The only spot," David added.

After we had been seated, our waiter came to the table. "You two are hearty; you braved this weather. This must be some special night? It must be big for you two to come out tonight."

David just looked at me. "Yes, to both—we are hearty and, yeah, brave, too. And it is a very special night—we have a date."

I smiled at my favorite date.

We ordered our meals and our waiter grabbed the menus and left.

"Did that man say 'brave and hearty,' David? If only he knew."

"He wouldn't want to know. And I know what you're going to say—that was another sign. No more talk of signs, please."

I'd been pointing out all of the BELIEVE signs all over town.

"David, I don't think it is a coincidence that Baltimore has this campaign this winter. I feel good about it. I think this is a reminder that we have chosen the right hospital and that we just have to have faith that things are going to work out okay. There are too many coincidences for this not to be true. Is any of this making you feel any better, or…?"

While I was growing my list of visual "signs," my husband was getting more and more unnerved that we were here, that we were going to Johns Hopkins, and that he was going to have a transplant.

"I'll feel better in June when this is all over. That is when I'll feel calmer," David answered.

"We have a busy day tomorrow," I said.

"Yes, we will. I want to stop talking about this," my husband said.

"Let's just enjoy our dinner, then," I said.

"Everything is going to be okay. I feel it, I know it, David," I said, as I grabbed my husband's hand and squeezed it. "I just know it."

"I hope so," David said.

To Baltimore for a Cure

Optimism, Hope and Electronic Solitaire

Since its opening in 1973, the Sidney Kimmel Cancer Center has led the world in deciphering the mechanisms of cancer and developing new ways to treat it. The strength of its research and treatment programs was recognized early on by the National Cancer Institute, and it became one of the first to earn comprehensive cancer center status and recognition as a "Center of Excellence." Patients who visit the Kimmel Cancer Center have access to some of the most innovative and advanced therapies in the world. Because Kimmel Cancer Center research scientists and clinicians work closely together, new drugs and treatments developed in the laboratory are quickly transferred to the clinical setting, offering patients constantly improved therapeutic options.

The Harry and Jeanette Weinberg Building was built in 1999 and was the cancer care hospital for the Kimmel Center. It was spacious and beautiful, and it sparkled now. The fifth floor of the Weinberg Building would be David's new home until we were free of this disease and discharged.

We settled into Hopkins. I filled the room with pictures of the boys and reminders of home. We also brought David's snack collection, a few magazines, a couple of books, CDs, a couple of funny movies, and some games for the long days we were anticipating. The first few days of testing went smoothly, and that went a long way to calm David's nerves.

"Does it seem any different?" I asked of David's new chemo regime.

"No, not really. But the radiation was a little strange. The doctors said that I'm certain to lose my hair this round." David was unusual in that he still had hair from his Geisinger chemo days.

"Well, I'll take bald as a great thing. Besides, I'm sure you'll look just as handsome bald," I assured my husband.

This was a time for optimism and hope. I was praying hard that David would have both, or at least one. While David was in the hospital, I would spend the days and evenings with him, then return to our apartment to sleep, as the hospital did not allow family members to "room in" (sleep overnight) on the chair in the patient's room.

"What've you got there?"

I was sitting in the chair beside his bed, fiddling with a small box and bubble wrap. The bubble wrap and clear tape covering the item securely made it nearly impossible to open without scissors. I was fighting with the package when I went into my handbag and looked for the sharpest object—a pen. I started stabbing the bubble wrap with the pen.

"Honey, you all right?" David asked cautiously, concerned that maybe I'd finally gone over the edge.

"Ah-ha!" I said, creating a hole

"This...," I said, working to create a larger hole with the pen. *Where did they think they were sending this thing? To the moon?* "This...," I said, squeezing it free of the bubble wrap and holding it up for David to see. "This, honey, is your electronic Solitaire game. It was in one of those boxes from that sweet Methodist Church group in Richfield."

I was still shaking the box with my left hand and dropping the batteries onto my lap. "It, of course, is for you, but would you mind if I played it?"

"If I said I did mind, would you hurt me with that pen?" David teased.

"DAA-vid, of course not, honey; I'd look for something sharper," I laughed.

No matter the circumstances, David and I were always trying to find humor. Laughter was a frequent and welcome guest at our house. And although we were dealing with this most unwelcome intruder, leukemia, we still looked for every opportunity to sprinkle our days with giggles and guffaws.

"No, go ahead. I can't imagine you watching this game with me." David knew he would have to tie me to a chair to get me to watch a sporting event.

"Thanks, honey. Now I will just pop these batteries in right here... and voila!" The Solitaire game played an electronic tune and was ready to go.

Ring...

Ring....

The phone rang constantly. The outpouring of love and concern was not lost on David. He was very appreciative of the calls to wish him luck.

"Hello?" David said. "Well, hello, Mother."

"My husband sounds great, almost normal," I thought. *"Oh, please, dear God, please let him stay that way."*

"No, things are good. I'm watching the game and it looks like my wife is going to play Solitaire. …My chemo is done. … Yes, the radiation, too. It wasn't too bad. It looks like we are on for the twentieth. The transplant is the twentieth. … Yes, Missa called. They should be here soon. … Oh, okay. I will. Bye, Mom. I love you and I'll see you on the twentieth. … Hi, Dad. We are okay. The food is still bad, but I have been sending Mary to Subway to get me BLT subs, minus the lettuce and tomatoes…Yeah, I know," David laughed.

"Yes, I am glad we chose it, too. It's a really nice hospital and the room is beautiful. We have a nice view of the parking deck. Mary and I figured that when the boys come down, we can visit with them on the parking deck, since it's so close and kids aren't allowed on the floor. … Yeah, we got it worked out. … Okay, Dad, I'll see you and Mom on the twentieth." And David put the phone down.

"I like that idea of seeing the boys on the parking deck. That will be great," David said, clearly missing our sons already.

"Maybe we can do it for New Year's. Yeah, that would be great," I said.

"Yes, it would."

"You know, it really will be a beautiful Christmas gift. The best Christmas gift ever—for you to be healed. This is the Season of Miracles."

Bleep… bleep… another digital tune… *whirr…* The shuffling of the deck, and my first hand of Solitaire was dealt.

"Ooh, I got it working. I think I am going to like this little game." And we both laughed.

The Day Before…

"So, how's everyone doing at home?" David asked when I came in the morning before transplant day.

"The boys are doing great with Heidi. And Heidi seems to be okay with Mom and Dad. And that says a lot." My parents decided to move into our house while we were gone, so there would be the least interruption in the boys' routines. Our children were covered in love.

"One of our neighbors has volunteered to plow our driveway all winter, so the home front is taken care of. And I've been keeping everyone posted by emails. We've had a lot of messages at the apartment, but by the time I get home, it's too late to call, so I have been sending out emails so everyone knows what's happening."

I showed him the email Denise had sent the night before:

From: ttdmkel@aol.com
Sent: Thursday, December 19, 2002 8:45 PM
To: Mary M. Tiffin
Subject: Hi there

Hello, Mrs. Tiffin.

I didn't know if you're checking messages. Wanted to let you know I'm praying, praying, praying for David. How're the new digs? Do you need anything? Loved the article about David. Did you see it? It was beautiful. I'll send it to you if you'd like. The only thing is, you've lost a lot of weight. Are you eating? (I know I sound like a Jewish mother. We have those roots, you know.) Anyway, hope all is going as planned. Thinking of you. Let me know if I can help out in any way.

Love & xoxo,

Denise

The Day Before…

A BLT, Minus the L and T... Extra B

"Right now, I feel that things are pretty much under control or as much as they can be," I told my husband. "We just need you to hurry up and cruise through this and be better again."

"Well, I think I am going to do some laps," David said, grabbing his IV pole and moving toward the edge of the bed.

"Great. Let's go."

We walked twenty-five laps around the unit, the spinning wheels on David's pole creating a gentle whirling accompaniment to his exercise. He made it a goal to take at least twenty-five laps every day and to work out in the small gym on the floor. So far, he'd made it. When he settled back into bed, David said, "I want to be in as good of shape as possible for this transplant."

"You're in good shape. I never thought I'd say this, but thank God for all your years at UPS. All that exercise will pay off."

"Yeah, who knew that all of that time, work would come in handy?" David said as he settled back into bed.

"Hey Dave, how was your walk?" Susan, his nurse, asked.

"Good. I did twenty-five laps. Does that equal a mile?"

"I do believe that is right. Let me check it for sure, but yes, I'm pretty sure. But keep it up, Dave, you're doing really good work." Susan, tall, thin, and smart, was originally from Texas but was now a "traveler," which meant she took nursing positions at hospitals around the country. So while she was new to Hopkins, she was not new to bone marrow transplantation, having worked on similar units in other hospitals for the past ten years. Susan was a great information source in addition to being a cheerleader for her patients. We really liked her—she made us feel comfortable.

"But do you know what I would really like right now?" my husband asked, looking in my direction.

"*Oh, no, not again,*" I thought.

He read my mind and smiled.

"I could really go for a Subway sub with bacon, lettuce, and tomato, minus the L and T, extra B."

Looking to Susan for a little help, I said to him, "All that bacon and mayonnaise, that can't be good for you. Don't you think we should think about your cholesterol? David, I don't want us to survive transplant only to have you die of a heart attack." Again, I looked to Susan for backup, but she was not biting. "Besides, they must think I'm a nut ordering a six-inch BLT sub on whole wheat with no lettuce or tomato."

"Oh, I wouldn't worry about that. The Subway staff knows folks here have special diets, so don't let that be a concern. And I don't think y'all are the first BMT patients to frequent our Subway. And since bone marrow patients can't eat fresh fruits or veggies, I'd like to think that they have gotten requests like that before. And the wheat bread—good move, Dave," Susan winked as she was collecting his vitals.

David looked at me as if to say, "HA!"

I got up from my chair and put my game down. "Okay, I'll be back in a little while. I am going to stop and see Big Jesus first." Kissing my husband and nodding to the chair that held the Solitaire game, I said, "And don't play my hand. I've got a good game going on."

"Thank you, Honeybabyloversweetie."

I was happy to hear the return of my nickname. Finally, my husband seemed to be relaxing a little.

Susan, who was charting in the computer in David's room, piped in, "Hey, that's cute, y'all."

"That's my wife," David said.

"Bye," I said, leaving the room.

"Mary, one more thing…," David called after me.

"Yes?" I poked my head back in.

"Tell the Subway guy, this time, a little extra mayo. That last one was a little dry." David smiled.

"Ahhhh!"—and I headed out to see Big Jesus... and Subway.

Situated in the historic Billings Administration Building, Big Jesus, or "Christus Consolator"—a ten-and-a-half-foot-high marble statue of Jesus—rises beneath the building's historic dome. Presented to the hospital by donor William W. Spence, it is a replica of a piece done by the Danish sculptor Bertel Thorvaldsen. The Hopkins piece was made in 1896 by Professor Stein of the Danish Royal Academy of Arts. This iconic landmark is a stopping-off point for sightseers, a starting point for Christmas carolers, and a gathering place for employees meeting for lunch.

For more than a century, the statue has left an indelible first impression on both patients and staff. Long a source of solace and hope for patients and families, the Christ statue also has meaning for hundreds of employees. For many, it signifies healing, hope, and compassion; for others, it means faith and tradition, and even freedom. For me, it was a daily stop to greet the challenges of the day in prayer for my husband. Big Jesus was the great consoler for me.

Big Jesus was also close to the food. The Hopkins hospital cafeteria was in the Nelson Building. In addition to Cobblestone Café (its cafeteria), the building housed a coffee bar, a pizza place, a bagel shop, a sushi counter, and Subway. I ordered David's sub.

"So you want a six-inch Bacon sub with nothing but mayo on it." He'd just listened to my whole "six-inch BLT minus the... yadda, yadda, yadda..."

"With extra mayo," I added.

"With extra mayo," the sandwich artist repeated.

I grabbed the sub, and a cup of coffee for me, and headed back to the Weinberg Building.

"The Picasso at Subway knows your order now," I said as I was gowning to enter David's room.

"You know, I really think we need to put a limit on these things, David," I said as I passed him the artery-clogging sandwich.

"Hey, if they are good enough for Jared, they are good enough for me!" he teased, reminding me of the commercial. Then, "Thanks, honey. This is really good. I really like this hospital, but I am not too crazy about the food," David said, clearly enjoying his sandwich.

"You're drinking coffee this late at night?" he asked, examining the cup. "Won't that keep you up tonight?"

"Nah, I should be okay." I was so exhausted by the end of each day that I could drink six cups of espresso and still fall asleep.

"The game is over and I am starting to feel kind of tired. I'm just going to close my eyes for a few minutes, but I can still hear you if you want to talk," he said.

"No, honey, go ahead and rest. I have a really good hand going here," I said, smiling and gesturing with the game.

"My wife," David laughed.

Bleep, bleep, whirr, bleep went the game.

"I won again!"

"My wife," David said again with a smile.

Whirr... And I dealt another hand.

Get It Done and Move On...

David was often too nervous to talk about the transplant, so we didn't. When I sensed that he was nervous, I would go into my mind reading mode and talk enough for the both of us. My bringing it up to him only made him more nervous. It took some time, but I learned not to do that. So I was surprised when he said, "You know, I really wish I didn't have to do this."

"Oh, yes, I know, David. I really wish so, too."

"I don't know... I thought that if we had to go to transplant it would be after years of trying other things, not after a couple of months."

"I know, honey. I'm so scared, too. But I have been doing research on this, and Hopkins has been doing this for forty years, so it is not new to them."

"Still... "

"I am viewing this as something we need to do, get it done, and move on with our lives," I said.

"Okay," David said, but not convincingly.

"Besides, the goal is for us to retire in North Carolina and see our grandchildren. We have to do this to see our grandchildren." We'd spend the first nine years of our marriage focusing on our hopes and dreams. If we conceded on those dreams now, we would be conceding to Leukemia.

"You mean, so *I'll* meet our grandchildren."

David's words pierced my heart. I knew my husband. I knew how he thought. I couldn't afford for him to enter a self-defeating spiral of negative thoughts.

"David, do you remember when your friends busted on you for saying that 'we were pregnant'? You didn't say that *Mary* was pregnant, but that *we* were expecting. In the same way that *we* got married, *we* built a house, *we* had children, now *we* have stinkin' leukemia. Good or bad, we do it together. And I hate it, too, so much—more than anything. But together we are much stronger than any disease. David, with God's help we will survive this, you'll see. Please trust."

"I'm trying."

"Did I talk too much again, honey?" I asked my sweet, wonderful man.

"Yes. Honey, you really need to learn when to zip it," David said with a smile.

"Dang. Less is more, less is more," I quipped.

David reached out to me and gave me a big hug. It was the first time in a while. I realized that he was trying to shut everything down.

"We'll be okay, David."

"Shh."

"Did it again, didn't I?"

"Yup. Stop talking." Note to self: I REALLY gotta learn to shut up!

I leaned away from him and gave him the zip-my-lips motion.

"Good. Thank you." We chuckled.

I had known it deep in my bones—I knew that David's sister, Melissa (Missa), would be his donor. And even though Hopkins tested Patrick and Scott, his older and younger brothers, for compatibility, they found Missa to be the closest match. Melissa would save her brother.

In a bone marrow transplant, the patient is prepped for the transplant by the administration of lethal doses of chemotherapy and radiation. This is done to eradicate the diseased—in David's case, the leukemic marrow and prepare the body to receive new marrow. The goal is to eliminate all that is cancerous in the patient and then rescue him with donated healthy marrow. Often, this delicate procedure has patients teetering on the precipice of life until the donor's marrow rushes in to save the day and life of the patient. One of David's doctors described it as the miracle of medicine. He could not explain how or why the donor marrow knew what to do, but it would graft, grow, and proliferate to save the patient from a sure death.

We knew David's disease was so aggressive that the transplant would be very difficult.

Once I understood how this worked, I had been even more certain the marrow would come from my sister-in-law. Missa and David were close. Not in an outward, overly demonstrative, let-me-fall-all-over-you-and-get-in-your-business close, but in a quieter, more respectful way. Missa has always had that calm reserve you could always count on; she loved deeply, but without a lot of fanfare.

I also thought that Missa resembled David the most. So it made perfect sense to me. David spent his youth tormenting his younger and only sister, and she spent her life dealing with three brothers. This next day, Melissa would give life to her big brother, and David and I were going to owe her big time.

In a Word, Anticlimactic

The transplant was just minutes away. Our priest friend had been in to say a prayer, as had the hospital's Chaplain, Norm. We knew that everyone at home was praying for us. We felt ready. This was a momentous day for us. It would be the start of David's new life.

Goo Goo and Pa, Missa, and her husband, Bill, were with us, and we sat in the room while Kevin, David's nurse, hung Missa's marrow on David's pole.

Dr. Hanson, the attending Blood Marrow Transplant (BMT) physician, informed us that it would look very much like a transfusion. We all sat and watched as Melissa's marrow was infused into David.

After almost four hours, around five p.m., Kevin disconnected the empty bag and said, "There, you're done."

"That was it?" I asked

David looked at me; I looked at him. Expecting something, anything, more.

"That's it," Kevin confirmed.

"Well, that seemed easy," David said.

"Yes, it is generally very uneventful," Kevin added.

I looked at David and my in-laws. "I feel like we should do something. Set off fireworks, play some music. This is your new official birthday, honey."

"Okay," David said.

"Well, what do we do now?" my father-in-law asked Kevin.

"Now we just wait for David's counts to recover," Kevin answered.

Hopkins had educated us on the BMT process, but now that we were in transplant we were feeling lost. It was like those childbirth classes—you learn all those breathing techniques, but when push comes to shove, you wind up holding your breath. And just like at the birth of my sons, I was holding my breath now. How long would it take for his counts to rebound and for us both to breathe again?

I'm Sending Out Emails

"Excuse me, Mary."

I had been attending morning mass every day at the Basilica before going in to see David at eight-thirty. This morning, I stayed longer to finish my rosary. I was kneeling in a pew near the front when I heard a gentle but familiar voice beside me. I looked up to see the benevolent face of Father Rob, the priest who had just said the mass.

"Oh, hello, Father Rob."

Father Robert Jasome was young, around thirty-five, and was an administrator in the Diocese of Baltimore. When the Very Reverend Cardinal Keeler was out of town, Father Rob would celebrate the mass in the Basilica.

"Please excuse me for interrupting." Father Rob said gently, "but I was afraid that I would miss you. The Cardinal and I are wondering how David is doing."

I'd met both after mass almost two weeks ago. Both men projected a loving calmness and peace, no doubt a result of their call and ministry.

"Oh, no problem, Father, thank you. It's been well over a week since the transplant and we still don't have any counts, meaning no good cells. But we have been assured by the Hopkins staff that this is normal," I answered.

"Well, we will continue to keep him, you, and your sons in our prayers."

"Thank you, thank you very much. And, Father Rob, would you be so kind as to thank the Cardinal for mentioning David in mass on transplant day? I told David, and he found great comfort in that."

"Of course. Please let us know if we can help in any way," Father Rob added.

"Thank you again, Father," I said.

The priest genuflected and left the church.

Going to daily mass helped center me and prepare me for the day ahead. I'd already become a regular with this very small but devout and congenial group of faithful city Catholics. I was starting to feel a real sense of community in the Baltimore community, and I was so grateful for that.

Zipping my coat, I left the Basilica and drove to the hospital. I grabbed a cup of coffee at the juice bar on the first floor of Weinberg and was at David's bedside by eight forty-five, fifteen minutes later than my usual time.

As we were growing up, our faith was as much a part of our lives as our eye or hair color. Faith was just part of who I was. As a child, I was taught that if you pray hard and consistently, God will listen and respond. I had the movie *Cinderella* to thank for teaching me this lesson. Well, sort of. We were all gathered in the living room of our New York City apartment watching Leslie Ann Warren being swept off her feet by the guy from General Hospital, that is, Prince Charming. Like most little girls of that time, I loved the movie.

"Oh, isn't she beautiful!" my mother said about Cinderella as she danced with Prince Charming at the Ball.

"Yes, she is sooo pretty," we echoed.

"She's lovely," my mother said. My dad made a sound as a form of acknowledgment. "What makes her so pretty is her beautiful smile and her long neck," Mom assessed.

"That must be the definition of beautiful," I thought to myself.

So when I would pray for things of beauty—because I was a little kid and did that kind of thing—my prayers generally asked God if he could deliver on the long neck and beautiful smile. And for many years, post my awkward preteen years, if I were to receive a compliment, it would generally be about my smile. This left me with the understanding that "Ask and you shall receive" (Matthew 7:7) meant, succinctly put, "God delivers." (If I'd only known God was so efficient, I would have asked him for thin thighs without any exercise!)

With David in the hospital, because this prayer request was much more important than a young girl's prayers for physical attributes, I was praying much harder—but I still expected God to come through.

By the time I gowned, gloved, and masked up, there were already a number of clinicians with David in his room. He was sitting in the chair with his gown part way down; his entire torso was exposed and a small group of doctors were looking very closely at his chest.

Raising my eyebrows, I gave David the "What's up?" look.

"No, I don't think so," one said as they backed up.

"It's still early," another said.

"Mary, I'm glad you are here. Last night, David developed this rash on his chest"—pointing to a downward-facing triangle about fifteen inches wide at the top. "We're not sure what this is. It may be a reaction to his medicine or it might be the start of GVHD, or graft-versus-host disease. If David starts GVHD this early, it will put us in a difficult spot. But I am thinking that it probably isn't," said Dr. Ted Mattsui, the most senior member of the team in the room. "But for now, we are not going to do anything other than keep an eye on it."

"Anything else new?" I asked, feeling I should have been there earlier.

"Nothing other than this rash, and we are waiting for his counts," Dr. Mattsui confirmed.

"Okay. Thank you, Dr. Mattsui," I said as he and his team prepared to leave our room.

"I really like this guy," David said of our newest doctor, Dr. Mattsui. "He told me that they change rotations every two weeks and he will be our doc for the next two weeks. We won't see Dr. Hanson anymore; Dr. Mattsui is on, and I really like him."

"Yes, we have really great doctors here," said I, Doctor Mom, examining his chest.

"So what's it look like up close?" David asked, pointing to the red skin on his chest.

Turning his body toward the window to get sunlight and getting really close, I said, "Let me see. ... It looks like really bad acne, small pimples bunched together, that is what it looks like."

"Okay." David shrugged.

"You know what's funny—the rash is in the shape of Superman's chest crest. Now it's official—you are Superman David; you have the crest."

"I told Dr. Mattsui I was feeling kind of funny," David said.

"How do you mean, 'funny'?"

"Kind of hot, sick to my stomach, not really comfortable."

"It's day eight. I wonder if Missa's marrow is starting to kick in," I said.

"Dr. Mattsui wanted to see my chest. Maybe it is related."

"Okay, maybe it is"—not really sure what to say.

"Dr. Mattsui said he'll be checking in on me later on."

Ring... Ring...

"The phone's been ringing all morning. I don't feel like talking," David said, trying to get comfortable.

"That's okay, we don't have to answer it. People mostly want to know how you are doing, and I'm sending out emails. Ignore the phone."

"Honey, you were late today," David said. I glanced at my watch, I was 10 minutes late.

"Yes, David, I was…"

"Please don't be late."

"I'm sorry, but let me tell you about my visit after mass." And I shared my visit with Father Rob.

"We'll have to thank Sister Karen for making the introduction with Cardinal Keeler," David said. Sister Karen Wilson, was a dear friend to David and me. When she had heard about David's illness, she and her religious sisters at the Convent of Saints Cyril and Methodius in Danville started praying for us. She also spoke to her friend at the Archdiocese in Baltimore to let them know when we would be in town. We found relief in knowing that we had prayers around the clock with the Sisters.

"David, I feel that we're really blessed. We have a great supportive community at home; here, we have the best doctors in the world; and we also have wonderful support here. Don't you feel so lucky?"

"I don't know."

"Just think, if we would have had ALL twenty years ago, it would be a much different story for us, but now with all of the advancements in fighting cancer, I think we are lucky," I added, trying to get my husband to see a brighter side.

"No, it would be better if I had leukemia twenty years from now—THEN I would feel lucky."

I could have kicked myself in the butt. I'd been so bent on keeping David positive, I totally missed that he wasn't up for another pep talk. "Right."

"Listen, honey, I appreciate what you are doing. But I'd rather talk about anything other than transplant and leukemia," David said.

"I once again committed the marital sin of over-talking to this poor man. When the hell am I gonna get it?"

David had had enough of these talks; I would keep them to myself or share them with others. For now, David didn't need to be constantly reminded of what he was facing.

Kojak or Yul Brenner?

It was a sweet sight. A small black woman, no taller than my seated hulking husband, gowned, gloved, and masked. In her small hands, the cleaning lady was holding David's hands, and both had their heads bowed in prayer. Jeanita Carney was a member of Hopkins Environmental Services Department and had the responsibility of keeping David's room clean. Through her frequent presence in David's room, they struck up a friendship sharing stories of family and faith, and she was a great information resource on Baltimore, her hometown.

I stayed outside the room, careful to not interrupt this intimate moment between friends.

"Amen," I heard Jeanita say.

"Amen," David replied.

I watched as David opened his eyes, raised his head, and looked up.

Jeanita, a gentle soul, still holding his hands, said to him, "David, we've gotten to know each other these past few weeks and I feel you're a God-loving man. You're as good as there is. Our Lord hears the prayers of a righteous man. Now, don't you have no worries, trust in the Lord."

"Thank you, Jeanita."

"Well, look who's here," Jeanita said, spying me at the door.

"Hello, Jeanita. Hello, sweet husband, how's it going this morning?" I bent toward David and gave him a kiss. "You're looking handsome, I must say!"

"Not great," David replied, grabbing his pole and walking toward his bed.

"What do you mean by that?" I asked.

"I don't know. I feel kind of different, kind of shaky. I might want you to get me a sub in a little while. I threw up this morning, and I want to see how my stomach feels."

"Oh, that stinks."

"Yeah, it does. They gave me Zofran, but I still feel bad."

"Well, David, this chemo is a lot stronger, and maybe that radiation is wearing on you. But we know that it is working, because all your hair is gone. You've never lost all your hair before."

"What do you think of the look?" he asked, posing.

"You mean the Kojak or the Yul Brenner?"

"I was thinking someone more in this millennium, like Michael Jordan or Shaq."

Jeanita was smiling and laughing. "That's funny," she said. "Y'all are funny. It's cute."

"Honey, I think I am going to take a picture of you, you look so good. I want to show everyone how handsome you look. ... Hey, feel like a walk? Maybe that will make you feel better."

David grabbed his I.V. pole and we started his laps around the unit.

I started a pattern that whenever David was quiet or sleeping, I would prepare my emails to let everyone know what was going on and to encourage them to pray. I decided to include the picture in the day's email.

From: Mary Tiffin
Sent: Sunday, December 29, 2002 12:49 AM
To: David's List
Subject: Handsome Even BALD

Hi Guys,

At almost nine days post-transplant, David is now in considerable discomfort. Nothing out of the usual for transplant patients, but nothing that we had experienced thus far. The doctors have said that the first two months are the most critical. Guys, we really need those prayers.

Anyway, I came home this evening (Saturday) to pick up my parents and the boys. We will be leaving tomorrow to spend the week at the apartment in Baltimore.

The boys will be able to "visit" with David from the parking lot across from his room. It's a perfect view. David's parents got us walkie-talkies to talk to the boys (cell phones are not allowed on the floor).

Christopher, Michael, and the baby will see him several times each day. I'm sending this photo of David because he looks beautiful! (I say "beautiful," you say "handsome") Even when BALD!!! I hope that you can view it upright; I am having a "Mary" moment (lifetime, actually).

Please, oh please, pray harder. Thanks.

BELIEVE.

XOXOX,

Mary

From: Maynard, Ed
Sent: Monday, December 30, 2002 12:17 AM
To: Mary M. Tiffin
Subject: Re: Handsome Even BALD

Man, he really is handsome!

Praying as I type this email.

You are an excellent wife and mother. Truly remarkable.

Ed

From: Kim Edwards
Sent: Monday, December 30, 2002 5:33 PM
To: Mary M. Tiffin
Subject: Re: Handsome Even BALD

Hi, Mary.

I am surprised how good David looks. And I agree with you, he is as handsome and beautiful

as ever!!! How is his sister doing? Thanks for the photo.

We are sorry to hear how uncomfortable he is. I hope that won't last too long. I know how hard it is to be around someone who is in pain. You feel so helpless. Hang in there, Mary!! David will be back to himself in no time.

Our prayers are with all of you!!

Here's to a happy and healthy 2003!!!

Love,

Kim

From: Martin Smith
Sent: Monday, December 30, 2002 5:33 PM
To: Mary M. Tiffin
Subject: Hi

Hi Mary,

We were so happy to receive your email. We've all been thinking about you and praying for you and David each day.

Unfortunately, I missed your friend Mara's call. Marty took a message and said that David was having some kidney problems, a fever, and rash. He also said that you were asking for heavy-duty prayers. [Please know, Mary, that you are constantly surrounded by prayer.] Very heavy-duty!!!

I have also called Maureen, Susie Brickman, Monica Shatler, and the word has been passed to kick the prayers up a notch. Continue to believe, Mary. God is on your side.

Keeping you close in thought and prayer,

Annmarie and Family

P.S. You're right, David looks beautiful!!!!!

Praying Like Crazy

"Things are getting a little ... I don't know ... uncertain. We just don't know what to expect, Johannah."

I was sitting in the apartment and decided to call my cousin Johanne. I didn't get a chance to wish her and the family a happy 2003. I was nervous, so I called her.

"Well, what did the doctors say?" Johanne asked.

"That this is all part of the transplant. But I'm on edge here," I said.

"How is David?"

"Physically, really uncomfortable; mentally, I think it's starting to show. He's nervous—I can see it in his face, his eyes. We stopped joking and being ridiculous." Pause. "Nervous, nervous," I added.

"Did you tell him that?"

"Oh, God, no! I'm Little Mary Sunshine; only rainbows and happiness out of me. You know, typical over talking, babbling incoherently half the time, I'm so annoying. But we can't afford for him to get depressed or to think we can't beat this. I must keep those thoughts away from him. David needs to keep his head in the game, and I won't talk about any of this stuff in front of him. I'm emailing to update everyone. I'll only email."

"Oh, honey, I wish I was there to help you," Johanne said.

"Thanks, Johannah, but we're really counting on these docs and God right now. Please keep praying."

"We are, honey."

"Thanks, Johannah. I can't talk about it anymore or I'll have to run to the potty."

"Denise said you have gotten skinny, really skinny. Honey, are you eating?"

"You try eating at a time like this. Besides, the food is gross. Anyway, enough of me. ... I hope everyone at your house is okay."

"Yes, Mary Mary, everyone is fine. We love you and David and are praying like crazy."

"Thanks, Johannah. I gotta go. 'Night."

"'Night, my girl."

"Bye." And I hung up. *"What would I do if I did not have my family and my friends?"*

From: Mary Tiffin
Sent: Thursday, January 2, 2003 10:45 AM
To: David's List
Subject: David Update

Hi All and Happy New Year.

It's been a rough couple of days, so I am glad to say goodbye to 2002 and, "HELLO, 2003!"

I am going to ask you to keep those prayers coming.

So here is the update. David is experiencing a good deal of discomfort and pain. He has mouth sores (mucositis), spiky temperatures, and a really bad rash. (Laur, they say it's too early for HVG but have biopsied anyway.) These are all to be expected. The doctors are changing his meds to make him more comfortable as we wait for Melissa's marrow to take over and counts to rise.

Those problems don't bother me as much as the deal with his kidneys. They are acting kind of wacky, but a nephrologist is coming in to talk to him today in case we need dialysis. Please pray that his kidneys start working.

One nurse told me last night it's one step forward and two steps back. A very slow process. I don't see them discharging David to the apartment within the next three weeks. He definitely will not return to Winfield before June 1.

On the really *great* side, at the suggestion of David's brother, Scott, and very diligent sister-in-law, Brenda, the Hopkins IT Department has started something brand new (actually, David is the first and only). They have provided a laptop with an eye-cam and wireless connection to communicate with the Brenda-provided laptop and iCam. They are doing this so David can see and communicate with our boys in Pennsylvania. David will be able to help Chris with his homework when he feels better.

Wasn't that unbelievable from Scott, Brenda, and Hopkins?

I have been playing with it and it is very cool. The director of IT was so good to work with, and they want to do a paper about David's experience. Every day, we are more and more thrilled that we chose Hopkins. We really love and have great confidence in this place.

Okay, guys, that's the story. Please pray hard—pretty scary stuff happens on this floor. I so appreciate your prayers.

Take care, and a wonderful New Year to you all.

BELIEVE.

Mary

From: Linda Brown
Sent: Thursday, January 2, 2003 11:19 AM
To: Mary M. Tiffin
Subject: Re: David Update

So good to hear from you! We'll continue to keep David, you, and the children in our prayers. The laptop and the iCam are a really cool idea. It's amazing what can be accomplished when people put their heads together. We had a nice holiday season. The snow on Xmas day was beautiful. A pleasant reminder to slow down and be thankful for the many blessings in our lives (including snow plows). We spent New Year's Eve with my childhood friends, Patti and Christina (and their partners and extended family). What fun sharing stories and just laughing.

I think of you so often. I wish there was more we could do to help you, David, and the children. Your friendship means so much to me. Many, many years ago when my mother was sick, she had a circle of friends who would constantly remind her of how much they loved and cared about her (and us). It has always stuck with me. It meant so much to my mom to get a card, call, or visit from Kate (she brought ice cream and lasagna), Ann, Mary, my Aunt Marion and Aunt Ruth. My challenge is to be there for you, like they were there for us.

We'll continue to keep praying and sending happy thoughts!

I believe!

LB

From: Saddles40
Sent: Thursday, January 2, 2003 3:19 PM
To: Mary M. Tiffin
Subject: Re: David Update

Dearest Mary and David,

Every waking moment, you, David, and the boys are in our prayers. As we pray at night together, before we even begin, Nicholas says, "Don't forget David." How could we ever forget him? We love you guys dearly and we wish we could be closer to give more support. All we can do is pray, but that is a very powerful thing to do.

As I read your email, I felt as if I was reliving what Karen emailed to me about her husband, Ed. He had the sores in his mouth and the rash all over his body. All of his organs shut down and it took a little bit longer for his liver to get better. But he made it and is doing well. He just had his one-year anniversary from the bone marrow transplant. I know that seems very far away for you, but you have to hang in and know that there is a light at the end of the tunnel, and you are to stay focused on that light.

Can you give me a phone number and a good time to call you? Please tell David we love

him and we are praying for him. You will have a great 2003!

Hugs and kisses,

Patrice, Peter, and the Kiddies

From: Mary Tiffin
Sent: Thursday, January 2, 2003 5:08 PM
To: David's List
Subject: Please Say A Quick One

Hi, guys.

Got somewhat distressing and inconclusive news. Could you please say a quick prayer (or longer if you have the time) that David is not starting graft-versus-host disease already.

I'll keep you posted.

Thanks, guys.

Mary

From: Kim Edward
Sent: Thursday, January 2, 2003 5:49 PM
To: Mary M. Tiffin
Subject: Please Say A Quick One

Mary,

We will pray very hard!!!

We hope to hear good news soon!!!!

Love,

Kim

From: Dave Burnside
Sent: Friday, January 3, 2003 10:30 AM
To: Mary M. Tiffin
Subject: Re: David Update

Hi, Mary.

Thanks for the update.

Yes, really scary stuff happens on that floor, and right now it may be one step forward and two back. In the big picture, though, have faith that it will be two steps forward and one back. Just

imagine the beautiful June day when David comes home!

You are in all my prayers.

David Burnside

You'll Get Through This...

"Laur, I'm not taking calls in the room. I don't want to make David any more nervous than he already is by talking about this stuff in front of him. I got your voice messages, and thank you for being such a good friend."

"No problem, Mare. So what's going on?" Laurie Bergenstock and her husband, Bob, were a nurse and doctor couple who had been our very close friends for the previous eight years. Bob, a hematologist, and Laurie, a research nurse, were very helpful in the very early days of David's treatment. With him in transplant, their advice and friendship was even more crucial.

"David's kidneys are failing," I said.

"Oh, I am sorry about that….. What do David's docs say?" Laurie asked.

"That this sometimes happens."

"Okay, then I would go with it. Mary, you trust these guys, and until they are alarmed, just try to accept this as part of the process, as hard as it may be," Laurie encouraged.

"Yeah, I just need to work through it with you because I want to be calm when I talk to David about it. Both you and he know how I feel about this kidney stuff." (I was referring to my mother's illness.)

"But that was different. Your mother's kidney was necrotic," Laurie responded.

"You're right, but this may be worse. My mother had an immune system. David has nothing to back him up right now. Can you just talk to me about how it works? The docs explained it to us, but I was too distracted to get it all. Please explain it."

"It's kind of like recycling your blood, Mare. The machine takes it out, filters (or washes) out the impurities or waste, then puts it back in. David will need access, he will need a dialysis port," Laurie explained. She was great at this, making the confusing simple to understand.

"Okay, that doesn't sound so bad, but why the bad rap?"

"Well, it is something that needs to be repeated and scheduled, like every other day. If it's not repeated, the impurities build up and the patient dies. That's why."

"Oh. Thanks, Laur."

"Listen, Mary, you like these guys? You still feel good that you're at Hopkins?"

"Oh, yeah."

"Did the doctors say that David would be on dialysis for the rest of his life, or is this part of the transplant?"

"They didn't say...." I wondered.

"Well, that would be something to ask them, then. And honestly, Mare, it sounds like you don't have a choice. And if I know you two, you always do what you need to do—and it sounds like you need to do this. You'll get through this, Mary. You will," Laurie said.

"Thanks for the help, Laur. Love you and good night."

"'Night, Mare. We love you both."

"'Night, Laur. Thanks to Bob, too." As I said good night, the knot in the pit of my stomach returned and would remain.

Can Your Church Pray for David?

David being incoherent was unnerving. It wasn't so much the fact that he was confused, but the way he looked. For the first time in this illness, David looked truly scared. It was absolutely breaking my heart. His eyes were pleading with me to help him. Was his confusion scaring him, or was he worried that something more dire was happening? What was I saying—this was all dire.

"David, it's okay. Your kidneys are not working right; you are feeling confused because of your kidneys. This happened before when you were newly sick. They can fix this, don't worry, honey. They can fix it."

David would not respond.

"It's okay, David. I'm here, I won't let anything happen, I promise," I whispered to David.

I pulled my chair closer to his bed and watched him sleep, and prayed. Rick, David's nurse for the day, went about his duties quietly tending to David's needs and the alarms of his pumps.

"S'cuse me, Mary, would you mind if I cleaned your husband's room now?"

It was Jeanita. "Oh, hi, Jeanita. Sure, come in."

She entered and stood at the foot of David's bed. "Looks like my friend is struggling some," Jeanita observed.

"Yes, he's having some problems. The doctors say it's a build-up of toxins—I think they said 'uremia,' or something like that—from his kidneys not working properly. They say dialysis if things don't turn around," I said.

"Oh, I am sorry, Mary. And I feel bad, real bad, for Dave. I have a relation who was on dialysis for several years. I know it's hard."

"Jeanita, do you think you would mind praying with me? I'm feeling really bad right now. I am trying to be strong, but this is hard stuff. He's such a good, good man, he really doesn't deserve this . . ."

"I know he is a good man; you can just tell by talking to him. He listens to you when you speak to him, and he listens with both his ears and his eyes. I noticed that. Most people, they don't give you the time of day," Jeanita said of her new friend, my husband.

"He does that because he listens first with his heart. That was the very first thing I noticed about David Tiffin, and the first thing that I fell in love with almost twelve years ago." I stood up, and Jeanita came over to my side of David's bed.

"Let's pray. Dear Heavenly Father, we are calling on you today for your help, Lord. We ask, Lord, that you visit with our brother David, lying here in this bed here in the Johns Hopkins Hospital, Lord. Our brother is in such great need of your care, Lord, healing that only you can give, Lord. We ask that you bring healing to his body, strength to his soul, so that he can be a witness to your greater glory, Lord. We ask this in your Holy Name. Amen."

"Amen," I repeated. "Thank you, Jeanita. Can I ask you to ask your church to pray for David? I am feeling that we need to get more prayers."

"Sure, baby," Jeanita replied.

"And can I give you this prayer reminder of our family?" I pulled out one of our Christmas cards.

"That's such a nice photo. David showed me this. Your baby is so cute and he is a tiny thing. How old is he?" Jeanita asked.

"Stephen is seven months old now."

"Oh, he's such a little thing, and so cute."

"Thank you. I miss him; I miss 'em all," I said.

"Well, David will be better, baby, you know who is in control here. Just remember the doctors are helpers to the Almighty. God will be doing the healing. You keep the faith, keep praying."

"I will. Thank you, Jeanita, thank you so much."

"David will be better. He has to be."

From: Mary Tiffin
Sent: Friday, January 3, 2003 11:10 AM
To: David's List
Subject: Update

Okay, David is going down the dialysis route.

We are still waiting for the word on the skin condition.

Please keep praying. Believe.

XOXO

From: Mary Tiffin
Sent: Saturday, January 4, 2003 10:31 AM
To: David's List
Subject: David Update

Okay . . .

So we changed our mind on how we feel about dialysis, and we now like dialysis.

The doctors are still out on their decision about the skin condition, but have decided to start treating him for graft-versus-host disease.

They had indicated that if it is GVHD and they refrained from treating it now, then David would most likely be inpatient for "many, many months" fighting the disease. I am glad they made this decision.

Please continue to remember him in your prayers, because we really need them now.

Thanks in advance,

Mary

We Need More Prayers

From the apartment that evening, I decided to return some phone calls.

"Oh, hi, D. I'm sorry that I haven't returned your calls. It's been… it's been… a little out of control," I said, talking to my best friend from Lewisburg, Denise.

"Mary, you never need to apologize. I just wanted to make sure you were okay. You've been conspicuously quiet and we've been worried. You know it's not like you to be quiet," Denise said, trying to make a little joke.

I'd been exhausted coming home the last few nights. I was unable to listen, let alone return calls. What do I tell people? How can I tell people? It barely made sense to me and it was happening right in front of me. How do I explain it to anyone else? But I was always happy to talk to Denise.

"I know, I know. I just didn't know what to say and so I thought it would be better to say nothing," I said.

"I understand," Denise said. "So what are the doctors saying today?"

"Dr. Mattsui is really concerned about David's mucositis. That's the name of the ulcers starting in his mouth and going all the way through his GI tract. It appears that it's so bad that it's cutting off his airway. They think they will need to intubate him. This means that David will be on a ventilator, but not because he has poor lung function; it's because they need to create an airway. The doctors say it is only until he gets some counts, and then the mucositis should improve and he should be able to come off." I exhaled. I couldn't believe I was saying that about David.

"Oh dear, that sounds serious. I am sorry, honey."

"It is, it is, Denise, and that damn rash doesn't appear to be getting any better at all. We need more prayers, D. Could you ask more people to pray, please? We need more prayers."

"I will, Mare, I will."

"That's all I have from here."

"Is there anything else I can do for you?" Denise asked.

"Could you please tell everyone that I really appreciate their calls, but I just can't talk right now? I just can't talk, but I will keep them posted. We are so thankful for all of them. Will you tell them that?"

"I will, Mare."

"Thanks, D. Good night."

"Love you, Mare. Hang in there. Good night."

"Love you. G'night."

From: Mary Tiffin
Sent: Wednesday, January 8, 2003 11:36 AM
To: David's List
Subject: David Update

Hi, guys.

It's been a busy time with the many doctors at Hopkins. So here is the deal—David is now on a ventilator in addition to the dialysis. He is in critical condition.

Please pray that his counts will recover and that we will be able to get off life support. I still have absolute faith that we will get through this and that God will give us our miracle.

Thank you for your beautiful prayers and consoling friendship. Please keep praying.

Mary

From: Maria Wolf
Sent: Wednesday, January 8, 2003 12:08 PM
To: Mary M. Tiffin
Subject: Prayers

Mary,

Just wanted you to know that we are all praying harder than ever (if that is possible) for David and that God continues to give you strength and optimism. David is so blessed to have you by his side.

I have been posting your emails because everyone is concerned, and the more people who know what's happening, that's more prayers being offered. I hope you don't mind.

Well, just wanted you to know that I'm thinking about you and praying for both of you.

Love,

Maria

From: Shelby.lammerdorf
Sent: Wednesday, January 8, 2003 12:37 PM
To: Mary M. Tiffin
Subject: Re: David Update

Dear Mary,

So glad to hear from you. You hold on strong and know that we all have faith that God will give you this miracle. We love you very much.

Shelby

From: ttdmkell
Sent: Wednesday, January 8, 2003 2:56 PM
To: Mary M. Tiffin
Subject: Prayers

Dear Mrs. Tiffin,

Spoke to your mom earlier and have been praying fervently every hour. Your faith is an inspiration to us all, Mare. I BELIEVE as well that a miracle will occur. We need to continue to pray and trust.

Love and prayers. Wish I were there to give you a big hug.

Denise

From: SADDLES40
Sent: Wednesday, January 8, 2003 11:00 PM
To: Mary M. Tiffin
Subject: Re: David Update

Hi, Mary.

Pete here. My heart and soul are in my prayers for David Tiffin. They will be heard.

Be patient. It is a long process and probably many more bad days before they will get better. I love you, my precious, and want you to know you are always on my mind.

Pete

From: Jyummie
Sent: Wednesday, January 8, 2003 7:39 PM
To: Mary M. Tiffin
Subject: Re: David Update

Mary,

Know that we are praying for David and for you. Catherine's calendar actually says "BELIEVE" for this month. Makes my spine tingle. We love you with all our hearts and wish that we could make it better.

Love, love, love, and faith.

Johanne

From: Brenda Patterson
Sent: Thursday, January 9, 2003 9:34 AM
To: Mary M. Tiffin
Subject: Dave

Good morning, Mary.

I've been thinking about you guys continuously. A group of us prayed for Dave and the family last night at our prayer meeting. My heart goes out to all of you.

Our desire is that God would perform a miracle, but we don't know what His plan is. We need to find comfort in the fact that God knows the whole picture and knows what's best. Our thoughts and prayers are with you without ceasing. Please continue to keep us informed.

Take care, and God Bless.

Brenda

From: IBGIB
Sent: Thursday, January 9, 2003 8:49 PM
To: Mary M. Tiffin
Subject: Beautiful Cousin

Well, that could go for either one of us, but I do mean you, Mary. I think and pray for you all very often. I'm so sorry you are all going through this. I wish I were closer to you.

Yes, it is David I pray for, but as my cousin and that beautiful little angel girl that I remember, you get my prayers, too. Thank you so very much for the article and the note.

I don't know how you have a moment. It meant so much to get it. Your part about it being very hard... his recovery... well, I'm so sorry. I just know that he will be alright. I just know it. You have such a wonderful relationship. As the article says, "So cute and the kids are beautiful." I won't make this too long because I know that you have much mail to go through. Updates would be great, but only if you can.

Love, love, love, love,

Darlene Potter

From: Mary Tiffin
Sent: Friday, January 10, 2003 11:15 AM
To: David's List
Subject: David Update

Okay, guys,

Okay, so here is where we are. Twenty-one days post-transplant and still no white blood count. It's hair-raising.

I am all up for suggestions on better ways to beg God.

All other vitals are stable—still very critical, but stable.

BELIEVE.

Mary

From: Michele Fegan
Sent: Friday, January10, 2003 3:05 PM
To: Mary M. Tiffin
Subject: In My Prayers

Follow-Up Flag: Follow Up

Flag Status: Red

Hi, Mary.

I know you don't know me that well (Brenda's aunt), but I have been keeping up with updates on David through Brenda. David and, well, all of you are all in our prayers!!!!!!!!!!!!!!!!!!!!!!

I can't even imagine how hard it must all be! (I say a rosary every day on my way to work!!!)

I wish you and the kids well through all of this also.

Mich

From: Jyummie
Sent: Friday, January 10, 2003 3:32 PM
To: Mary M. Tiffin
Subject: Re: David Update

Hi, Mary, Mary.

Catherine was just saying as we were driving in her car, "I wonder when we're going to get the 'BELIEVE' bumper sticker from Mary." Sure enough, there it was when I opened the mailbox. The article is amazing and your letter even better. You must know that I love you the best of all my cousins—I always have. You are in my heart and thoughts always. If you need me, just ask. I will do my best to be there for you. We all continue to pray for David. The bumper sticker is going to go on Catherine's car. I plan on wearing the shirt as often as hygienically possible.

I am sending you a huge hug, and my thoughts in the morning and our last thought at night are of you all.

Johanne

From: Marchsport28
Sent: Saturday, January 11, 2003 12:06 PM
To: Mary M. Tiffin
Subject: Re: David Update

Hi, Mary.

I called you last night. We are praying for you and David. We just have to keep our faith strong. I know your mom and dad are there with you. You need them for support. We will check back with you tonight.

Love you,

Donna & Marcus

A Visit with Big Jesus

I was beginning to lose track of time. When did everything get so quiet? Was it a week? Nine days ago? When did my sweet husband stop talking?

My daily routine had changed little: mass in the morning at the Basilica, coffee, gown, gloves and mask, and wait in the room for the next twelve hours, waiting for David's counts to rebound. Only the spinning "whirr" of the dialysis machine and the gentle "pphhning" breath of the ventilator. No TV, no Solitaire game, no reminders of our optimism; everything quiet since David entered his medically induced coma.

What a difference a few weeks made. My lively and engaging conversations with David had been replaced with intermittent exchanges with nurses, physicians, and hospital staff caring for my husband. The mood in David's room had changed from optimism to a cautious, measured hope with the addition of the new life-saving equipment.

Gowned, gloved, and masked, I sat and watched the daily routine of the nurses caring for David. Some I care for more than others. David's nurse this one day was John. With five years in Bone Marrow Transplant, John brought experience, but not good energy. He was the most negative nurse on the unit, and I didn't like when he took care of David. With David on the vent, I felt as if John was ready to throw in the towel, forget about him, write him off.

"John, David is a really strong guy, he'll get over this," I said, trying to defend my husband and to get this guy to see his worth.

"He's in a bad spot," John said.

"But you don't know this man. He's unlike anyone you have ever met. He'll get through this, you'll see."

"Oh, I will, will I?" John said doubtfully.

"Just do me a favor—keep an eye on him. I'm going to run out and make a call."

"Of course," John said, and went back to checking his email.

I was so put off by this guy that I decided to go for a walk. I needed to visit with Big Jesus; I had to see this Christ statue.

When I returned, John was not in the room. His shift was nearing its end and he was giving his report to Maria, one of our favorite nurses. She would be David's nurse for the night.

"It's going to be a much better night, David," I told my sleeping husband. "We have Maria tonight."

When I got back to the apartment, the blinking answering machine showed that we had nine messages. *"Oh, jeeze... I can't listen,"* I thought. *"Worse yet, I just can't call everyone back. Going through all this stuff one time is hard enough, I can't do it over and over again by talking on the phone to nine different people, I just can't. I really need to find a way to let everyone know what is happening and how we appreciate everything that they are doing."* I pressed "delete" on the answering machine, jumped in the shower, and went to bed.

From: IBGIB
Sent: Sunday, January 12, 2003 10:44 AM
To: Mary M. Tiffin
Subject: Re: David Update

Mary,

Thanks so much for the update. You said you are all up for suggestions on better ways to beg

God? Well, when we get to that point, we have to give it Him... or Her... or faith of the universe, or whatever. Or maybe it is that we have asked and He's heard. When you think of it, how many times does God have to be asked? I was told recently: ONCE. Can you imagine any of us doing that? But really—and you know that this is true, Mary—if it's God, once is enough, and He knows what we want. Let go just a little. No, don't give up, but it's like falling backward and not knowing who will catch us or if we will be caught. Faith, but know you will be caught.

Know that no matter what, know that you will be caught—you will be held and embraced, and in all this madness try to feel that now.

With great love always,

Cousin Darlene.

Focus on feeling that—just feel it. Maybe that's what God wants you to do now.

From: Jody Hutchinson
Sent: Monday, January 13, 2003 8:09 AM
To: Mary M. Tiffin
Cc: Debby Porter
Subject: Re: David Update

Dear Mary,

Hi, it's me, Cousin Jody. As you know, we have been praying for David and you and the kids fervently, but I wanted to reach out and touch you, so I asked Debby to forward your message on to me. Would you please add me to your update list?

I have thought about yet another angle on prayer. Maybe you have done this and know how powerful it is that we all pray at exactly the same time. (Yes, it was even mentioned in the news article you sent me.)

What if all of us on your update list stop everything, every day, at some designated time (maybe nine p.m. or so?) and simultaneously pray for David for five minutes. Maybe we can all close our eyes and focus on him surrounded by God's love or whatever else you think. I'll leave it up to you to pass this along if you wish, but Harteltons's will be doing it at nine until we hear differently from you.

We love you.

Jody

From: Seth Zieber
Sent: Monday, January 13, 2003 10:40 AM
To: Mary M. Tiffin
Subject: Re: Fwd: David Update

My wife and I continue to pray, as well as our prayer chain at our church, First Presbyterian in Lewisburg. We believe a miracle can still take place.

From: Mary Tiffin
Sent: Monday, January 13, 2003 3:51 PM
To: David's List
Subject: David Update and BELIEVE Story

Okay, everyone,

So David is still in critical condition, but I'll take critical, especially since he was in much worse shape on Saturday.

Now, for everyone that I didn't explain the "BELIEVE" story to...

Before we were admitted, David was required to come to Hopkins for pre-admission testing. On one of the trips, we were driving from the Marriott to the hospital and we were talking about the disease, our faith in God, our faith in the hospital, and the feeling that we were "meant to be" here in Baltimore.

As we were having this conversation, we both couldn't help but feel a little nervous. It's heavy-duty stuff, you know.

And what to our wondering eyes should appear but these interesting "BELIEVE" signs. They were on buildings, taxi cabs, cars, buses, billboards, etc. They were *everywhere* and very hard to miss.

I said to David that God knows we are visual and that He was trying to tell us something. He provided sooo many signs because he knows that I am a little on the thick side ("A little?" you say). And they *keep* appearing on all of these locations, especially when I feel nervous and need an emotional or spiritual lift. It's been a long struggle, but I have to keep BELIEVING.

So that is the story. Please BELIEVE and keep praying.

XOXOXO,

Mary

From: Cicilla 829
Sent: Monday, January 13, 2003 12:46 PM
To: Mary M. Tiffin
Subject: Our Hearts are with You

Dear David and Mary,

We think of you both constantly, and the boys, too. We pray for your health and happiness and welfare. I can't even begin to imagine what you must be going through.

Just know that we love you, and whatever we can do to help, we will do. Many people ask how you are doing, and we always urge them to continue praying.

Miracles do happen and we do BELIEVE!!!

Surrounding you with love and light,

Pamela

4:44

Ring . . .

Ring . . .

"Mary," a voice said.

"Yes?"

"This is the hospital," said the voice.

I looked at the clock. It displayed 4:44 a.m. *"Why are they calling me so early?"* I thought, wanting to go back to sleep.

"Mary? MARY! HELLO, MARY! ARE YOU AWAKE?!"

"Yes," I replied, waking up.

"You need to come to the hospital. Your husband, David, has taken a turn," said the voice.

"What? Huh... What?"

"Your husband, David... We think you'll want to be here at the hospital."

"Oh, David, yes, yes, I'll be there right away!" *"Oh, my God, get up, get moving, get dressed. Please, dear Jesus, protect my sweet husband. Please protect David."*

I threw on some clothes, grabbed my coat, and was out the door. By the time I got to the floor, maybe fifteen minutes after the call, several doctors were in the room, attempting to stabilize David.

"Your husband has had an event. He either had a pulmonary embolism, a heart attack, or is in septic shock," said a pulmonologist I had never met before this evening. "Whatever it was, it will be very difficult for your husband to survive the evening," he went on to say.

"A heart attack? No way!" I was thinking. *"David's heart is perfect."*

"Your husband's body has suffered a horrible assault, and it would be very difficult for a healthy person to survive this, much less a patient as compromised as your husband," the doctor continued. "I'm not certain if he will survive this evening."

While the doctor was speaking, I was praying—praying so very intently that David would survive or that the doctor could be wrong.

"... Do you understand what I am saying, Mrs. Tiffin?"

"Thank you, Dr. Heinsile"—reading his jacket—"I understand. May I go see my husband now?"

"Yes, I think that we are done in there. That would be fine. Mrs. Tiffin, I am very sorry."

"Tonight is not the night that David Tiffin will die. Tonight is just not the night. It's way too soon," I told myself.

When I returned to the room, I committed to taking an active role in this fight. I started to dig into our bag of tricks. I grabbed the boom box that we had taken to the hospital, plugged it in, and found the right CD.

David loved Earth, Wind and Fire, and "Shining Star" was his favorite song. I pressed REPEAT on the Box.

"David, honey, I know that you are in there. You have to fight, fight really hard— fight through this, follow the music. Listen to me, David. Don't go toward the light, go toward the Music. I'm playing your song." I planned to keep him connected to this world for as long as I could. I cranked it up *loud*!

So I prayed and listened to the CD with David over and over again. *"The song that promised a shining star as the pathway to seeing what your life can truly be . . ."* blared the CD player.

"Mary, do you think we can lower the volume on this now?" asked his nurse, Kathy, at eight-thirty a.m. "It may be disturbing other patients. The doctors will be rounding soon, and they will need to examine David without the music."

"Oh, my goodness, of course. Do *you* think he is better?" I asked Kathy, who had been with us during the entire night.

"I'll let the doctor's check, but from what I can see, he looks like he is back to normal to me. But I can't make that call, I'll leave that to the docs."

"We did it, David," I whispered to him, with a kiss on his forehead. "I knew you would."

From: Mary Tiffin
Sent: Monday, January 13, 2003 3:07 PM
To: Jody Hutchinson
Subject: Re: David Update

Jody,

What a beautiful idea. I have forwarded your email to all on my list so that we will all pray at nine p.m.

Could the prayer be that David's sister's marrow will engraft and that his counts will rise?

We are still in heavy-duty critical condition, but the prayers are helping and I BELIEVE that they helped him from the brink this past Sunday.

Mom and Dad are here with me now. The hospital called me in at four forty-four a.m. Saturday morning when they felt that David had a pulmonary embolism (blood clot).

We prayed like maniacs, and he is holding his own.

I will, of course, add you to my email list for all updates. Thank you so much for your email.

We send our love.

XOXOXO,

Mary

From: Saddles40
Sent: Monday, January 13, 2003 4:40 PM
To: Mary M. Tiffin
Subject: Re: David Update

Okay, Mary, nine p.m. it is. We will all say prayers together.

We do BELIEVE.

Patrice

From: tandk
Sent: Monday, January 13, 2003 4:45 PM
To: Mary M. Tiffin
Subject: Re: David Update

Mary,

Prayers at nine—our family is in! We'll be praying.

Karen

From: Jyummie
Sent: Monday, January 13, 2003 5:00 PM
To: Mary M. Tiffin
Subject: Re: David Update

Mary, Mary,

We'll all be praying in Connecticut!

XOXOXO,

Johanne

From: Cicilla829
Sent: Monday, January 13, 2003 5:03 PM
To: Mary M. Tiffin
Subject: Re: David Update

Yes, Mary, we will pray at nine p.m., and I will offer it to those in the String Studio who are so inclined, because they all care for you as well.

Love,

Pamela

From: BProbst
Sent: Monday, January 13, 2003 5:10 PM
To: Mary M. Tiffin
Subject: Re: David Update

Dear Mary,

I will be praying for David and you from Arizona each evening at nine (EST). I have also asked my mother in Toms River to pray for you, and she has promised to as well. Wish we could do more.

Your childhood friend,

Bill

From: Michele Fegan
Sent: Monday, January 13, 2003 5:17 PM
To: Mary M. Tiffin
Subject: Re: David Update

This is a great idea. Our entire family will be praying in Maryland for David at nine p.m.!

Mich

From: Ernie Klemper
Sent: Monday, January 13, 2003 5:19 PM
To: Mary M. Tiffin
Subject: Re: David Update

Mary,

I like this idea. We're in, and I will ask some friends at St. Pious to join in as well. Stay strong!

Ernie

From: Ken Sanger
Sent: Monday, January 13, 2003 5:22 PM
To: Mary M. Tiffin
Subject: Re: David Update

Mary,

We will be joining you in prayer in Montoursville. Please let us know if there is anything else we can do to help.

Ken

From: IBGIB
Sent: Monday, January 13, 2003 11:27 PM
To: Mary M. Tiffin
Subject: Re: The BELIEVE Sign

That is amazing and real.... WE ALL BELIEVE.... WE ALL LOVE YOU.... AND WE WILL PRAY AT NINE P.M.

Love to the beautiful boys, and Mom and Dad and the whole family, and especially David.

Love,

Darlene

9:00 pm Prayer Power

"Mary, he's the number one pulmonologist on staff," our nurse, Lori, said with a smile. "And he is super smart." She was speaking of Dr. Rex Shah, a new physician who was called in to see David. "He was in to talk to you a little while ago and I told him you just stepped out."

"Figures. The only time someone looks for me is when I am at the coffee bar. Drats. I just needed an extra cup today."

"Oh, no problem; he'll stop by again. He was rounding."

Young, but really experienced, Lori was a nurse we were always happy to see. She had a sunny disposition and was really good with our constant questions. David enjoyed it when Lori was assigned as his nighttime nurse. They would watch comedies and laugh. David would joke about his movie dates with Nurse Lori. I was so grateful that he was able to laugh. We liked Lori; she made us feel comfortable.

But our laughter ended when David entered his medically induced coma. And there was nothing funny about the frightening events of the other night. Lori went about her job quietly and calmly, efficiently responding to the pumps and machines when they signaled for her attention.

Her sense of calm over the environment was good for allaying my fears and helping me remain positive. I felt that Lori had a connection to us, and she cared about how David did in this process. Whenever I saw Lori on duty, I felt more at ease.

David was considered critical enough that he also required one-on-one care, which meant that a clinical person was in the room with him around the clock. With both Lori and the one-on-one, I felt comfortable enough to slip down to the coffee bar for another cup of coffee.

Opening the laptop on the little table that had become my temporary workstation, I was sipping my coffee as I was waiting for my laptop to boot, and talking to Lori about the parking garage, when a young physician of about thirty-five walked into the room followed by two younger physicians.

"Mrs. Tiffin?"

"Yes, I'm Mrs. Tiffin," I said, gloved hand outreached to greet this newest of doctors.

"I'm Dr. Shah. I am on the pulmonology team."

"Oh, hello, Dr. Shah. I have heard good things about you."

"Let's step outside the room, even though we know that David is sleeping. We want to respect him. We really don't know how much, if anything, he can hear in a state like this."

"Wow, he is great," I thought to myself. Aloud, I said, "Thank you, thank you, for being sensitive to David's needs, Dr. Shah."

In the hallway, Dr. Shah started to recap the night of David's near-death event. "Mrs. Tiffin, I have been asked to check on your husband. Two of my colleagues were attending this past Saturday night when your husband had his unfortunate incident, Drs. Heinsle and Wolford. I have consulted with the two physicians, reviewed your husband's chart, and read the notes."

"Yes, I remember the doctors… and, of course, the night."

"And after consulting with them, I want to make clear your understanding of your husband's state."

"My understanding?"

"I want to make it clear to you that your husband is very ill. Do you understand? A bone marrow transplant is very difficult on the body."

"Oh, really? No kiddin', doc."

"And frankly, your husband is not rebounding the way the medical staff anticipated. I think that you need to think about the short-term or long-term implications. This transplant is taking a tremendous toll on your husband. Can you see this?"

I was stunned. *"Who is this guy? Well, of course I can. I'd have to be blind to miss this."*

"David survived the other night, but I am not sure what will happen from here. I am concerned that you are not being realistic with your expectations for your husband. Do you understand what I am saying, Mrs. Tiffin?" Dr. Shah articulated slowly, as if I were slow and hard of hearing.

"This guy thinks I am an idiot. Oh, that's funny, and not funny at the same time…. Stay cool,

Mary," I told myself.

I was processing his bad news and his assault to both my lack of understanding and my intense need to stay hopeful, so I was behaving in a way that was very uncharacteristic of me... I was quiet.

"Mrs. Tiffin?" as in 'knock, knock'.

"Mary, get back in the game...".

"Dr. Shah, uhh, I see. Let me help you with your understanding, may I?"

"Of course."

"I'm sensing that you think that I might be missing the gravity of the situation?"

"I just want to make sure you are clear on the expectations."

"Of course, I sense that you think that I am some sort of dimwit, a dolt, perhaps a little off?" To myself, I thought, *"The hell with cool."*

"Oh, no, that is not what I am saying. I merely want to align your expectations."

"Allow me, then, to tell you from whence we came, and then I'll discuss my expectations.

"In choosing Johns Hopkins, we went through a selective process to choose the most appropriate facility, the best transplant hospital. We interviewed several, reviewed statistics, and read studies. Ultimately, we selected JHH for its brilliance and experience. In preparing for transplant, David and I made a commitment that we would be joining the medical staff to form a team committed to David's wellness. As part of his wellness team, we would bring four unrelenting tools in our arsenal: the first, our love and devotion to each other; the second, our positive outlook; third, our faith and belief that all things are possible; and the last item was our commitment to fight for wellness with every ounce of energy we had. These are the tools we have. And as part of this team, we vowed to uphold our end of the bargain, never reneging on any of those items, as we expected you remain brilliant, Hopkins' most compelling tool. So you stay smart, and I will stay positive and have hope. Got it?"

He looked at me, stunned.

I continued. "So what you see as a lack of understanding or unrealistic expectations is our us holding up our end of the bargain. Do *you* understand, Dr. Shah? David and I are just team players. You do your patients a great disservice by misinterpreting their skill set for ignorance. And to answer your question, yes, of course, I see that David is very ill, critically ill. He is being sustained by machines. If there is a power outage in that room, without a backup generator,

I lose my husband. Dr. Shah, I get it. I expect you to bring good judgment and clinical knowledge; you can expect me to stay positive. Now, do *you* have any questions, Dr. Shah?"

"You're an overly optimistic person; too optimistic, I believe, for this situation."

"Dr. Shah, why don't you let me determine the amount of optimism I want to extend toward our experiences, and I'll let you determine yours. Again, do *you* have any questions?"

"No; we will continue to follow your husband," he replied, nonplussed by my comments.

"Thank you, Dr. Shah. We truly appreciate your wisdom."

I walked back into the room exhausted.

"What was *that*?" Lori asked.

"Oh, you heard it?" I hadn't been paying much attention to what was happening. "I guess he thought I was a dope, Lor; that I didn't know that David was critical. Like I can somehow gloss over the fact that there are lines and tubes coming out of my husband's body. Like all of this"—motioning to the equipment surrounding David's bed—"is easy to ignore . . ."

"Yeah, I'm sorry."

"He got my panties in a twist....I think he was trying to give me a reality check, and I checked my reality with him. He might be smart, but his bedside is pretty crappy. I apologize if my conversation with him puts you in a difficult situation."

"Don't let him bother you. He is just doing what he feels he needs to do."

"I get that, but the next time, I hope he sends someone else."

Later that evening, Dr. Mattsui came in.

"Mary, I came in to talk to you about your conversation with Dr. Shah. I heard about your conversation. And I wasn't very happy with the way he spoke to you. He doesn't know you, so he doesn't understand that, even though you are aware of what is happening, you remain a very optimistic person."

"You don't need to apologize. I told him about our position. I hope he understands now. I'm just not ready to throw in the towel. David is not ready to give up, and I believe if there is life there is always hope. And I have great hope for David. He'll pull through, you'll see."

"I know you feel that way. And we are not ready to give up. We will continue to fight as long as David does. His survival of the other night was unusual;

he was really lucky. But his body can only take so much. He cannot endure repeated episodes of the other night; it's too much for the body. He has to have his counts rebound."

"I understand that, Dr. Mattsui. I feel that we were blessed the other night, and I'll go with that."

From: Marlene Roreback
Sent: Tuesday, January 14, 2003 12:03 PM
To: Mary M. Tiffin
Subject: WE ARE BELIEVING

Hello, Mary.

My name is Marlene Roreback of New Life Ministries. I take care of our email and website.

(Just wanted to let you know that, since I am responding from my work email address.)

All of New Life Ministries would like to thank you for the updates on David. Please rest assured that we have been praying for him continually and we, too, have complete faith that he will be completely healed. I have notified everyone in the ministry to pray for David at nine p.m. each night, as you requested. I believe this is wise, as there *is* power when many people pray together.

Just wanted to let you know that my son, Matthew, who is in first grade with your Christopher, and my daughter, Chelsey, have been praying for your entire family each morning and night since David became ill. They have never missed a day! I know the people of St. Monica's have been faithful in their prayers, also.

Mary, please let us know if there is anything else that NLM can do to help you and your family in any way. We would all like to let you know how much of an inspiration and blessing you and David have been to all of us and our families through your ordeal. Your unshakable faith and trust in the Lord are just AMAZING. Your strength and courage have touched the lives of more people than you know in ways that you can't even imagine. To so many of us, the two of you have been a MIRACLE.

Please continue to keep us posted and we WILL keep believing!

In Christ,

Marlene

From: Mary M. Tiffin
Sent: Tuesday, January 14, 2003 2:36 PM
To: David's List
Subject: Update

Hi, guys.

Here is the update on David. We are still in a holding pattern. David is critical but STABLE. Oh, how I love that word.

But here is an amazing story for all of our nine p.m. prayers. I'll start by saying that now, we all realize that David's recovery is critically contingent upon the white blood count. You will probably recall the prayer last night was for David's counts to rise with Melissa's marrow kicking in.

His white blood count was 6 yesterday (we entered the hospital at 7,600). Shortly after nine p.m. last night, his counts rose to 80!!!! This was definitely a high for us. We haven't seen numbers in that vicinity for more than three weeks!!!! So do you get it? Isn't that ecclesiastically cool?

I ask that if you could, please, oh please, oh please, remember him in prayer again at nine p.m. so that we can get him to where we really need to be.

So that's my story, and thank you in advance.

XOXOXO,

Mary

From: Kim Edwards
Sent: Tuesday, January 14, 2003 2:51 PM
To: Mary M. Tiffin
Subject: Re: David Update

WOW!!!! That is great!!! You can count on the Edwards prayers every evening at nine p.m.!!!

Hope to speak to you soon.

Kim

From: Michele Fegan
Sent: Tuesday, January 14, 2003 4:07 PM
To: Mary M. Tiffin
Subject: Re: Fwd: Re: David Update

That is GREAT!!!!!!! I'll definitely keep praying. I think at this point, you/we have a private ongoing "party line" to the Man upstairs!!!!

Mich

From: Jyummie
Sent: Tuesday, January 14, 2003 5:53 PM
To: Mary M. Tiffin
Subject: Re: David Update

Hi, Mary, Mary.

Alex and I were just on eprayer.com and requested prayers for David. The Pope will probably reply, but it will be in Italian…. Who cares!!! It will still work!!! I got one more person at work to pray for David today.

Love and kisses and keep the numbers rising.

Johanne & Alex

From: Bernie Miller
Sent: Tuesday, January 14, 2003 11:10 AM
To: Mary M. Tiffin
Subject: Re: David Update

GO, DAVID!!! We will be rooting for you tonight at nine o'clock. GOD BLESS YOU!!

From: Mary Tiffin
Sent: Wednesday, January 15, 2003 11:26 AM
To: David's list
Subject: Your Prayers are WORKING

120!!!! 120!!! 120!!!! WE ARE AT 120!!!!!

Thank you, thank you, thank you. God bless you all. Keep praying.

XOXOXO,

Mary

From: Kim Edwards
Sent: Wednesday, January 15, 2003 11:45 AM
To: Mary M. Tiffin
Subject: Re: Your Prayers are WORKING

YIPPEE!!!!!!

Kim

From: Bprobst
Sent: Wednesday, January 15, 2003 2:33 AM
To: Mary M. Tiffin
Subject: Re: David Update

God does still work miracles. I will continue to pray for David's recovery and the continued rise in his white cell count.

Bill

From: Mary Tiffin
Sent: Wednesday, January 15, 2003 11:58 AM
To: David's List
Subject: David Update

Dear friends,

What a difference a couple of days makes.

On Saturday, things were so incredibly horrible and the doctors were talking about stuff like Advanced Directives and saying that David probably will not come back. They also mentioned that they do not recommend CPR if his heart also goes, as everything else was not working. CPR on him with failed organs is cruel and inhumane.

Now, the doctors are saying it's amazing that he survived/recovered from Saturday. The pulmonary doctors indicated that his recovery was amazing. His primary transplant doctor indicated that it was almost like Saturday did not happen and that David is once again ROCK STABLE—still very critical, but ROCK STABLE. The nephrology (kidney) guys said his kidneys recovered nicely and he is making urine (he will be so embarrassed that I am talking about his urine) and that he is off dialysis for at least the day.

So, I want to tell you about your prayers. Shortly after our nightly nine p.m. vigils, David's counts rose to 80 on Monday and 90 on Tuesday. We have never seen these numbers. They are so exciting but not as exciting as now.

His counts are now 120, which is beautiful and amazing. Thank you. Thank you for your vigilant prayers.

80... 90... 120... Urine!!!!!

Boy, the things that excite me these days (and it used to be jewelry).

Remember, the prayer is Melissa's marrow will engraft and that she will grow white blood cells in his body.

We still have a very long way to go, but this is the first step. Thank you in advance.

XOXOXO,

Mary

Going on Sight

During those quiet mornings of David's coma, my rounds would start with a review of how the previous night went for David—I'd check to see what medications were hung for him on the poles by his bed, review all the settings of his pumps and machines to see if there were any changes, and then assess David. I am visual and have been able to catalog his skin in my memory, but as a back-up, I've been keeping notes and making sketches about the areas it covers.

David's rash, once an inverted triangle of dots on his chest, quickly spread to cover his entire torso and then his arms and hands. At first it looked like a rash—red speckled dots. Within days, it turned to a solid red color, then it darkened to purple. They were calling it "Red Man Syndrome," a hypersensitive reaction to Vancomycin, an antibiotic that David was given. But the "rash" continued even after the drug was discontinued. Now as I looked at it, I thought it was getting even darker on his chest, black in spots, like he was burned.

With David asleep, I relied on what I saw each day to gauge his status and to let these changes speak to his condition. His skin has become a bellwether for his fragile condition.

These past few days, I was feeling okay with the medications and was growing accustomed to the sounds of the life-saving equipment—the dialysis machine whirring and purring, the ventilator pphhning and pfffting, the monitors beeping, and the pumps chiming. All the devices working together to create a symphony of a life suspended, an unexpected opus creating a lullaby for my dear, sleeping husband.

While the machinery was a concern, it had become a comfort. I was growing more alarmed by this rash. I was not certain if there was ever a conclusive answer on what exactly it was. I made a note to show it to Dr. Mattsui as he rounded. About forty-five minutes later, the rounding staff of physicians led by Dr. Mattsui, which includes the charge nurse, Rick, along with David's nurse for the day, and Annette, the social worker, entered the room.

"Good morning, David. Good morning, Mary," Dr. Mattsui greeted us. I was so appreciative of the fact that he said hello to David even though he was asleep—he could still be listening.

"Hello, all," I returned the greeting.

"So what are your concerns today?" Dr. Mattsui asked. He'd become accustomed to my rapid-fire, I-gotta-get-this-out-before-I-forget type of questioning, so he often got to that right away.

"I've been watching this and I don't think the rash is getting any better. If anything, I think it's getting worse," I said to Dr. Mattsui as I lifted the sheet to reveal David's arms and then his legs. The rash that had started on his chest was spreading down his arms and legs.

"The last time we checked this, it was covering about 80 percent of his skin," Dr. Mattsui confirmed with Dr. Alvarez, one of the physicians, a Fellow, who was accompanying him.

"Yes, but I am thinking that looks like more than that. I think it looks like his entire body," I said.

Turning to David's nurse who was also at the bedside with us, Dr. Mattsui asked, "What do you think, Rick?"

"The rash covers David's entire body except for his buttocks. Some areas are worse than others. His chest, which as I understand from Mary and the chart was the original site, is perhaps the most acute or severe. But his body is covered," Rick offered.

"I am going to write orders for a different type of bed, one that is used with patients with skin issues. We don't want to worry about bed sores or other problems," Dr. Mattsui said. "And we will continue to watch it and treat him as we are."

Dr. Mattsui then reviewed where David was as compared to yesterday. David's healing was on hold until he got counts. "We are about in the same place as yesterday, just waiting for his count recovery."

"Okay, Dr. Mattsui, you know what I am going to ask now." This kind physician had learned my routine, that I would figuratively hold my breath when they offered the not-great news, because invariably I would ask for the silver lining. "So did anything good happen today? Was there anything to celebrate? Did we have even the smallest victory anywhere, Dr. Mattsui?"

"Well, his renal numbers were slightly improved. Slightly. That would be a good thing."

"Great, so we'll celebrate that win. Thanks, Dr. Mattsui."

"Sure. So we'll just continue and wait," Dr. Mattsui said.

"And I'll take the victories wherever they are. You said yourself, Dr. Mattsui, it's tiny steps; we are taking tiny steps."

After Dr. Mattsui and the team left, I sat down to prepare an email to our growing list of supporters.

From: David Burnside
Sent: Wednesday, January 15, 2003 12:55 PM
To: Mary M. Tiffin
Subject: Re: David Update

> Climbing numbers are the greatest thing you can have. They bring tears to my eyes.
>
> Looking forward to an absolute neutrophil count of 1,000 soon!
>
> I am so happy for all of you. The prayers will continue.
>
> David Burnside

From: Lisa Robinson
Sent: Wednesday, January 15, 2003 3:43 PM
To: Mary M. Tiffin
Subject: Re: David Update

> Mary,
>
> I am so happy for you! I am thinking of you guys always!
>
> Love,
>
> Lisa

From: Bernie Miller
Sent: Wednesday, January 15, 2003 3:47 PM
To: Mary M. Tiffin
Subject: Prayers

Mary,

Hallelujah! Go David! We continue to pray... and BELIEVE.

Blessings to you.

Bernie & Debbie

From: Jyummie
Sent: Wednesday, January 15, 2003 6:09 PM
To: Mary M. Tiffin
Subject: Re: David Update

Keep that good news coming. The second thing I do when I get home is to check for messages. I do say "hello" to my family first... HA HA.

We are wowing and being very thrilled, as Junie B. Jones would say—Chrissy would love these books. I have people praying at nine p.m. each night. We are on a roll, and the road to recovery is looking brighter and brighter.

Keep the faith.

XXXOOOXXX,

Johanne

Like a Really Bad Sunburn

The phone was ringing as I unlocked the door of the apartment.

"Hello."

"Hi, Mare," Laurie said.

"Hi, Laur."

"So, how is it?" she asked.

"It's gotten a lot worse, Laur. It was only on his chest before and now it's spread all over his body. His body is really red."

"Oh," Laurie said.

"They've never seen it before. Everyone is coming in to look at it. It's very unnerving."

I could hear Laurie talking to her husband at the other end of the line. "How red, Bob wants to know," Laurie asked.

"Like a really bad sunburn. You know, that dark, dark red," I said.

"Let me see what I can find out at work tomorrow. I'll talk to some doctors and email you."

"That would be great. I'm pretty beat, Laur, and the morning comes really quickly. 'Night, Laur."

From: IBGIB
Sent: Wednesday, January 15, 2003 9:35 PM
To: Mary M. Tiffin
Subject: To My Beautiful Cousin

I say that so easily because they always said we looked alike. How terrific this news is. Thank you, God. We will pray and keep praying at nine p.m., YES. But whenever else we can, too. Besides us, that family of ours in heaven also has a hand in it: Mom and La La and Aunt Evelyn, and of course your Grandma, and my Aunt Minnie, who, when I was very young, was dishing out ice cream for me and Lee. She asked me, "What flavor do you like?" "Chocolate," I said. Then she asked Lee. "Vanilla," Lee said. Soooo, she gave me all the chocolate and gave Lee all—and I mean *all*—the vanilla. So she does things in big ways.

Love, and love to the boys and your beautiful parents and the gang.

Darlene... YOUR beautiful cousin.

From: Jane Mossart
Sent: Wednesday, January 15, 2003 10:16 PM
To: Mary M. Tiffin
Subject: Thanks For The Update on David!!!

Dear Mary,

What wonderful news! Those counts are astounding, and what a roller coaster you must have been on these last several days. I am so glad that you have included me in your call for prayers. Charlie, Max, and I pray for David and your family every night, and I have been including David in my morning offering each day. I also offer every Mass I can attend for him and make a spiritual communion for him whenever I receive Holy Communion. I asked my parents to keep him in their prayers (theirs are so powerful), and, of course, my sister Carol and family, too.

Something Father Nessel said in his homily at Sunday Mass stayed with me, and your family came to mind at the time. He was talking about trusting God, and without trust in God there will be chaos. Certainly, the recent events of your life (and David's) appear chaotic, but I heard the peace and trust in your voice on the phone today and I read it in your messages. You are truly an inspiration, Mary, and I feel very grateful that I have gotten to know you even just a little bit.

Take care of yourself, Mary.

Love in Christ,

Jane

From: Laura Santucci-Burley
Sent: Wednesday, January 15, 2003 10:23 PM
To: Mary M. Tiffin
Subject: Re: David Update

Hi, Mary, Dad, and Mom.

Here's my first email to you. It's ten eleven Wednesday night and everyone is asleep. Everyone is so very excited to hear David's counts are on the rise. We did our nightly prayer tonight for David; you, Mary; Mom; and Dad. Ethan is the official prayer starter. He says Our Father first and then says his personal intention for David. It is just precious and sweet. And then we say our own intention for David, you, Mom and Dad. Tomorrow, Olivia will be the prayer starter. I have to go to work tomorrow, but I will call you when I get home. I'm hoping to hear a 200 count. Until I speak to you tomorrow, think positive, have faith, and trust in the Lord that everything is going to be okay. Bye for now. Be strong!

Love and kisses,

Laura Ermina

Really Need Those Prayers

The doctors' rounds started with a report on how David did the night before, then they reviewed his blood work. They had been drawing blood at scheduled points during the day to check his total blood counts and gasses, and also to check the functioning of his major organs, including his liver and kidneys. The clinical staff had been keeping a close eye on David's I&Os, or the ins and outs. This is a measurement of the amount of fluid he is taking in and that which his body is releasing. I had been told that bone marrow transplant is a fine balancing act, and had been witnessing the delicacy of keeping a patient suspended this way.

This review was done with the team, led by the attending physician, charge nurse, fellow physicians, bedside nurse, social worker, and an occasional ancillary person or two, like the chaplain. It was generally done outside the room, with a computer on a mobile stand. I know that they review this way because I had overheard the process on a number of occasions. When their review was complete, it would be time to meet with the family.

"So, Mary, our concern today...." started Dr. Mattsui while he was rounding on David, "is still his skin."

"I've been watching and measuring it, Dr. Mattsui. It's also on his legs and feet, besides his face," I added.

"So, essentially, his entire body. That is a significant concern because it is a primary site for infection. And since he is so severely neutropenic, David's skin condition poses the greatest threat so far," Dr. Mattsui informed us.

"The biggest threat so far?" I thought. *"Bigger than the other night when he had his 'event'? I thought that was the biggest threat. This is bigger?"*

"What part? His chest? His arms? His legs? What part should I worry about the most?" I asked, the lump in my throat returning.

Dr. Mattsui very gently lifted the sheet covering David. "Can you see how his skin looks open, almost raw? Our skin is our largest organ, so not only do we watch David's kidney, heart, and liver functioning, but now we have to keep a careful eye on his skin. An infection can start anywhere. We will be doing our best to keep it clean. In addition, we need to confirm that this is not graft-versus-host disease. And I've asked Dermatology to come back in. I know that they took measurements before, and I'd like for them to consult."

"Oh, okay. I guess we need to pray for his skin. Thank you, Dr. Mattsui."

"And let's not forget the mucositis issue. We're still waiting for his mouth, throat, and GI tract to show signs of improvement. Okay?"

"Yes, Dr. Mattsui, we'll focus on that as well."

"In the meantime, I am going to write orders for a different type of bed to better support his skin. And I will make sure that Dermatology gets up here today."

"Thank you, Dr. Mattsui," I said, feeling deflated as I fell back into my chair. *"Looks like I'd better get our prayer friends started again."*

From: Mary Tiffin
Sent: Thursday, January 16, 2003 4:28 PM
To: David's List
Subject: David Update

Hi, all.

Once again, what a difference a day makes. Today was not as great as the early part of yesterday.

Although we were buoyed by David's count rising, we were quickly reminded of the next hurdle that we have to cross—that being graft-versus-host. Our doctor informed us that we are not yet halfway there, but the rest of the journey will be tricky and hard to navigate. David will probably not be released until this summer.

We went from being really excited about the rise to really, really, really scared. I mean *really* scared.

But with God, all things are possible, so once again I ask that you turn to prayer. I promise to repay you and pray for you whenever you need or want, but please pray heavy duty.

Could you please use this prayer at our nine p.m. vigil (or something like this):?

"Heavenly Father, I call on you in a special way. It was through your power that David was created. Every morning he wakes, every breath he takes, every moment of every hour he lives under your power, I ask you to now recreate him. Please remove his bad cells, encourage his good cells, cleanse him from infection, and heal his skin and GI tract.

"Free him from suffering so that he will regain his strength and have a total healing, that he will be able to honor and praise you forever.

"We ask this in your name. Amen."

David is still on the ventilator and heavily sedated. WE REALLY NEED THOSE PRAYERS.

Thank you all.

XOXOXO,

Mary

From: Brenda Tiffin
Sent: Thursday, January 16, 2003 1:33 PM
To: Mary M. Tiffin
Subject: David Update

How is it going? Melissa just told me that David may not be able to leave the hospital until June. Is that correct? Why? What is that based on?

I just wanted to tell you how proud I am to know you and David. I think that you both are very strong and have done an amazing job so far!

From: Mary Tiffin
Sent: Thursday, January 16, 2003 4:13 PM
To: Mary M. Tiffin
Subject: David Update

Hi, Brenda.

Because David has not followed the typical bone marrow transplant path—if there is one—it does not seem that there is a discharge date in sight. The ventilator, dialysis, and his delayed counts have really complicated matters for us. There is no discharge date on the horizon. I feel safe with him here; as long as he gets better, I don't care if we are here for a year. I just want him to get better.

From: Jyummie
Sent: Thursday, January 16, 2003 9:22 PM
To: Mary M. Tiffin
Subject: Re: David Update

We continue to pray. I'll be wearing my "BELIEVE" shirt to work tomorrow. It's jeans day for me. I saw a rainbow in the sky this morning and I talk to David on my ride in each day. I'm happy to hear that you are going home to see your babies. Trust that the doctors and nurses will take the very best care of David. You are a constant part of my thoughts.

My love as always,

Johanne

From: Carla McClintock
Sent: Thursday, January 16, 2003 9:26 PM
To: Mary M. Tiffin
Subject: Hope

Mary,

If you could add my email to your list, I would greatly appreciate it. I wanted to send this verse to you all week. "I know the plans I have for you," says the Lord. "They are plans for good and not for disaster, to give you a future and a hope." Jeremiah 29:11.

Love and prayers,

Carla McClintock

As I read these emails and responded, I was thinking, *This email list is growing and growing. I can't wait to tell David when he wakes up about how large his email list has grown. Initially, as we were headed down here to Hopkins, I sent it to fifteen addresses plus our work addresses. Now, David's list has 213 email addresses on it.*

"David will be amazed that these people asked to be included in our updates and want to know how or what to pray for."

Some Amazing Strength

David had become a patient of interest for many clinicians. Since David's survival and rebound from "the event," his room had become a clinical destination for staff not directly associated with his care but also for those who had heard about David's highly unusual survival of the other night.

I was typing at the laptop when a gowned, gloved, and masked trio of physicians I did not recognize entered. "Mrs. Tiffin?" the center doctor inquired.

I got up from my chair and went to meet them before they reached David's bed. "Yes, that's me. I'm Mrs. Tiffin."

"I am Dr. Delacorte, from Pulmonary, and these are two fellow physicians, Drs. Green and Mukhtar. We work with Drs. Heinsile and Wolfender."

"Oh, yes, hello, gentlemen."

"We came to examine your husband. How do you think he is doing?" they asked quietly.

"Um, well . . ." I turned and looked at David. "He's resting quietly. He's just taking his time, I guess."

"Mrs. Tiffin, your husband has exhibited some amazing strength. He is very resilient."

"David is an amazing man with a tremendous amount of reserve. But he has an even greater will to beat this disease. He would tell you that if he could, but since he can't, I'll do it for him: This man is flat-out awesome."

Dr. Delacorte smiled. "Yes, I'd say he's awesome, too. I'd like to examine your husband."

"Sure, go ahead."

Moving aside, I granted access to the space that I appeared to be guarding. I went to the side of the bed opposite Dr. Delacorte and team.

"I'll just take a listen," Dr. Delacorte said, pointing to David's chest.

He removed the stethoscope, cleaned off the plastic disc, leaned over, and placed it on David's chest. He moved it around and gave the fellows a few nods. They, in turn, took out their stethoscopes and did the same thing. After they were done listening, they stood up and rehung their devices around their necks.

"So?" I asked.

"So your husband's lungs, except for a little—I mean a very faint little—rattle, sound clear," Dr. Delacorte said. "But I'd like to do a procedure called a bronchoscopy to check. I understand that David has had one of those before."

"Yes, he has, and it is okay to do another one to check."

"This is a good thing. We want the lungs to sound clear."

I grabbed the pink stethoscope that was hanging from one of the poles on David's bed, cleaned off the disc, and asked the doctor, "Would you let me hear what you mean? I want to understand what you are saying." I put the pink stethoscope on.

The doctors looked at each other, unsure how to respond.

"Are you a medical person, perhaps a nurse or something?" Dr. Mukhtar asked.

"No, but I am Dr. Mom. So show me, would you, Dr. Delacorte?"

Dr. Mukhtar looked at me, not knowing what to say.

"Sure," said Dr. Delacorte with a smile. He placed the bell and disc end from the stethoscope that I was wearing on the upper part of David's chest. "Now listen here," Dr. Delacorte instructed. "Can you hear the air move in and out?"

"Yes, I think I can."

"Now listen down here," he said, moving the stethoscope to David's upper abdomen. "What do you hear?"

I was listening really hard. "Nothing. I don't hear anything."

"Listen again," Dr. Delacorte prompted. "Here, try this area," he offered, moving the position of the bell. "Now do you hear anything?"

I listened really hard. Still nothing… wait… like from down a long hallway, I heard a little cracking sound, and the more I listened, the more I heard the pattern.

"Oh, I think I hear, like, a cracking sound," I said to the doctor.

"Yes, that's the rattle. From what I understand, that was very pronounced the night your husband became very critically ill. Now it appears to have abated. A very positive sign."

"What would you say happened, then, to turn things around?" I asked.

"Well, we're not really sure. But from what I can see, whatever happened to your husband the other night appears to, at least for now, have reversed itself. It seems that he has returned to his baseline. I can't tell you exactly how or why it reversed itself; it just did."

"Well, I've got a feeling on that ... But this is great. And thank you for showing me. Now I can check his rattle."

"We'll return to do the scope. A member of the team will continue to monitor David, and I wish you luck," said Dr. Delacorte.

From: Mary Tiffin
Sent: Friday, January 17, 2003 10:08 AM
To: David's List
Subject: David Update

Hi, guys.

David is once again stable. Although his white blood count is 12 (huge bummer), it appears that something is happening that's positive. His skin looks better and not as charred.

It also appears that his mouth (mucositis) may be recovering a little. Since David's problems are so extensive, we have a lot to recover from before he can get off the ventilator.

Actually, he was off his dialysis yesterday, so that was a good thing, and all of his cultures came back negative.

He is having a procedure (a bronchoscope) today to check for pneumonia or a respiratory infection. So please pray these procedures come out okay.

I'm actually going home soon to spend the weekend with our boys. Our doctor recommended it. I can't wait to see them. I miss them more than I can say, so I probably won't be doing updates from home.

Thank you for your vigilant prayers and support. It really means so much to the both of us.

Please remember: nine p.m.

XOXOXO,

Mary

Dealing with the Moment

I was sitting in my chair getting ready to respond to a few emails when Nurse Lori poked her head in the room. "Mary, there's someone here to see you."

"Someone to see me?"

"Yeah. He said he's a friend from home."

"Oh, I wonder who that could be?" Aside from our parents and Missa and Bill, the only company we had was hospital visitors. I got up from the chair and went to the door.

"Well, hello there, kid!" said the man who looked like one of my co-workers.

"Wow, that looks like Lannie," I thought to myself, *"but what's he doing here? Interesting—my eyes are playing tricks on me."* Aloud, "Hello," I said, not wanting to be rude. "Lonzo?"

"Yes. Can I come in and visit? I came to see you both, not just you!"

"Oh, sure. Sorry, I was just taken aback that you're here—out of context and all."

"Oh, sure. I was at the landscaping show and I thought I'd drop over." Lannie and his two adult sons had a weekend landscaping business.

Pointing to the sign about isolation precautions, I said, "You just have to wash up, gown, and glove."

"No problem." Lannie went directly to the sink on his right and started washing his hands. "So I shocked you, didn't I?"

"Yeah, I guess you can say that. I didn't expect to see you here. It didn't register... I am happy to see you here, but I didn't expect it. This is so different from where we are, it's like we have landed on the moon, so don't take my fuzziness personally."

Lannie and I had worked closely together for the past ten years. He managed the team of technicians who would program and install the systems I sold. He was a trusted friend and co-worker.

"I saw you trying to figure that out. Yeah, my father-in-law was here a few years back, and that is why I knew you would appreciate the visit." Lannie was dressed and ready to head in.

When we walked into the room and he laid eyes on David, Lannie was visibly shaken. "Jeeze, what happened to him? Was he in a fire?"

"Huh? What do you mean, Zo?"

"His skin, it didn't look like that before he was sick…"

"Oh, yeah." For the first time, I realized that I'd been seeing David's skin every day and really watched the progression. It was gradual for me, but for someone who hadn't seen David, this was indeed radical and probably pretty disturbing.

"Yeah, his skin… Well, they are not really sure…"

"It looks really painful," Lannie said, twisting his face and trying not to look any longer.

"I guess because I'm here every single day, I might not have noticed it so dramatically. I think it's been gradual. And yes, it does look horribly painful."

"It looks charred. Poor guy," Lannie said, truly sad for David. "What d'you think'll happen? Do you think he will need a skin graft or something like that?"

"I don't know, Zo. I'm pretty much dealing with what is happening in the minute. David's skin is just part of the problem. I don't know; I guess, I'm just hoping and figure that it will improve like everything else has and will. Zo, I'm still so very hopeful that we'll get through this. And since he is sleeping, I'm also hoping he doesn't feel anything."

"Well, everyone in Lewisburg misses you. The company, your customers—they're asking about you and David. I hope that things turn around soon, so you can come home. I bet you miss those boys," Zo said, to change the mood.

"Yeah, Zo, I sure do, but this is what we have to do so we can have a future with our boys."

"Understood. Well, I'll leave you now. If there is anything that you need, or your parents or Heidi need back home, just let us know, okay?" Zo offered.

"Sure, Zo. Thanks for everything, and hi to everyone. Just ask them to keep praying, please."

"Will do. You know you can get claustrophobic in these things—the mask and the gown. It doesn't bother you?"

"No, I guess I hadn't noticed. Drive carefully."

"See you."

David's skin looked charred. The red turned a little darker each day, until now, it was black. Having lived through the progression, it was not alarming to see. But from Lannie's reaction, I saw that it was disturbing and shocking to see. But Zo's shock reaction was like that of other new people who entered David's room. Red, charred or not, I saw only David's strength and goodness.

From: Bernie Miller
Sent: Friday, January 17, 2003 2:32 PM
To: Mary M. Tiffin
Subject: If You Need Anything

Dear Mary,

We appreciate the updates concerning David. We will not panic if we don't receive them when you are home. We continue to pray. Please know that if you need us for anything, we will be there for you.

We BELIEVE.

Debbie & Bernie

From: IBGIB
Sent: Sunday, January 19, 2003 8:23 AM
To: Mary M. Tiffin
Subject: Beautiful Cousin

Yes, it is your look-alike again. Yes, we will pray and this will work. I'm sorry for all that you are all going through. I know that there will be a wonderful outcome—you will see. Vicki just told me a story about her friends just like yours and all is well now ... so hang in. We are all with you, catching you when you fall—feel the embrace.

Love,

Darlene

Just Like Us

David was a great conversationalist. He could talk to anyone about anything, and, as a result, he made friends easily. He was naturally very comfortable and had, as my mother often says, the "gift of gab." Our son Christopher is very much like his dad, so our house had always been lively and spirited, not often a place of quiet reflection. So this absolute quietude from my husband was just another loss that I blamed on this nasty disease.

I was so grateful that this hospital had great employees, otherwise, with David sleeping, I would have felt totally isolated during this experience.

"Hello, there!" came a voice from the door.

I recognized it immediately—Norm Donaldson. So I got up to go to the door to greet him.

"Hi, Norm. How are you?"

"I am well, but I think the more important question is, how are you two doing?"

"Oh, we're okay. Hanging in there. I'm still 'a lady in waiting' of sorts, holding tight for a strong count recovery. Do you want to come in?"

"Actually, I am headed to a meeting at one of the other campuses, but I wanted to tell you that I met someone yesterday, and the two of you may be a great support to each other," Norm offered.

"Oh, really. Who's that and why do you think that?"

"Her name is Diane Maul, and her husband, Mark, is also a BMT patient. She, like you, has young kids, around the boys' age," Norm described.

"Oh, the poor woman; poor family." I thought it was bad that we had to endure this, and I hated to hear that there was another family with young kids in the same struggle.

"Exactly, and that is why I think you two should meet. Here," Norm said, pulling a piece of paper out of his pocket. "I told her about you and I thought you'd want to connect. She reminds me of you in many ways. I think you will enjoy each other. This is her mobile number. Why don't you call her?"

"Oh, I will."

"Well, I gotta go. I just wanted to make that introduction. We're still praying, and we will pray you both outta here," Norm said as he was leaving.

"Thanks, Norm, thanks so much for thinking of us." I took the slip of paper and went back to David's bedside.

"David, can you believe there is another family in this hospital now like us?" As I sat down, I thought, *"God, that stinks for them."* And I was wondering where in the process her husband was. Is he just starting? Or is he sleeping like David? The physicians had said over and over again to me that David's progression through transplant was not the normal process, that somehow we fell off the normal grid. So what would I say to this woman if her husband were healthier? *"Oh, don't worry, we are not your average?"* How could she gain any comfort from meeting me? The only thing I could think of was that it looked like we both drew the short straw.

The thought of me sharing this with someone who was also living it seemed overwhelming. I slipped the paper under my laptop. *"Maybe tomorrow, maybe I'll feel more encouraging tomorrow…"*

I wasn't given the option of delaying our meeting.

There was another knock at the door.

I knew her. Not that we had ever met before, but as soon as I saw her face I knew we had a moment of instant recognition. Norm had been right. We shared the same walk. I saw in Diane's face the efforts at optimism, the attention to remaining steadfast in this world while wanting to retreat into a world of sadness and self-pity. And I saw in her, faith. All at a glance. She was my twin. Instinctively, we hugged, she feeling the same. At that moment, because of this shared experience, Diane Maul and I became fast friends. I invited her in and listened as she told the tale of the journey that she shared with her husband, Mark.

From: Diane Maul
Sent: Sunday, January 19, 2003 9:21 AM
To: Mary M. Tiffin
Subject: Sunday Prayers

Good morning, Mary.

It was so nice to hear from you and I am glad you are getting a chance to enjoy the boys. I have only seen my children about one week a month since October, and that has been one of the hardest things for me. Especially as our littlest one is learning so many words right now. Every time I seem him he is like a different boy, and I feel like I have missed it all!!

My friend Ann feels so burdened for both of us and our families, and sent an email last night to the whole praying community at the Heidelberg Army base in Germany requesting special prayer for David during this time. As you know, there are really few people who totally understand this process and what all the counts and days mean—and she is one of them.

We have gotten good news this weekend that they are going to let us finally leave Baltimore! Mark's counts have been holding steady for a week and they feel he can be treated in N.C. until our sixty-day check-up. I am a little nervous about him being around all the kids, but we'll have to pray for special protection from infection. He still really can't do much except move between the couch and bed—he is extremely tired and is not eating well. We hope to get out of here on Tuesday if the counts hold.

We are finally getting out of the Park Charles after all these months. I wondered if I could drop some food and kitchen things down at your apartment—unopened things that we have not used and will not fit in our car. I will probably leave them at the leasing office on twenty-four and will let you know when I do so. A local church has been supporting us and brought much more than we needed.

Mary, stay strong and on the rock of Jesus Christ; he will uphold you with his right hand in your trouble.

With prayers for your precious David,

Diane

From: Ann Winn
Sent: Sunday, January 19, 2003 9:45 PM
To: Mary M. Tiffin
Subject: A Friend Sent Me More Prayers

Dear Mary,

You don't know me, but we share a mutual friend—Diane M. She indicated to me that you and your husband, David, were in quite desperate need of prayer. Please know that there is a group of faithful servants praying for a divine and miraculous healing in the Heidelberg Base in Germany.

"Confess your faults one to another, and pray one for another, that you may be healed. The effectual fervent prayer of a righteous man availeth much." James 5:16

Prayerfully,

Ann

Believe... Believe... Believe Again

When people talked about transplant being difficult, they could never quite accurately describe why it was so hard. But now, with more than a month post-transplant, I had found that it wasn't just the toxic doses of chemo or radiation, nor was it the fact that the patient has essentially no immune system, and it wasn't even the fact that you had to host and grow another's cells in your body.

But it was all of these singularly deadly events, combined with all of the pitfalls that you never want or expect to happen. That is why transplant is so difficult. I had decided that when Goo Goo and Pa come to see David, I would go home. I needed a break from the constant daily fear. It was time to regenerate with our babies. I needed to be around the boys.

From: Mary Tiffin
Sent: Tuesday, January 21, 2003 5:33 PM
To: David's List
Subject: David Update

Dear wonderful family and dear friends,

Okay, so I spent a couple of days at home with the boys. It was wonderful to see them. I miss them so much.

Now, David. The totally EXCITING news is that he is officially off dialysis. His kidneys have recovered, although the doctors thought that it might take up to a year post-transplant—so we keep praying.

Regarding his numbers, David was basically as I left him—stable, with very low counts. Our nine p.m. prayer tonight (if you wouldn't mind) is again for his counts to rise and for God to protect him from infection.

I am really hoping to write with some really great count news. Well, thanks once again.

BELIEVE.

XOXOXO,

Mary

From: Kim Edwards
Sent: Tuesday, January 21, 2003 6:43 PM
To: Mary M. Tiffin
Subject: Re: David Update

Hi, Mary.

Glad to hear that you spent some time at home with the boys. I am sure they were very happy to see you!!! How are they handling all of this? It must be really tough on Chris.

Yippee for David getting off dialysis. I would think this is a huge step in the right direction!!

Keep sending us good news!!!

Love,

Kim

From: Mary M. Tiffin
Sent: Wednesday, January 22, 2003 12:38 PM
To: David's List
Subject: David Update

Hello, everyone.

Okay, we are in desperate times and we need desperate measures. The doctors are talking to me with concerned eyes again.

David's counts dipped to 24 while I went to the chapel a little while ago. Why do I keep harping on the counts, you may ask? Well, his white blood counts are critical to his recovery. They have to come up.

So what do you think about this prayer for our nine p.m. prayers? If you like it, could you please print it and we will say it at nine p.m. (EST).

"Heavenly Father, we call on you right now in a special way. It was through your power that David was created. Every breath he takes, every morning he wakes, and every moment of every hour, he lives under your power.

"Father we ask you now to touch him with that same power. For if you created him from nothing, you can certainly recreate him. Fill him with the healing power of your spirit. Cast out anything that should not be in him. Mend what is broken. Root out any unproductive cells. Grow his sister's white blood cells. Rebuild any damaged areas. Remove all inflammation and cleanse any infection.

"Let the warmth of your healing love pass through his body to make new any unhealthy areas, so that his body will function the way you created it to function.

"And Father, restore him to full health in mind and body so that he may serve you for the rest of his life.

"We ask this through Christ our Lord. AMEN."

Thanks, guys, and remember—BELIEVE.

With love and gratitude,

Mary

From: Carol Crabtree
Sent: Wednesday, January 22, 2003 10:15 AM
To: Mary M. Tiffin
Subject: Re: The Card

I just wanted you to know just how much I am thinking of you and caring about you. I am praying for you and asking for God's strength for you. My heart goes out to you, and I can only wish there was something more I can do! I would do anything you need. Just ask, okay?!!! We love you both!!!!!!!

From: Ann Winn
Sent: Wednesday, January 22, 2003 11:33 AM
To: Mary M. Tiffin
Subject: Praying with Everyone

Hello, Mary.

It's Ann from Germany. I just wanted to let you know that there are twenty of us gathered at nine p.m. (Eastern Standard Time) to pray for David's healing; to pray as you request in your emails. I am confident that, as we storm the heavens with our prayers, God will hear the prayers of this righteous man. Please stay strong. And we are BELIEVING in Heidelberg, too!

Love and prayers,

Ann

From: Mary Tiffin
Sent: Wednesday, January 22, 2003 9:39 AM
To: Friends
Subject: Michael Size Sighting

Dear girlfriends,

So yesterday, my heart was very heavy and I was most despaired of. It was hard to see David yesterday. It was just hard, and I was deeply sad.

I won't get upset in front of David. That happened once while he was still lucid and I will never do it again.

Anyway, on the way to the hospital this a.m., I saw a little fella walking with what I assumed was his father, and he was the perfect Michael size. It made me miss my babies, and I cried and cried.

Could you please ask God to give me a little more strength in handling this? I could really use it.

Thanks!

XOXOXO,

Mary

From: Barry Krishner
Sent: Wednesday, January 22, 2003 10:31 AM
To: Mary M. Tiffin
Subject: Prayers

Hi, Mary.

Just wanted you to know that you and your family are in our prayers. My wife, Karen, also passed some of the background information on the 9 p.m. prayer vigil on to some other folks at her workplace (Penn State).

May our good Lord hold you, your husband and children so very close in a warm embrace of peace and confidence in your faith.

Barry

From: Frank Fedora
Sent: Wednesday, January 22, 2003 11:02 AM
To: Mary M. Tiffin
Subject: Re: David Update

Mary,

Thanks for all the updates. I really look forward to them every day. Of course, each day we are all hoping that the "news from Mary" will have a positive tone to it.

Karen, Marc, and I are praying every night at nine (same time "Pokémon" starts!) for David. I have been wearing a "St. Christopher Protect Us" medallion that I had when I was a kid. I haven't worn it for YEARS, but it feels great to have it on. I will wear it for as long as it takes. I guess it will be working double-time on February 4 when Tom Gretchen gets his transplant. He will be admitted to the hospital on January 27.

If you think Chris would ever want to come and hang out with Marc, just have him give us a call. Karen has a home game on Friday around five thirty, and if he wants to come to that just let me know.

I guess I'll let you go for now. Have a great day.

Frank

From: Shelby.lammerdorf
Sent: Wednesday, January 22, 2003 2:24 PM
To: Mary M. Tiffin
Subject: Re: David Update

Mary,

I have sent your prayer to our friends and asked them to pray with us at nine each evening. The girls have also taken their copies to their school buddies and asked for their prayers. We all have faith that David will get better, and ask God to give you strength through all of this.

I also want to ask if it would be okay with you that I go and visit, even if it's only to see you for a few minutes. Also, know that our doors are open for you all. If you need to get out, want company, talk to someone... I will come and get you. If your family is visiting and needs a place, please let them know to call us. If you want the kids to stay with us, we would love to have them. We love you all very much, and if there is anything we can do to help, please, please, please let us know.

From: Jyummie
Sent: Wednesday, January 22, 2003 5:36 PM
To: Mary M. Tiffin
Subject: Re: David Update

Hi, honey.

We will certainly pray. I am so sad that you are sad. You have been so strong through all of this. I certainly admire you and only hope that I could be half as positive and strong as you have been, should I ever have to face what you are facing. I still talk to David each day, and I see things in the clouds to eat up his bad cells. We are pulling for him and praying for you. It's okay to be sad, it really is. This is a sad time. Call me if you need me.

I love you.

Johannah

From: Mary Tiffin
Sent: Wednesday, January 22, 2003 6:37 PM
To: Jyummie
Subject: Re: David Update

Johannah,

I was talking to God earlier, saying, "Hey, I could really use some help here. I am sad, really in a big way sad. Just give me something, anything—a post-card, a letter, a whack on the head!" when who should I run into but my favorite little, hip, Catholic priest, Father Sal. He was sweet and consoling, and I felt better.

We talked about God's will and how I really could give God 100 strong, in-fluencing reasons why my idea of his will are actually pretty good (keeping in mind that I am in Sales). Father Sal prayed with David. I was excited to show him my impressive collection of borrowed relics. Our room is a regular mini Vatican East.

After the novelty of his visit had worn off, (maybe two hours later)—and remember, I am crying sad—I asked God the same question—when who should knock on our door?

Knock, knock. "Hello, Mary."

There stood my favorite Episcopal priest and his friend Norm M. He brought a survivor friend along to meet me and to again pray with David. It was a wonderful visit. Nate is a great guy and has been a source of strength through this.

So there have been many highlights through the day, but the really big highlight will be David's big numbers—you'll hear me screaming for joy from Maryland to Connecticut.

So, I am doing a little better now. Thank you for your concerns. I love you, YO-HAWN, and I am so thankful that I have always felt that you were my official big sister.

I tried to get Aunt Carol to spill the beans about my adoption—at forty-one, shouldn't I know my heritage? Aunt Carol held firm to the family story that I was born of my parents.

Well, I am going to do a little reading now.

XOXOXOXOXO,

Mary

From: ttdmkel
Sent: Wednesday, January 22, 2003 10:06 PM
To: Mary M. Tiffin
Subject: 9 PM

Hello, Mrs. Tiffin.

What a beautiful prayer you composed for nine p.m. I will say it each night with faith and trust in the will of our Lord. I also pray for you, too, Mar. You've got a wonderful soft side, but you're strong like your mom ☺. (I really wish she'd let us bring dinners over! Let me know when we should start. I've got a list of folks who really want to help in any way.)

I'm glad David knows you're near. You're giving him strength to keep up the fight—he probably doesn't want to get yelled at again ☺. Glad to hear you will be coming home for the weekends. It will do you a world of good, but can't imagine how hard it is to leave either place.

Stay strong, girlfriend; you've got God and His Son by your side.

XOXO,

Denise

From: Mary Tiffin
Sent: Thursday, January 23, 2003 1:12 PM
To: David's List
Subject: David Update

So the white blood count is 6 today... 6. Just 6.

Please pray that we get these numbers up.

They are doing a bone marrow biopsy today at one p.m. Please pray for David at one p.m. Please pray that the results will yield good results, with his sister's marrow grafting and making cells.

Thanks. BELIEVE

XOXOX,

Mary

From: Mary Tiffin
Sent: Thursday, January 23, 2003 4:08 PM
To: ttdmkel
Subject: Re: 9 PM

Hello, Mrs. Kelcher.

Thank you for the kind note. They did David's bone marrow biopsy at one p.m., and I went to say a Rosary while they were doing it and I have faith that everything will be okay.

Oh, my dear, I must confess that I did not compose that prayer. I am not that ecclesiastically gifted (even though I had my Cardinal appointment—I can't help but throw my Catholic weight around—bless you, my child). It was a prayer sent to me by a friend, which I modified for my sleeping one. It is actually my favorite prayer in times of sickness.

Well, Denise, I will gladly accept dinners when I return to Lewisburg's suburb of Winfield. I want to get Christopher back involved in soccer and violin once

David is lucid and ambulatory. I know that with the boys, my job, and travel back and forth, dinners would be most appreciated. I'm just not there yet.

I actually thought David would be awake now, so I was planning a February return to work, but that hasn't happened yet. I think you should know that I will keep you posted on where I am.

My love to your sweet family.

BELIEVE.

XOXOXO,

Mrs. Tiffin

From: Steve Sattison
Sent: Thursday, January 23, 2003 3:18 PM
To: Mary M. Tiffin
Subject: Re: The Tiffins

Mary,

How are things going? Please let me know if I can be of assistance and if you've had a chance to make the webcams work for your family. I have kept your family in my prayers and hope things are getting better.

Steve

From: Mary Tiffin
Sent: Thursday, January 23, 2003 4:20 PM
To: Steve Sattison
Subject: Re: The Tiffins

Hi, Steve.

We really appreciate your email. My husband is, unfortunately, on a ventilator and is heavily sedated. We are definitely having a hard time.

We need to pray that his sister's marrow is engrafting and we have to get those counts up. When that happens, we are going to start talking to the boys in Pennsylvania.

Steve, thanks for your help and prayers.

BELIEVE.

Mary T.

From: Steve Sattison
Sent: Thursday, January 23, 2003 5:30 PM
To: Mary M. Tiffin
Subject: Re: The Tiffins

Thanks. I was hoping that there would be better news. I had a recent expe-rience that reminded me to check with you guys. I had asked my dad to add you to his list of people he prays for. My dad had left the Church for many years, but several things in his life caused him to return about ten years ago. Since then, he goes to church just about every day and prays for an hour for all those he can.

After the holidays, I was home one evening and received a phone call from my mom. Dad had a heart attack and has had a rough time over the past few weeks with recovery and various medicines. In addition, was the discovery that he's had a stroke at some point and is at risk for more.

He had bladder cancer last year, so it's been a difficult time for his health. He's sixty-seven and pretty well set for whatever happens to him. While I was visiting him in the hospital, he asked me to check up on you guys. Funny thing having him lying in a hospital bed, about to go into surgery, and asking about people he has never met. It made me appreciate him that much more. I told him I'd make sure that I checked in.

Steve

From: Diane Maul
Sent: Friday, January 24, 2003 9:08 AM
To: Mary M. Tiffin
Subject: Have Courage

Mary,

I am so burdened for you and David now and was up much of the night praying. Remember, Abraham and Sarah didn't get their son until they were 100 years old! God has a time for everything, and we pray that it is his will to heal David sooner rather than later! He and you have suffered enough already. Take courage that you are bringing many closer to the Lord through your faith.

"For I am the Lord your God, who takes hold of your right hand and says to you: Do not fear; I will help you." Isaiah 41:13.

If I didn't have so many of my own problems, I would come up there and sit with you! I thought Jim said your kids were coming down this weekend. I hope that works out for you. I was so torn when my kids were in town—wanting to be at the hospital and home with them at the same time. We continue to pray for your strength and wisdom, Mary. If you have time, read Psalm 86 today. I thought some days it summed up my thoughts!

Keep us posted. Blessings,

Diane

We Aren't the Giving Up Type

I wondered how much longer? "When, David, will your body kick in? In my heart, I believe that you are strong enough, but there are so many things that can happen to you? Every day, it's more of the same." Each day David slept, his marrow slept, we waited. I got the feeling that people here were expecting us to give up, to throw in the towel.

Somehow on the night of the fourteenth, David's code status got changed to a "Do Not Resuscitate" (DNR). I found out about it almost accidentally through our nurse last night. Before heading up here this morning, I went to the Social Services office and got several sheets of different-colored construction paper. With magic markers, I wrote out intentions: that David is unequivocally, undeniably, FULL CODE. This meant that the staff was instructed to intercede if David's heart stopped beating. There should be no confusion now.

From: Mary Tiffin
Sent: Friday, January 24, 2003 11:40 AM
To: David's List
Subject: David Update

Hi, all.

This will be the last update for this week. I will be going home to take care of the boys when David's parents arrive later.

This may be excruciating for you to hear all this talk about counts, but imagine, if you will, how it feels to us. It's so painful.

Today we are at 70. Still, nothing to write home about, but it's a little better than the 6 of yesterday. I feel that my life is revolving around those numbers.

The early information on the bone marrow biopsy didn't tell us anything. We are looking for the molecular stuff. Please pray that Melissa will engraft and start growing.

They are going to do a CAT scan of David's lungs. They are afraid that he might have pneumonia now. It's always something.

So what can I ask you to pray for? I don't know. How about to pray that his lungs are healthy and that he doesn't have a serious bladder infection. He's got blood in his urine. Please pray. Pray, pray, and pray.

BELIEVE.

XOXOXOXOXO,

Mary

From: Marty Kik
Sent: Friday, January 24, 2003 12:22 PM
To: Mary M. Tiffin
Subject: Re: David Update

Dear Mary,

Your son was an angel in Mass.

Your parents were very well received by the class afterwards.

You are loved!!!

Let me know if you need anything for the boys over the weekend.

XOXO

Love and prayers,

Mary Forester

From: Mary Tiffin
Sent: Friday, January 24, 2003 3:49 PM
To: debbymay
Subject: Re: Have Courage

Diane,

So how are you guys doing in N.C.? I continue to pray for Mark's complete recovery.

I am so uplifted by your emails. I am having another super-low day. David is now urinating blood and has a temperature.

I am overwhelmed by emotion. Even though my faith is strong, I am still so sad.

Every day, I beg God to help me, Diane. I know that He has, and continues to, but I still feel overwhelmed. The love of my life is lying in bed so sick, and I am so thankful that he doesn't know what's going on. So thankful.

I wrote you an email yesterday, a repeat of an earlier version that I am not sure you ever got, but in it I thanked you for the cloth. I have been laying it on David when I pray.

Well Diane, we wish you a very blessed day. I am going home tonight to be with the boys. I can't wait. It feels like I am going on vacation!

BELIEVE.

XOXO,

Mary

From: dianem
Sent: Friday, January 24, 2003 4:58 PM
To: Mary M. Tiffin
Subject: Re: Have Courage

Mary,

My heart is just breaking for you. I remember the one night I left the hospital and I just cried for an hour in the car. I couldn't even go up in the apartment and see my family. Mark was so sick that night, in complete misery, and I couldn't even stand it for him. I felt so helpless. I knew it was a time we just had to get through, but it was so horrible. I prayed and prayed and prayed and couldn't sleep.

Even with all that, I never had to go through what you are handling. It is a very hard moment to be in. I am not a fearful person, and I truly rely on God to take the burden of fear from me. I think you are this way, too, but the sadness is there even if the fear isn't. My overwhelming feeling was that, with God, I could handle life without Mark, but I didn't want to.

I hope that David is mercifully feeling no pain, as I can't imagine what he would feel without the medicine. I am worried for you, Mary, and wonder how you have the strength to make all the decisions that you need to. I know what it is like to sit in that room and wait for counts and test results.

I hope that you will be able to really enjoy your weekend with the boys, their every smile and snuggle.

"It is the Lord your God who goes with you; He will not fail or forsake you." Deuteronomy 31:6.

Blessings, Mary, as you travel home.

Love,

Diane

From: Carol Raynard IC US
Sent: Friday, January 24, 2003 5:46 PM
To: Mary M. Tiffin
Subject: Re: David Update

Hello, my sweets.

I've been following David's journey very, very closely.

I've been trying to give you space, but I really just want to touch base with you (yet another voice) to tell you how much we are praying and thinking about you guys.

You "sound" like you are hanging in there and that you are maintaining perspective.

I love your spirit and your devotion to David. I also know that David is worth every minute of it!

If you can add me to the email list, that would be great; otherwise, don't worry, Jo Jo's keeping me in the loop.

You know, it's funny—I have always loved Johanne, but it's David's illness that's bringing us closer (we spend a lot of time talking these days).

Again, we love you. Please take care of yourself. Enjoy those beautiful boys, and rest!

Hugs and kisses to all of you.

Your Husband is Kind of a Celebrity

I woke up this morning feeling unnerved. This would be a day of change. It started off wrong at the apartment. Under normal circumstances, I always made sure I had enough coffee and cream on hand so that I could have a cup before my shower. This morning, I ran out of cream, so I did not get to enjoy or even have my morning pick-me-up.

And to really interrupt my mojo, I learned Dr. Mattsui was now off the inpatient service. He had told me yesterday that his floor rotation would be ending last night. During this BMT process, we had started with Dr. Anderson for a few days, then he went off service. Dr. Anderson was replaced by Dr. Taylor for a few days, who was just filling in for a traveling physician, and then we had Dr. Mattsui. We have been through the most difficult part of the transplant with Dr. Mattsui. Not only was he a very good physician, but he was also a kind-hearted man who seemed to really care about David. I became fearful of losing him as our attending. Who would be next? What if we got someone who is not as diligent or compassionate?

I began feeling scared and nervous for David; for us. I started praying that this new doctor will come in with hope in his eyes. I arrived at the hospital, greeted my sleeping giant, assumed my normal spot in the makeshift desk by David's bed, opened the laptop, and started reading and responding to emails. Within the hour, a physician walked into the room alone, without any fellows, nurses, or any other ancillary staff, and quietly introduced himself and gave me his business card.

"Hello. My name is Dr. Ari Levinson. I'll be assuming your husband's care." Dr. Levinson was of medium height and build and had a nice face. Maybe eight years older than me, he was relaxed and comfortable, almost like he was visiting. When he spoke, in addition to David's treatment and experience, he noticed that we had sons and spoke of his children, so I was grateful that he recognized what was so important to us. He described the plan of care for David, which was basically waiting for his counts to recover and letting his body do what it needed to do. Dr. Levinson said that he had heard about our nine p.m. prayer times and was interested in it. I told him how it started and what has been happening since it started. Dr. Levinson said that we could schedule blood draws for ten p.m. to see how our nine p.m. prayers were working. I thought that was amazing and wonderful, and thanked him very much for it. The day had started out really poorly but got instantly better after meeting this physician.

"Well, David, that is a relief. I like our new doctor. This will be a good day after all," I said to my sleeping husband. I sat down at the computer and returned to my emails, then heard a knock on the door.

I opened the door to see a man in a religious collar, gowning and gloving.

"Oh, hello, Father. Won't you come in?" I said.

"Hello. Are you Mrs. Tiffin?" he asked.

"I am."

"I am Rev. Phil Simmons. I am not a priest; I am wearing the collar so I can visit patients. I lead a congregation of the faithful in Towson, a town in Baltimore County," he said with a nervous laugh.

"Huh," I thought, but somehow was not alarmed.

"Your husband is, I don't know how to say this, but kind of a celebrity," the reverend said.

"Excuse me?"—still not alarmed.

"Some people are calling him a miracle man," the man continued.

"Oh"—Thinking, *"So you wanted to see him for yourself?"*

"Rev. Simmons, my husband was miraculous even before we came to Hopkins. He is an unusually good man. In the twelve years that I have known this man, there has not been one single day that I have not thanked God for his presence in my life."

"Our congregation is praying for him on Sunday, and he is on our prayer chain."

"Thank you. May I ask how you heard about David?"

"One of our members is employed here at the hospital and may have assisted your husband in some capacity, and this person indicated that David was seeking prayers. This member has been keeping us posted. We are so pleased that God is responding to our calls. It is gratifying to witness His love."

"Thank you, Reverend. May I give you a photo of our family for your congregation as a reminder?" I said, offering him a Christmas card.

Taking the Christmas card, he said, "This is a nice picture. You have a lovely family. All boys?"

"Yes, all boys," I said, about the picture.

"A blessing."

"Yes. And if you have email, I can email you updates for your congregation?"

"Oh, I don't have email. I try and stay away from the computer. But my secretary does; she takes care of all of that stuff."

"Do you have her email address?"

"Let me see, it's something like 'kburrows at saint john church.' Or is it 'Kathy Burrows at st . . .'? I am not sure; I can't remember."

"Here, let me put my email address on the back of the picture, and you can ask Kathy to send me hers so I can add your church to our David Update list. How does that sound?" I asked.

"That sounds good. Would you like me to say a prayer now for your husband?" Rev. Simmons asked.

"Please." The reverend said a prayer and prepared to leave. "Thank you for stopping by, and will you thank your congregation for us? Tell them we really appreciate their prayerful compassion."

"I will, Mrs. Tiffin. God bless." And he left.

I turned and spoke to my sleeping husband, "Wow, honey, that was a nice visit. What do you make of that? Another church praying. You are a celebrity. Sleep well; everything is going to be okay. We're covered."

I returned to my chair feeling comforted that we had an even bigger group praying.

"And David, I told you those seventy-five extra Christmas cards would come in handy. I am handing them out like a politician.

"Now let's see what the pray-ers are saying." And I opened my email.

From: Todd Christy
Sent: Sunday, January 26, 2003 4:36 PM
To: Mary M. Tiffin
Subject: Our Hearts Are With You

Dear Mary,

Hi. I'm Kris, and I am here in my home today with my sisters, Marlene and Jodie; my mom, Carol; hubby, Tom; kids, Jake and Emily; and Grandpa Aaron. My sisters and I, when we were young, lived with Aaron and Mary. We always remembered "the letters from little Mary" that Gram would read to us. Today, your letters are more touching than ever.

Aunt Jody and Uncle Don have been keeping us posted, and we want you to know that our thoughts are with you. Grandpa asked me to tell you he has been praying for David and his wonderful family. If there is anything he can do, please let me know.

All our thoughts and prayers are with you, David, and the children.

With much love,

The Hartletons

From: Mary Tiffin
To: David's List
Sent: Monday, January 27, 2003 12:01 AM
Subject: Living On A Prayer

Okay, dear family and friends,

So here's where we are today, in case you haven't heard.

David has pneumonia.

And to make matter worse, we are still without any white blood counts.

BOOOOOO. HISSSSSSS. Talk about really crummy news.

But there is always an interesting side of the story.

While speaking to David's doctor today, even though he related the news about the pneumonia, there was positive news. The GVHD (graft-versus-host disease) team came in and were very pleased with his skin, so that appears to be under control.

The CAT scan revealed a substantial section in David's left lung being affected. The doctor went on to say that he was *surprised* that David was doing so well with his breathing, in light of the fact that he had pneumonia. (He was off the ventilator for three hours the other day, for goodness' sake!!!)

"Surprised?" I asked.

He said, "Yes."

"Protected," I responded.

He went onto say that most people would not have made it to this point (Day 35) without counts, and he had actually been expecting pneumonia much earlier. The doctor now feels the pneumonia is under control.

"Protected," I reiterated. Then I launched into my (and you all have heard it a billion times) "we are at Hopkins for your brilliance, but we know that ultimately God is in charge" statement. He kindly concurred and indicated that it is a balancing act, and said they were doing their best with the brilliance part.

If you could see darling David so close to the edge, so close to the light, you would know that your prayers are keeping him close. Your prayers are sustaining him.

With no white blood cells, no immune system, David is literally living on your prayers. We are at the precipice and hanging by a string.

Now are you ready??? Do you feel it coming???

Here it is, the prayer beg:

We want to thank you for all of the beautiful and selfless prayers offered, but could I ask one little thing? If you could, just *ask one more person* to remember David in prayer.

If you could, ask God to bring up those white blood cells and make his bone marrow biopsy be okay, protect him from infection, and cure his pneumonia.

We would appreciate it from the bottom of our collective, not yet broken (read "hopeful") hearts. We love you all and keep you close.

Well, guys, keep the faith, and BELIEVE.

XOXOXOXO,

Mary and David

From: Shelby.Lammerdorf
Sent: Monday, January 27, 2003 3:04 PM
To: Mary M. Tiffin
Subject: Re: David's Counts

WHAT GREAT NEWS, MARY - :) :) :) :)

We have a bigger group prayer tonight ! ! ! !

From: SADDLES40
Sent: Monday, January 27, 2003 6:42 AM
To: Mary M. Tiffin
Subject: Re: Living On A Prayer

Dear Mary,

I will call Kirsten's school today and ask to keep David on the prayer list always. Every morning in school they announce over the speaker whom they are praying for. It also goes home in the weekly newsletter. God always answers children's prayers.

As always, we are praying for you and yours.

Love,

Patrice

From: Mary Tiffin
Sent: Monday, January 27, 2003 2:41 PM
To: David's List
Subject: David's Counts

Wonderful all,

We are still waiting for the results of the bone marrow biopsy. Hopefully, around 5-ish.

I have been anxious to give you good news for such a long time regarding his counts.

I'll just put it this way:

140 140 140 !!!!!!!!!!!!!!!!!!!!!!!!!!!!!!

Can you tell I am out-of-my-mind excited? Your prayers are working. We are so blessed, and will let you know about the biopsy.

God bless you. BELIEVE.

XOXOXOXO,

Mary

From: Carol Ann Franski
Sent: Monday, January 27, 2003 3:09 PM
To: Mary M. Tiffin
Subject: Re: David's Counts

Dear Mary,

Wonderful news! I am so excited for you and David. God is answering our prayers, and the angels are watching over him. Keep the good news coming. Our prayers will continue faithfully for his healing. Amen.

Just to let you know, I did send the letter of introduction to Dr. Applebaum last night just in case you decide to contact him. Your news is really great, and I'm sure David will continue to do better daily. Keep the faith.

God bless. Love ya both!

Carol Ann

From: Terri Grasslie
Sent: Monday, January 27, 2003 4:32 PM
To: Mary M. Tiffin
Subject: David

Mary,

Loni has been passing David's updates to me. Mary, I pray for David, you, and the boys every day. All of our thoughts and prayers are with you.

So many people have been asking about you and David. David is a very, very loved and respected man. When I see people that David knew on his route, they ask about him and tell me stories about David. They are all good, wonderful, and helpful stories. Here are a few I can think of: Steve Heffner and Joan from Dr. Long's office, Tom Ebenhart, and Lisa Kern. This is what I remember and just wanted to let you know.

You may not physically be here, but you are with us always.

Your friend,

Terri

From: Jyummie
Sent: Monday, January 27, 2003 6:37 PM
To: Mary M. Tiffin
Subject: Re: No Subject

Hi, Mary Mary.

So happy to read your subsequent emails!!!! Carol's address is [carol.ray-nard]. It's about six thirty. Email if you can about the biopsy. I will check again later.

Another sky story to tell: I know it was a rough weekend for you, but on the way home Friday I was looking into the sky, as I do, and talking to David. I then saw a line (it was from a plane, of course). Then I saw another one. Then I saw random lines in the clouds the entire way home. I thought of that show that I really didn't like, "Who Wants to Be a Millionaire," and immediately thought of life lines.

I told David the sky was full of life lines and that they were all for him. Please tell him for me.

This afternoon the sky was calm. We got bad news about a young teacher's dad today. He died of an apparent heart attack. I was feeling very sad, and I started to yell at David and told him to start getting better—that we're waiting. Maybe I'll just keep yelling at him and his counts will get higher and higher.

Hope you have time to read this all.

I love you, I love David. Keep the faith and BELIEVE!

XXXOOOXXX,

'Yohawn'

Protect and Pray

My routine was the same, I would go to morning mass, dash to the hospital, get a second cup of coffee, run up to 5B, and wait for the sleeping David to recover. Always thinking that today would bring the breakthrough day. Most of my moments were spent talking to David, his nurses, or God.

Our lives were revolving around lab and test results. They would complete the test; I would wait.

I had been playing a game with David and the Christmas decorations. Since we had decorated before his snooze, they were a daily reminder of how long he had been sleeping. I had been waiting for David to wake up before I took them down. I vowed to keep them up until he could help me remove them. The longer he slept and hung in there with us, the more the decorations acquired a kind of magical quality, some sort of Christmas good luck charm. When people would come in and notice our little Southern North Pole, I'd make excuses for the "Christmas carry-over." But the truth was, I didn't want to jinx us; I just couldn't do anything to shift the weight on this delicate seesaw, so I kept everything exactly the same.

Silly, pathetic, irrational, superstitious—yes, all of those. But I couldn't see how it hurt. I was resolute that as soon as David started to stir, I would take them down. So, with the decorations looking so festive in an unfestive time in the dreariest, darkest time of the year, with my sleeping husband in this very hushed room, this was a time for reflection, prayer, and review. It was also a time to learn to wait and to find the value in acquiring physical and mental stillness.

I was not inclined to watch TV or read any of the books I had brought or that friends had sent. My little electronic Solitaire game, once an object of amusement and distraction, sat idly on the windowsill. I had no interest in the beep, beep, whirr of a hand electronically dealt. I sat and waited and watched, making sure no harm came to David, making sure that anyone who entered the room is gowned and gloved and following neutropenic precautions. If I couldn't make his cells grow, I could certainly protect him. And I prayed.

From: Mary Tiffin
Sent: Tuesday, January 28, 2003 12:46 PM
To: David's List
Subject: David Update

Okay, all,

Welcome to the Tiffin daily rollercoaster.

You may want to sit down when you read this. It's positive news, not bad news.

Okay, here is a wonderful story about the power of our prayers.

Yesterday, we met with our doctors, and they gave us the upsetting news that there was nothing in the bone marrow. Nothing... empty... nada... niente...empty. Not a cell in sight—no baby cells, no mature cells. Just bad, bad news!!!

That, coupled with the pneumonia, was just crappy—and there is no other word for it.

"Sepsis," he called the infection. Very large and looming.

When I asked if there was any positive news, the doctor said there was some interesting and optimistic news. There was an increase in his white blood count. It actually started out at 120 and then rose to 140.

They didn't know if it was real or a lab error, and they questioned the validity of those numbers due to the results of the bone marrow biopsy.

We also found out that there were neutrophils (mature and infection-fighting white blood cells).

We posed the question, "How can there be these neutrophils if the marrow was empty?"

We are in unchartered waters here at Hopkins. Most people don't make it to this point in this position.

The white blood cells are critical for the next step. There will be no step without this critical ingredient.

Well, here is the *big* news: we are at 450!!!!! 450!!!!! It is our fifth consecutive rise (we have never before had consecutive rises). The neutrophils are also rising. Since last night, David's white blood count has tripled. The doctors don't really have a good explanation for how he is growing cells without marrow.

I think we know, right?

Okay, here's the prayer. Just to make sure that we all understand, David is still dangling by a thread. (David still has a very high temperature, and the pneumonia is a huge concern.) We have seen the prayers work with the counts. Please pray that God will continue to protect him, raise his counts, and remove the infection.

Keep the faith and BELIEVE! Thank you.

XOXOXO,

Mary

From: SADDLES40
Sent: Tuesday, January 28, 2003 8:05 PM
To: Mary M. Tiffin
Subject: RE: David Update

Mary,

HOLY SHIT!!! That's awesome. This is PJ, by the way. Patrice would say HOLY MOLY. What is unknown to the medical community is easily explained. By some. I'll keep praying.

Petie

From: Mary Tiffin
Sent: Sunday, January 26, 2003 6:22 PM
To: Fred Appelbaum
Subject: Help

Dr. Appelbaum,

I am writing out of desperation.

I was given your name by a Hutch patient, Tamela Franski. I hope you don't mind me emailing you.

My husband, David, is an ALL allogeneic transplant patient at Johns Hopkins. His sister was his donor, and matched five out of six antigens, excluding the DRB1. He is forty-five years old and an incredible father to our three very young boys.

David is now thirty-five days post-transplant, and we still have no white blood counts to speak of. Do you have any suggestions?

Hopkins did a bone marrow test, and we will get the results of that tomorrow. I am desperate because David just contracted pneumonia and we need help.

You may return my email at the address above.

Thank you very much, Dr. Appelbaum.

Sincerely,

Mary Tiffin

From: Fred Appelbaum
Sent: Tuesday, January 28, 2003 1:22 AM
To: Mary M. Tiffin
Subject: Re: Help

Hi, Mary.

I'm sorry to hear about your husband's illness. Without a great deal more information, there is very little I can say about his case. The physicians at Johns Hopkins are very competent, and you should ask them what they think is going on and what their plans are.

If you would like to have your husband's physician call me, I would be happy to speak with him/her.

Fred Appelbaum

From: Mary Tiffin
Sent: Tuesday, January 28, 2003 3:39 PM
To: Fred Appelbaum
Subject: Re: Help

Hi, Dr. Appelbaum.

Thank you for your kind reply.

I am happy to report that since I last wrote, my husband, David's, WBC numbers are finally on the rise. We are at 450 today.

I wrote because I've heard that The Hutch had a lot of experience with delayed counts.

You are correct. The doctors here at Hopkins are extraordinary doctors and great people. We are very thrilled to be working with Dr. Avi Levinson and have great confidence in his experience and brilliance.

So thank you once again, and God bless you for the wonderful work you are doing to help in the frightening world of cancer.

Most respectfully,

Mary Tiffin

From: Fred Appelbaum
Sent: Tuesday, January 28, 2003 8:33 PM
To: Mary M. Tiffin
Subject: Re: Help

Hi, Mary.

I'm glad to hear your husband's counts are on the rise. Please give my best to Dr. Levinson. He is an outstanding physician and scientist.

Fred Appelbaum

A Call from Rome

I was coming back down the hallway, returning to the room, when Rich, the respiratory therapist, came to David's door and shouted to me, "Mary, hurry. You've got a call; you have an international call."

An international call? I wondered who would be calling. My traveling cousins knew to email me. I started to jog the remaining half-length of the hallway, not wanting to keep whoever was calling, waiting.

When I entered the room, Rich said, "Sorry. I don't normally answer the phone, but the desk clerk came in and said it was from Rome."

"From Rome?"

"Yes, that is what she said."

I picked up the phone. "Hello."

"Hello, Mary." It was a voice I instantly recognized.

"Oh, hello, Cardinal Keeler."

"Mary, is everything okay? Everything with David?"

I'd forgotten that I had placed a call to his office a day earlier when I was very distressed about David's condition.

I said, "Oh, Cardinal, David was so sick a day or two ago and that is why I called. I was calling to ask for you to remember him in your prayers. I was really afraid … I called your office… He seems to be slightly improving now."

"Yes, Mary, my secretary gave me your message. I am in Rome now with all the Cardinals. I haven't forgotten about David, and we are praying for him. So is he doing better?"

"Yes, a bit better."

"I'm glad that he is improving."

"Oh, thank you, Cardinal Keeler, thank you very much. I won't keep you."

"God bless you, Mary."

"And may God bless you, Cardinal Keeler."

"Thank you, Mary."

I hung up the phone.

I was so engrossed in the conversation that I didn't notice Rich watching me. "Was that Cardinal Keeler calling you from Rome?"

"Yeah, I guess he was.... So very kind of him, don't you think?"

"Listen, I am Lutheran, but I still think that is really cool. I mean, really cool."

"I guess we are just very lucky, very blessed."

"I guess you are. That's neat," Rich said, and he went on going about his duties with David's ventilator. "Well, it looks like I am about done here."

"Thanks, Rich, and thanks for grabbing me. I would have hated to have missed that call. Can I ask you a favor, Rich?"

"Shoot."

"Would you mind remembering my husband in your prayers? They are really important to us..."

"You got it, I'll pray for you and David."

"Thank you, Rich. I do appreciate it."

"Well, if they don't send me to David's room again, it was nice working with you today and I want to wish you both good luck. But I think you are looking for more than luck, right?"

"Yes, you could say that."

Rich grabbed his cart and pushed it out the door.

"Now, David, wasn't that sweet—the Cardinals are praying for you. We are so blessed." I sat down and pulled out the computer feeling so very, very fortunate.

From: Linda Paul
Sent: Tuesday, January 28, 2003 7:30 PM
To: Mary M. Tiffin
Subject: Re: David's Counts

Hi, honey.

I just wanted to drop you a quick line to let you know that I am thinking about you guys and have been praying for you. I hope that it is okay with you that I do things additional to nine p.m. and I have muttered a few Hebrew words. We all read the same first book, you know. If you need to chat, yell, scream, laugh, smile... I am always here for you.

Have a good night. Keep the counts rising!!!!!

Love,

Linda

From: Mary Tiffin
Sent: Tuesday, January 28, 2003 7:31 PM
To: Linda Paul
Subject: Re: David's Counts

Linda,

It was so nice to hear from you. OF COURSE, I want your prayers. God is God, right?

I have been thinking of you often, but am so very busy with David.

Well, honey, know that I am thinking of you and I hope that you are okay. It is easier for me to write about David's condition. When I *talk* about it, I get ill.

Take care of yourself.

XOXOXO,

Mary

Can You Hear Me?

Dr. Shah mentioned that they were not sure what the patients could hear, if anything, in a sleep state like David's. I continued to talk to him as if he could hear, listen, and would soon respond. Why wouldn't I? I mean, I felt like he could hear. So today, I started my day of bargaining, bargaining with the Sleepy Head.

"Hey, Kathy." I was happy to see Kathy as David's nurse. Kathy waved hello from entering numbers into the computer.

"Good morning, honey. Your wife is here," I announced as I entered the room. "I've been thinking about you, you know, lying there, playing possum. It's time to wake up, and as an incentive, I've decided to bring out the big guns."

David lay motionless, deep in the Versed/Fentanyl slumber, the only sounds coming from the machine supporting his life.

"So last night, when I decided that you were forcing my hand, I came up with this plan to sweeten and hasten your wake up time. David Tiffin, when you wake up from this you are getting what you always wanted!" I got closer to David so Kathy could not hear. "Honey, they think that with all you've been through, you might not be there anymore. I guess we'll have to show them, huh?"

In a normal voice, "So I'm guessing you are wondering what the big prize is? What is behind door number one? Well, David, you wake up and you are getting your Hoover Wind Tunnel. Now, how is that for exciting?"

Kathy looked at me. "David's dream is a vacuum cleaner? You're kidding, right?"

"Well, maybe 'dream' is the wrong choice of words. Let's just say he wanted one, okay? We just didn't want to spend 300 bucks on a vacuum cleaner." David did the vacuuming at our house and he was always investigating the newest in vacuum cleaning technology. First, he'd wanted an Oreck, and his most recent vacuum dream was the Wind Tunnel.

"I was thinking most guys would like big screen TVs or sports cars, not vacuum cleaners," Kathy said, and we both laughed.

"Wait, Kathy. What's that you say, there's more? A bonus prize? You're right! David, you wake up and you are going to get your dog! No more 'I'm allergic' whining from this wife. You pick out your puppy. Now, you can take that baby to the bank."

Kathy just shook her head and turned around.

From: Mary Tiffin
Sent: Wednesday, January 29, 2003 1:56 PM
To: David's List
Subject: David Update

Okay, all,

Boy, what a difference day makes!

The great news first: the counts are 660!!!! 660!!!

Our Christopher asked me to tell Daddy that he wanted his "blood pressure" to go to 660, and, true to form, David gave Christopher exactly what he wanted ☺.

So, now, at least we have something to work from.

David had a little "thing" going on with his urine, and Dr. Levinson mentioned that he was very concerned about that and we should pray for his kidneys and bladder.

Well, I know you are not surprised, but those are fine today.

Everything else that they were concerned about, like his blood pressure and most of his skin, are pretty good and not a huge concern.

So here is the new prayer focus. David still has a very high temperature, probably from the pneumonia. Please pray that his temperature gets under control and his body is free of any new infections.

Guys, we have come such a *long* way, but we still have a very long way to go.

Keep the faith and BELIEVE.

XOXOXO,

Mary

From: shelby.lammerford
Sent: Wednesday, January 29, 2003 2:46 PM
To: Mary M. Tiffin
Subject: Re: Fwd: David Update

Mary, what great news on David's white blood cells.

We had contacted these three large churches to pray for David and list him on their prayer list for several days. Maybe we should ask everyone to call their church also.

St. Anthony's in Falls Church, Nativity Church in Burke (the one where we baptized Kissie) and St. James in Falls Church.

I hope you are feeling better. We love you very much and send our big hugs and kisses to all.

Shelby

From: Cole
Sent: Wednesday, January 29, 2003 3:10 PM
To: Mary M. Tiffin
Subject: Support

Mary,

I didn't even know that I had your email address, but I found it today in my address book.

You have been ever on my mind and I have so wanted to talk to you, but don't want to call not knowing when it is a good time. I have been kept updated by Mara, who calls me every several days to let me know Dave's status. I wanted you to know that we are all praying very hard for Dave's recovery. I am also praying every day for your health and strength. I hope that you are taking care of yourself and trying to eat and rest a bit. Please know that you and Dave are in our thoughts and prayers daily.

With much love,

Wendy

Can You Hear Me?

It's a Girl!

I was writing thank-you notes and answering emails, and I lost track of time again. I wound up taking a later-than-normal dinner, heading down to the Cobblestone Café at around eight. I grabbed a slice of dried-up, left-out pizza and a diet soda. Sizing up my dinner choice, I realized that I wasn't in such a hurry to eat after all, so I swung by Big Jesus to say hello and a prayer for David. Seeing the Jesus statue at night was always so calming; there was never a big crowd around him and I found great solace in the quiet. I returned to David's room around eight forty. As I set my dinner down on the little table, I was surprised to hear someone in our room.

"Hello, Mary," said Dr. Levinson. He was a wonderful physician and man, one whom I quickly learned to trust and respect. He, like Dr. Mattsui, did not mind my constant barrage of questions or suggestions, and was sensitive to our perspective. He was the picture of brilliance and compassion.

"Well, hello Dr. Levinson. You're here awfully late. Is everything okay?"

With the door open, Dr. Levinson was leaning with his back against the door jamb.

"Everything is okay. I have a question for you. Do you see pink booties or blue booties?"

I really didn't understand what the kind doctor was saying. "Dr. Levinson, I'm not pregnant.... Is that what you are asking?" I asked, confused.

Dr. L chuckled. "Oh, no, Mary, that is not what I am asking. Pink or blue? You don't remember? The FSH test? We tested David's blood to see what it was."

"Oh, yes, you're right, I remember!!!!" I could sense that Dr. Levinson had some good news, but I didn't want to assume anything and be disappointed, so I waited.

"What is it, Mary, a girl or a boy?"

"I don't know, you tell me."

If the test results came back as male, it meant that the blood in David's blood growing from his marrow was originally his, not a good sign. If the test results returned as female, that meant Melissa's marrow had engrafted and was growing in David, a miraculous sign.

"I can't stand it, just tell me!" I prompted the good doctor.

"It's a girl, Mary, it's a girl," Dr. Levinson said, with a smile on his face.

Until that point, I hadn't noticed how excited our Nurse Susan looked as well. When Dr. L shared the news, she clapped.

I felt like I was going to fall over. This was the first bit of actual news we had received that the transplant was *actually* working. I had to sit down. This was good news; we had good news!

"Oh, my. Thank you, Dr. Levinson, that is the very best news. Thank you so very much."

"I got the results a little while ago and I had to come and tell you. I knew it would make your night. This is very, very good news, Mary. Congratulations on your girl!"

A wave of relief spread over me, I got up and gave Dr. Levinson a hug. "You have made our night. Thank you."

"Goodnight. I'll see you in the morning," Dr. Levinson said as he left the room.

"Goodnight."

I sat down for a few minutes and let it settle in. *"Thank you, dear God, for the gift of today, thank you for this good news. We so needed to hear something positive."*

I got up and went to David's bed. "Honey, we got a really great sign today. You heard Dr. Levinson—Missa is in there working. You hang in and do what you need to do. I really think we're going to be okay. Take your time and heal, but know we're going to be fine. You're being so brave and so strong. I love you."

From: Mary Tiffin
Sent: Wednesday, January 29, 2003 7:10 PM
To: lorribc, JYummie
Subject: DAVID NEWS FLASH

Okay, here is some GREAT and uplifting news. They did a genetic test on David and were thrilled to report that David's marrow is MELISSA'S.

HIP HIP HOORAY. I AM DOING A HAPPY DANCE!!!!!

HAPPY!!!!! HAPPY !!!! HAPPY!!!!

It's like they say—God may not come in your timetable, but He's never late.

They have very effectively wiped out David's hematopoietic (blood developing) system and replaced it with Melissa's. The doctor said they are thrilled.

Want EVEN MORE GOOD NEWS??? His white blood count is now up to 920!

So here is the new request from the doctor for prayer: Please pray for his GI tract and that things start to move down there.

This request is from me: Please pray that his fevers go away, and stay away, while he builds an immune system.

Thanks, and BELIEVE.

XOXOXO,

Mary

From: Eva Peterson
Sent: Wednesday, January 29, 2003 8:28 PM
To: Mary M. Tiffin
Subject: Prayers

Hello, Mary.

I took the liberty of sharing your update note with my daughter, Janice Dietzel, and with my neighbor, Jim Keller (retired from Lewisburg High School), and with my son, Andy, in North Carolina. The result is prayers offered at St. Joseph in Orefield (near Allentown), the Lutheran Church in Lewisburg, and by my son and some others in North Carolina. In addition to continued prayers by us at Sacred Heart parish.

Take care, and God's blessings in abundance.

Eva Peterson

But I Play One on TV

Dr. Levinson did not always round with the entire team as some of the other physicians often did. Occasionally, he came in after rounds to talk a little longer about what was going on with David.

"Today, and for the past couple of days, I've had concerns that David is not clearing the infection in his lungs. I am working with the pharmacy on other possibilities. But based on David's sensitivity to vancomycin and a few others we have eliminated, it appears that we've used every drug available to treat a patient in his condition. The fact that he still has pneumonia is troubling. This could lead to more difficulties for him," Dr. Levinson sensitively delivered.

"So, as I understand, he has fungal pneumonia, and current broad-spectrum prophylactic antifungal hasn't affected it at all?" I asked.

"That is correct. We also have to be concerned about the other issues that David has at the same time," Dr. L answered.

"So have you given any thought to caspofungin—Cancidas? From what I understand, it is kidney- and liver-friendly," I offered.

Dr. Levinson looked surprised and asked, "Mary, what do you do?"

"Excuse me?"

"For a living? What do you do for a living?" Dr. L asked.

"Oh, I play a doctor on TV . . ."—I'd been dying to say that line since David and I got there—"Well, I do a little of this and a little of that."

"Really, what do you do?"

"I'm in technology. I'm a network specialist in the broadest sense, meaning in my career and personally. I have a very large group of friends with many different areas of specialization. A couple of my friends made the caspofungin suggestion," I answered.

"Caspofungin? I'll talk to pharmacy," Dr. Levinson said.

"Well, I did kind of say something to them earlier today when I noticed that David wasn't responding so quickly. I hope you don't mind—just for them to kind of research it," I said sheepishly, with a smile.

"I'll consult with them," Dr. L said.

"Dr. Levinson, I really don't want to appear pushy, but please understand that in this bed is not just a bone marrow transplant patient, but a kind, generous, warm and loving soul. A person who sends flowers anonymously to lonely old ladies who are getting cancer treatments, a person who would go out of his way to someone in need, a person who does his acts of kindness without the expectation that he will get something in return.

"He is a fair, decent human being, a one-in-a-million kind of guy, much more beautiful on the inside than his handsome and hunky exterior. And you know what, Dr. Levinson? For as close as we are, David has never spoken to me about his fears with this disease. He did not want me to be scared. He is always putting me and others before himself. David is that kind of guy. The world needs more Davids, not fewer.

"That is why I am trying so hard. In that bed is my entire life. He is my children's father—and, believe me, with me as their mother, my sons need him. I need him; he is my best friend and partner. I can't imagine living my life without him. I just need to know that you won't give up on him. I need you to keep on trying. Please, it's important to us. And me maybe 'pushing the envelope' with you all, is just me being my husband's best friend and advocate. I can't let him down. And if sometimes I sound pushy or rude, I apologize—that is not my intention. I am not trying to be rude; I am trying desperately to keep this man alive, as if I can do it by my sheer will and determination."

"Mary, I appreciate you saying that, but you didn't have to say that. I have not found you to be rude. Instead, I see you and have used the term 'Steel Magnolia' to describe you. You are doing what you need to do for David. You have been a tremendous advocate. So, there is no need to apologize. We are not giving up; we'll keep trying. And, one more thing—if anyone can keep him alive by sheer will and determination, I'm betting on you, Mary."

From: Mary Tiffin
Sent: Wednesday, January 29, 2003 4:02 PM
To: Laurie Bergerstock
Subject: Cancidas

Hi, Laur.

I just spoke to the pharmacist and will be talking about Cancidas tomorrow. I just spoke to you about David's pneumonia and his rising temperature. I love the people here.

XOXOXO.

BELIEVE.

Mary

From: Laurie Bergerstock
Sent: Wednesday, January 29, 2003 9:25 PM
To: Mary M. Tiffin
Subject: Re: Cancidas

Hi, Mary.

Did the bronchoscopy reveal a particular organism? In the study I was involved in, it looked at Cancidas in patients with neutropenic fever. It is approved by the FDA for candidiasis and invasive Aspergillus in patient's refractory to other antifungals. You can find information on the Net at www.cancidas.com. If they are asking you to participate in a trial with the drug, I would not be afraid to do it. It is showing to be a safe drug! We want to protect those kidneys!!!

I am going to call you.

Love,

Laur

From 13 to 4,775

In my free time, I would occasionally do Google searches on Acute Lymphocytic Leukemia bone marrow transplant survivors, and it certainly didn't do a lot to boost my morale. The sites that I visited were not sources of inspiration or hope.

Frankly, the survival statistics were not good for David's disease. I recognized that, but, statistically speaking, someone must survive in the 30 percent post-transplant survival group.

Someone has to be in that group, and David had as good a chance as anyone—better, actually, since his baseline health and fitness had been so strong before leukemia, I would tell myself. So I continued, as hard as it was, to search the Internet to find one survivor, just one. I wanted to know that there was someone out there who had gone through this process and survived; someone who had come out on the other side.

There were many transplant survivors, but we had yet to meet, or even hear, of one with David's type of leukemia. I wanted to find one for him to meet so that he had a connection when he woke up.

When the search came up empty again, I returned to my emails. Hearing from our friends and family was always uplifting and a source of inspiration. There were responses to the emails about David's rising counts.

"So, every time I walk back by this door, I see you seated at that little table typing. Are you doing work?" Dr. Levinson asked as he walked into David's room.

"Well, I don't know if I would call it my normal job, but I'd call it work. And I do other things as well."

Dr. Levinson drew closer and was standing behind me now, looking at the screen. "So what are you doing?"

"This, Dr. Levinson, is my email list for David."

"I think I've heard a little about this list."

"So, you know every day when I ask you what we should pray for? When I say, 'Dr. Levinson, what is our prayer prescription?' and you tell me, 'It's David's lungs… his skin… his urine…,' I come to this laptop and tell the praying friends to pray."

"Oh, I see. And is the Cardinal one of your praying friends? A little birdie told me that he called you from Rome."

"Yes, I guess you could say the Cardinal is a praying friend, but I don't email him—I call instead. I am not sure how he feels about email. Here check this out." I opened up a new email message and clicked on the address book icon, and scrolled until I saw the words "David's List." "See this? See this David's List? When we were first admitted, there were about thirteen names on it, but check this out now." I double-clicked on the highlighted words, and addresses started to fill the screen.

Dr. Levinson's eyebrows raised and then he watched the names scroll.

"At their request, I have added people since we arrived. Some of these people we know, others we've never met."

"And they heard about you here?"—still trying to figure it out.

"I guess friends have told friends, who have found us. It's been very touching."

"It looks like a pretty big group"—watching me scroll through the addresses.

Keeping my finger on the ball of the mouse and rolling it up and down, I said, "So, just yesterday I tried to count them, and I kept getting different numbers. My eyes were getting all funky and I was losing count. But of all the email addresses, some are representatives of groups, so the number actually came out to somewhere between 4,600 and 4,775 praying supporters."

"You have that many people?"

"So when I ask you for a prayer Rx, it is because I am getting our praying friends queued up to pray."

"That is really something."

"It is, it's a tremendous blessing. And I feel the need to tell folks how we are doing."

"So you type."

"You got it. I tell them by email. Many of these names represent a praying group, so, at last count, I know we have between 4,300 and 5,000 praying for David at nine p.m. Eastern Standard Time."

"It helps create a lot of peace for me."

"So, Dr. Levinson, I know Jesus isn't your man, but you are a God guy, right?"

"Yes, I think I understand what you're saying—when I say I'm not a Jesus but God guy," Dr. L answered, with a smile.

"Do you remember when I asked you to repeat labs at ten p.m.? Well, just like you do experiments as a man of science, I am doing an experiment as a woman of God."

"Okay, that's very interesting. I am interested in the ten p.m. labs also."

"Thank you, Dr. Levinson."

"No, thank you, Mary."

After Dr. Levinson left, I returned to the computer.

From: IGBIB
Sent: Wednesday, January 29, 2003 10:26 PM
To: Mary M. Tiffin
Subject: Hee Ha

Great news, Mary.

Thanks for sharing and thanks for those beautiful children. Christopher's request to his dad and the way David's body responded—amazing! I have always felt that Christopher was very special, and now I know. I can't wait until we meet—all of us—still praying and thanking God and angels and guides.

Love to all.

BELIEVE.

Darlene

From: Linda Paul
Sent: Thursday, January 30, 2003 8:25 AM
To: Mary M. Tiffin
Subject: Re: DAVID NEWS FLASH

Yay! Yay! Yay! Yay! I am doing my little happy dance for you, too! See, your token Jew friend helps ☺.

Kisses, wishes, and prayers to all!

Linda

From: David Burnside
Sent: Thursday, January 30, 2003 6:38 AM
To: Mary M. Tiffin
Subject: Re: DAVID NEWS FLASH

Mary,

I'm so happy for all of you. To see 920 for the blood counts has tears dripping down my face.

As the counts rise, it gets easier to fight the infections.

The prayers continue.

Dave Burnside

From: Jan Reibsome
Sent: Thursday, January 30, 2003 10:49 AM
To: Mary M. Tiffin
Subject: Prayer

Greetings, Mary and David.

I am a friend of Jean Moohr's and have been getting all of the reports/prayer requests and praises regularly. I am praying and trusting an awesome God to meet your every need, calm every fear, give you both rest and peace in the midst of these storms, and heal David. I know that He is able to do—and far exceedingly, abundantly—all that we can ever ask or hope for.

"When your vision of God gets cloudy because of pain, keep looking. You're about to see Him more clearly than ever."

Mary and David, I believe that. Keep exercising those faith muscles, and the day will come when we rejoice in what God has done.

In continual prayer for you and your family,

Jan Reibsome

From: Roreback, Melanie
Sent: Thursday, January 30, 2003 2:39 PM
To: Mary M. Tiffin
Subject: Re: DAVID NEWS FLASH

Oh, Mary,

THIS IS FABULOUS!

What a wonderful God we serve!!! I can't wait to meet with the rest of New Life Ministries this evening to tell them the great news. There's going to be some heavy-duty praising and worshiping going on there tonight! But don't worry, we will still go on praying just as we have been.

Please know that I will also share the email from your friend Debbie with the girls tonight, and we will pray for Mark.

We'll keep the prayers coming, and WE DOOOOOO BELIEVE!!!!!

In Christ,

Melanie

From: ttdmkel
Sent: Thursday, January 30, 2003 4:32 PM
To: Mary M. Tiffin
Subject: Another Miracle

Hello, My dear Mrs. Tiffin.

ALLELUILA!!!! Oh, Mary, I've been thanking God all day today for answering this important step in David's recovery. What a miracle. Are the doctors amazed, or what? Our prayers are still with David, and you both are never far from my thoughts and prayers.

Well, my bunch of bananas is getting out of control down here—even Gracie gets into the act ☺.

We'll continue to TRUST and BELIEVE!

Love and XOXO,

Mrs. Kelleher

From: Mary Tiffin
To: David's List
Sent: Friday, January 31, 2003
Subject: DAVID UPDATE

Hi, all.

In the transplant business, there are great days and crummy days. Yesterday was a great day with rising counts and no temperature.

But in general, this has been a miraculous and beautiful journey.

Dr. Levinson said yesterday that we have a direct line to God. How did he know I was in telephones?!

Today, David's counts are 1,770 with 1,231 neutrophils. I am out of my mind excited.

The not-great news is that David has a swollen head. A big head. And they are trying to figure out what it is. They are doing an ultrasound to make sure it's not a clot. Please pray that it is just fluids. It's always something. And we are still waiting on the tracheostomy.

Well, guys, I'll keep you posted. Keep praying.

Those prayers are really working.

And please BELIEVE.

XOXOXOXOXO,

Mary

From: Pendeleton, Alexandra
Sent: Friday, January 31, 2003 11:50 AM
To: Mary M. Tiffin
Subject: Re: DAVID NEWS FLASH

Hi, Mary.

Chrissy has been forwarding me all the updates, and I have been forwarding them off to some special friends here at the office. Everyone I have asked has been praying for David, you, and the kids.

If there is anything you need me to do (at least from New York; my hours are crazy), I would love to help.

I am constantly thinking and praying for you. I love you and miss you and I hope to see you soon.

With all my love, thoughts, and prayers,

Allie

From: Mary Tiffin
Sent: Friday, January 31, 2003 12:38 PM
To: Pendeleton, Alexandra
Subject: Re: DAVID NEWS FLASH

My sweet cousin Ali,

Thank you so much for your email and for your offer of help. Just knowing that my New York cousins are thinking and praying for us is enough. Please just remember him in prayers as often as possible—we are really up against the wall right now, and Ali, you know I wouldn't ask for this if I absolutely didn't need it.

So, thank you, baby. And we will see you when we are all better, whenever that will be—and I hope it is not too far away.

XOXOXO,

Mary

From: Cole
Sent: Friday, January 31, 2003 1:10 PM
To: Mary M. Tiffin
Subject: Re: Hello

Dear Mary,

I just had to write to you and tell you something that happened at our church. I really didn't realize it until yesterday when a friend of mine pointed it out. Last Sunday, our preacher asked me about David. At that point, it was looking really bleak, and I told him that things were not going well and asked him to pray for David and his family for strength. He announced this in church, and then we prayed. He prayed that "a miracle would happen that would amaze the doctors and staff of the hospital." Then I spoke to you on Wednesday and you told me about the doctors beings amazed, but it didn't click (you know my thick head). The next day, I was talking to Gary

Espenshade, and he asked about David. I told him the news you had relayed. He immediately picked up on the "miracle" aspect and said how wonderfully God is working. I'm not saying that it was those particular prayers that worked (although we all want to believe that it is our prayer that is making a difference), but I believe that the multitudes of people who were praying for a miracle really made a difference! God was showing our congregation that prayer is effective and that we must pray in faith always.

Thanks for putting me on your email list. I so much appreciate getting the updates.

Love,

Wendy

"And we know that in all things, God works for the good of those who love him, who have been called accordingly to his purpose." Romans 8:28

From: Hanna Bulger
Sent: Friday, January 31, 2003 5:51 PM
To: Mary M. Tiffin
Subject: David!

Mary,

That's such great news about David's counts going up little by little each day!!!! Wonderful!!!

Somebody's listening ☺. I'm sure there's a long road ahead, but he's come miraculously far and I pray that it continues this way. Kidneys functioning on their own is really great, too! He's got a lot to fight for—not just the boys, but you, too. Please be sure to take care of yourself as well.

Believing,

Hanna J

From: JYummie
Sent: Friday, January 31, 2003 6:11 PM
To: Mary M. Tiffin
Subject: Re: David Update

Keep the good news coming. We all know it isn't like David to have a swelled head! HA HA.

We'll keep praying!!

XOXOXOXOXO,

Johannah

From: Mary Tiffin
Sent: Saturday, February 1, 2003 12:33 PM
To: JYummie, mariapita61
Subject: Miracles Abound

Hi, everyone.

Okay, so we are still in critical condition, but I feel that we are not as close to "the light" as we have been.

So here is the David update: David's WBC is 3,770!!!! All other vitals are perfect. Praise the Lord!!!

He still, however, has a low-grade temperature, and he's still puffy and has a biggish head. The docs think it's probably just fluids. Another miracle is that David's ultrasound is clear.

Provided his platelet level is high enough, they are going to perform his tracheostomy today. They need to get the tube out of his mouth, and this will be our next step toward waking him.

David is still sleeping, but he appears to be very comfortable. The doctors came in today and have said that David has broken many records here at Hopkins. There have been a lot of firsts.

When he does awake, he will be so happy that he was able to help the doctors here.

Mo is here with me now, and I know that David feels her presence. He has "blinked" in acknowledgment of our questions.

Okay, guys, here is the prayer prescription: Let's please pray for his GI and that the trach goes okay and his mouth heals well.

BELIEVE.

XOXOXOXO,

Mary

From: Diane Maul
Sent: Sunday, February 2, 2003 10:38 AM
To: Mary M. Tiffin
Subject: Fwd: Fwd: DAVID UPDATE

Mary,

Can you add Marty to your list? She is gathering prayers in her hometown of
Roanoke. Her email is attached. Thank you.

How is David and how are the kids?

XO,

D

From: Wolfanner
Sent: Sunday, February 2, 2003 2:52 PM
To: Mary M. Tiffin
Subject: Re: Miracles Abound

Mary,

Thanks for the great news. We pray it continues.

Stay strong!

Love,

Lana & Richard

From: Mary Tiffin
Sent: Sunday, February 2, 2003 5:08 PM
To: Ceccila62
Subject: Re: Just A Touch

Hello, Pamela.

How are you, my dear? Today was finally trach day, and David is now settled
into his room. He did well through the procedure.

It's amazing how good this side of critical can be. Every day it appears that
we are getting farther away from "the light." I thank God for that—and you

know what, Pam? It is God because there is no medical explanation for what has happened there.

We still have a very long way to go, but we have had some successes. Thank God.

David is amazing me, and I am so proud to be married to this man. He is amazing everyone here at Hopkins. It's really cool.

Thanks again, Pam. We miss violin.

XOXOXOXO,

Mary

From: Roreback, Melanie
Sent: Monday, February 3, 2003 9:05 AM
To: Mary M. Tiffin
Subject: Re: Miracles Abound

Hi, Mary.

Praise God!! This is so wonderful. We have been praying, among other things, that David's WBC would increase exponentially, and God has been doing just that. I believe that God is using YOU and DAVID mightily to touch so many other lives. The two of you are absolutely AMAZING, and both so very strong! When I shared the good news on Thursday night with everyone (WBC was at 940 at that time, I believe), we all cried (tears of joy!!). Then we immediately stopped and started praising and worshiping and thanking God like crazy.

We are all praying (my children, too—the first thing they ask me each night when I get home is, "Did you get an email today, Mommy? How is Mr. Tiffin?") and believing for David and also Mark. Please let Diane know that we are keeping him in our prayers as well.

Thanks, Mary. WE ARE BELIEVING. FAITH LEVELS ARE SKYROCKETING!!!

Love,

Melanie

From: Mary Tiffin
Sent: Monday, February 3, 2003 12:31 PM
To: David's List
Subject: DAVID News

Okay, everyone,

So here is the great stuff first: WBC 11,330. God is good!!!!

We are still waiting for a trach. They didn't get to do it yesterday, or the day before, or the week before, so we are waiting.

His skin looks great—no more discussion about the skin-eating bacteria.

Oh, we have had some bad moments, some really bad moments. All of the doctors have remarked how incredible (amazing) it is that his skin is so good.

Now here is the somewhat spine-tingling news. You know there is always spine-tingling news in transplant. Please pray for David's lungs. He has been on a respirator for so long, and when they suctioned him a few minutes ago there was gunky stuff in there. SO WE KNOW how powerful your prayers are. Please pray for that.

Well, friends, please keep praying. And BELIEVE.

XOXOXOXO,

Mary

From: Raynard, Carol
Sent: Monday, February 3, 2003 1:44 PM
To: Mary M. Tiffin
Subject: Re: David News

Hi, my sweets.

I am in Mexico as we "speak." Now my energy and prayers are coming from yet another place in the universe.

Love ya!

From: Ceccila62
Sent: Monday, February 3, 2003 1:46 PM
To: Mary M. Tiffin
Subject: Just A Touch

Hello, my beautiful friends!

We have our constant thoughts and prayers, and we know that God is working His "magic" in your lives. We do believe!!!

I can only imagine what it must be like for you to try to be everywhere and handle all of this at once. Mary, you will deserve a BIG vacation when David is recovered.

Jean Mowery asked me to let you know that she has thought of you alone there, and has offered to come down to sit with you through a weekend. She knows what it is like to wait by the bedside of your loved one, and she wants to help. I told her I would pass this information to you.

Well, my dear, take care of you, too. We are grateful for the news you share about David's recovery, and we will keep on praying—and also for your friend Mark.

Love and hugs to you both.

Pamela and Gus

Breathe Again

What a difference a budding immune system makes in fighting disease and lifting spirits. I began to wonder if we could be finally turning a corner here. I felt like I could breathe again!

From: Laurie_Bergerstock
Sent: Monday, February 3, 2003 6:00 PM
To: Mary M. Tiffin
Subject: Hi

Hi, Mary.

Just a quick note before I get into my day. I wanted to let you and David know that I have been thinking of you and I continue to pray. I will look for your update when I get home this evening. How did you make out with the antifungal? What is David on? Did you receive a box at the apartment? Gotta scram.

Much love,

Laurie

From: Mary Tiffin
Sent: Monday, February 3, 2003 6:00 PM
To: Laurie_Bergerstock
Subject: Re: Hi

Hi, Laur.

We are finally trached, and David tolerated the procedure very well. They are going to start weaning him off the vent sometime late tomorrow. Laur, I am so looking forward to hearing him talk again. He was on the ventilator for something like twenty-seven days. Yikes.

His WBC count is 11,330. So many things are going very well.

No more discussions of the pneumonia. David has a little temperature now, but has been fever-free for a couple of days.

Now, Laur, I tried to type you earlier but I have been having problems with my email. I wanted to thank you for being such a doll with your package. The blanket came in very handy—with the baby, Heidi packed everything so nicely, but forgot a blanket. The magazine and goodies were a great diversion down here. Thank you so much for thinking of me.

Well, Laur, I have to leave the room now. They are bathing David. You take care of yourself. Love you lots, Laur.

BELIEVE.

XOXOXOXO,

Mary

From: Laurie Bergerstock
Sent: Monday, February 3, 2003 7:59 PM
To: Mary M. Tiffin
Subject: Secretions

Hi, Mary.

Well, now that David has his white cells working, they are eating up those bugs in his lungs, thus gunk. Is he still oxygenating well? What is holding up the trach? Are they talking any time frame for the vent? What antifungal is he on?

So the blanket came in handy? The bright yellow was to represent sunshine. I'll bet Stephen was kept awake by that color! Ha.

Speaking of the boys, you mentioned they were with you. How are you managing? Who is helping you?

Sweet dreams. Love to all,

Laurie

From: Mary Tiffin
Sent: Monday, February 3, 2003 9:59 PM
To: amsmith, mschmidt
Subject: Christopher Off From School

Hi, Anna and everyone.

Just a quick note to let you know that the boys and my parents are down here with me. David had his tracheostomy scheduled for last week, but with the complications, it was finally done today.

The nurses and doctors are absolutely amazed. Thanks to all your beautiful prayers. They are quick to caution us that we have a long way to go. We are still in critical condition. We're critical but STABLE (my new favorite word).

Anyway, I am coming home tomorrow, probably Tuesday around one-ish, so I'll pick up Chris's homework—and his report card, of course.

Christopher will be back to school on Wednesday. Well, thanks, all.

BELIEVE.

XOXOXO,

Mary

From: Mary Tiffin
Sent: Monday, February 3, 2003 10:23 PM
To: Laurie Bergerstock
Subject: Re: Secretions

Hi, Laur.

We are doing okay. I am so thrilled that we have the trach. They were delayed because of the tight OR schedule.

All his I's and O's are great. His counts are great. His bili numbers are fine, and his creatinine and BUNs are inching down, so we are rock stable again. Hip hip hooray.

Okay, he's oxygenating well, his pulse oximetry is between 98 and 100, and his blood gasses are fine, if that's what you are asking.

They are going to lighten his sedation starting Wednesday, although he was pretty light today and "spoke" to me with his eyes. They gave him a bolus.

I am thrilled about stuff and looking forward to talking to David again.

Well, honey, gotta go home. Please give my love to everyone at your house.

XOXOXOXO,

Mary

From: Karen Fedorah
Sent: Tuesday, February 4, 2003 10:32 AM
To: Mary M. Tiffin
Subject: Thinking of You All

Mary,

Hey, it's Karen Fedorah writing, and I just wanted to pass along a hello and a smile because it's been so long since we've talked. I've been staying in touch daily through the emails Frank receives, and David, you, and the entire family are in our prayers constantly. I just wanted to tell you again that we're all with you in prayer and spirit and you are in our thoughts around the clock. Don't worry about writing back (I know that's why you send out the mass email). I just wanted to send along some hugs.

I'm amazed at you as well, Mary! You have been so incredibly strong through all of this. And, David, he's amazing. I know that it is his incredible will to live and the prayers that are doing it.

Please don't hesitate to call on us if you need anything. We're all praying. Our love to both of you!

Love,

Karen

From: Laurie Bergerstock
Sent: Tuesday, February 4, 2003 8:01 PM
To: Mary M. Tiffin
Subject: So Glad

Hi, Mary.

Thanks for the updates. I read them daily. Voriconazole is a relatively new drug, too. I am glad he is on it!!

Everything is sounding on the up and up. Let's keep going. I hope the weaning goes well. Keep me posted.

Love to both of you, and I think of you constantly. Tonight I am feeling a bit under the weather, so I am heading for the tub.

Good night.

Laur

Can't Wait to Talk with You

At the risk of jinxing us, I really felt that we may have turned a corner. I was beginning to see that there was a light at the end of this tunnel. I was excited to think of talking with David again. He'd been asleep for such a long time. I wondered what he's heard or seen at those times when he'd been so close...

You hear those stories about people seeing God or angels at the time of near-death experiences. I couldn't wait to hear what David said he saw.

From: Mary Tiffin
Sent: Wednesday, February 5, 2003 12:52 PM
To: David's List
Subject: David Update

Hi, all.

"God whispers to us in our pleasures, speaks in our conscience, but shouts in our pains. It is his megaphone to rouse a deaf world" —C.S. Lewis

Okay, so we are so roused!!!

I am happy to report that most of David's vital numbers are in the normal range. His platelets are on the low side, but we are definitely getting better.

Many of the docs here come in and just shake their heads. They can't explain how well he is doing in light of where we have come from. They feel that David is doing AMAZINGLY well.

Even though he is still on a ventilator and is still critical, we are inching farther from the light. I want to THANK YOU all for that, because it is your prayers that have worked.

So his GI tract is now working—another Hallelujah! They are going to do a procedure today to aspirate some of the fluids in his lungs, so please pray that it goes well.

They hope to be able to lighten the sedation enough so that he will wake by the weekend. I will be out-of-my-mind excited.

I am at home with the boys today and we will be leaving tomorrow, so I can be there without interruption in David's early days of waking.

Okay, guys, so that is our update. Again, thanks for all the prayers. The prayer prescription is that he will wake painlessly and without incident when the time comes. In addition, the prayer for his aspiration at two today. Thank you.

BELIEVE.

XOXOXO,

Mary

From: Jean Paulhamus
Sent: Wednesday, February 5, 2003 1:47 PM
To: Mary M. Tiffin
Subject: Re: David Update

Mary,

Just had to let you know how anxiously I await these updates every day. Lannie sends them on to me, and I send them on to my sisters, a girlfriend, and the church. We are all encouraged by how God is answering prayers on David's behalf. There certainly is no other way to explain it, is there? My sister called me this morning wondering where yesterday's update was. Co-workers were asking what was going on (at Sun Orthopedic. Jane (my sister) sends these out to Pittsburgh to a pharmacist friend who understands so much more of what you report. She just marvels and praises God for how He is touching David. Our faith has been encouraged and made stronger. To God be the glory and may the good reports continue.

Jean

From: snecarnes
Sent: Wednesday, February 5, 2003 2:32 PM
To: Mary M. Tiffin
Subject: Mass

Dear Mary,

We had Mass said for David yesterday at St. Peter's Church on Big Pine Key, Florida. There were six priests participating!! They like to come here on vacation, and when they do, they say Mass. Must say it was quite impressive. One priest we have gotten to know well, as he comes to the Murrays' for dinner often (the Murrays are my daughter-in-law's family, and we are staying with them). We are thrilled at David's progress and pray for him and for you.

Love,

Sally Carnes

Confident Enough to Wonder

I was beginning to feel confident in our hope. I was wondering what David's been doing in there this whole time and what he had experienced. When he became strong enough, I'd share it with him.

From: Mary Tiffin
Sent: Thursday, February 6, 2003 2:47 PM
To: David's List
Subject: EXCITING David Update

Hello, all.

I am so excited to tell you what I am about to tell you that I just can't type fast enough.

Let me start by saying that way back when David was first diagnosed with leukemia, he chose to go on a study or protocol. He did this because he was hoping the world of science and medicine would benefit from his participation and that he could help other patients struck with leukemia after him.

Then, when we came to Hopkins, he said the same thing—to paraphrase, "I hope that whatever they learn from me will help others."

You may recall my saying that Hopkins has never before seen a skin condition like David's (read- "this bad") in the thousands and thousands of transplants they have done.

The graft-versus-host team came in, and one of the prime members of that team is a woman by the name of Veronica Andrews. Since Hopkins has an internationally renowned GVHD department, Hopkins conducts seminars all over the world to assist in the treatment of GVHD patients worldwide.

They presented David's case at the seminar in which Veronica spoke. It just so happens there is a person in Miami who has experienced the same skin problem as David. The information the clinician received from Veronica was helpful for the person in Miami and now that person is headed in the right direction. Isn't that unbelievable!!! I am overjoyed.

Veronica said that David is a medical miracle. Isn't that just amazing? No, it's just God.

The other super-fantastic news is that David is waking. He is very light on the sedation and he knows that I am here. He has also been moving a little. It's a beautiful (I use that word a lot don't I?) thing. Well, guys, we can't thank you enough for all of your prayers.

If there is anything I can do for you—except give you my first-, second-, and third-borns—I'd like to repay you for the fervent petitions, and am up for suggestions.

The prayer Rx tonight is to allow David to totally wake and keep him free of infection.

God bless you all, and thanks again.

BELIEVE.

With ecstatic hugs and kisses,

Mary

From: Raynard, Carol IC US
Sent: Thursday, February 6, 2003 3:01 PM
To: Mary M. Tiffin
Subject: Re: EXCITING David Update

Okay, now I am in my office crying with absolute joy!!!

And yes, it's beautiful.

We love you and your boys, kiddo!!!!

From: Steve Sattison
Sent: Thursday, February 6, 2003 4:37 PM
To: Mary M. Tiffin
Subject: Re: EXCITING David Update

I am grateful to be included in the news about your miracle. Maybe I'll get to meet this amazing person one day.

Steve Sattison

From: Mary Tiffin
Sent: Friday, February 7, 2003 2:08 PM
To: David's List
Subject: GREAT David Update

Okay, guys,

This is a great email . . .

I am first going to take you back to January eleventh when we were called into the hospital at four forty-four a.m. when the doctors sadly informed me that David was very close to, if not at, "the light." Remember???

I generally don't like to remember, but we need to know where we are coming from in order for you to truly appreciate what I have to say.

Anyway, you may recall on that night we spoke to the pulmonary doctors, who said that, basically, they saw no way out of where we were. They said that David either had a pulmonary embolism (blood clot), heart attack, or septic shock—remember? When I asked Dr. Wolfender what I should pray for (which was the best of the worst), she said they were all equally bad, and all meant "the light." My response was, "Okay, then we just pray for total healing." I then asked Dr. Wolfender if she ever saw miracles in a state such as ours, and she gave me an unequivocal no.

Well, I saw the doctor today and I reminded her of the conversation from almost a month ago. I asked her if we were her first miracle, and she said yes!!! I told her that we were happy to do it for her. She said that it was really neat for her as well. Isn't that the greatest? We converted another skeptic.

Now some additional great news.

The doctors with the formerly long faces now have happy eyes (I assume they are smiling, as we are masked, so I can't see their mouths). Anyway, the mood has changed dramatically.

All of David's vitals are good.

His numbers are strong.

He has been using the ventilator as backup support for the past twenty-three hours. He is initiating his own breaths rather than the ventilator doing all the breathing for him.

They are using words like "impressed" in speaking about David. I always knew he was impressive.

So isn't that beautiful? And I have to thank God and you for your beautiful prayers.

Our new prayer is for him to have a safe weaning and that God continues to protect him from infection.

Well, thanks, all, and keep BELIEVING. I do.

XOXOXOX,

Mary

From: Janet Moser
Sent: Friday, February 7, 2003 2:21 AM
To: Mary M. Tiffin
Subject: Re: EXCITING David Update

Mary,

What joy! God is so good. I had tears in my eyes as I read your last two messages. Just think of all those doctors, considering science maybe really didn't have everything to do with David's progress.

Max (who is in preschool) told me that he prays for Mr. Tiffin during the circle time at school, which means that he offers his intention, and all eleven of those sweet four- and five-year-olds pray for David. The prayers of children are so powerful. Charlie tells me that he and many of his fifth-grade class-mates offer David's intention in their daily classroom prayers.

Praised be God!

Janet

From: IBGIB
Sent: Friday, February 7, 2003 1:24 PM
To: Mary M. Tiffin
Subject: Re: EXCITING David Update

Don't you know how much you have done for all of us, letting us be a part and helping?

And we all pray more now and we all have more faith than before. So you have given us this gift. Kiss David, beautiful David, for his cousins. And we hug you.

Always,

Darlene

From: Christine M. Gordon
Sent: Friday, February 7, 2003 5:25PM
To: Mary M. Tiffin
Subject: Re: Hello

I received and have ALWAYS BELIEVED!

I am so very moved to hear your encouraging news! Everything else becomes so trivial, doesn't it? Please, please, please, tell me what I can do—take the kids, send you to the spa, sit and hold your hand. Just let me know. I'll make rounds of Bucks County churches again and relight those candles.

Patrick has never forgotten Mr. Tiffin in his prayers, nor have we. Wonderful things happen every day—we just have to know where to look and when to appreciate them.

Let me know the best way and when to get in touch. Save your energy for your husband and kids. God will take care of the rest!

Thinking of you always,

Chris & Dan

From: Diane Maul
Sent: Friday, January 7, 2003 6:29 PM
To: Mary M. Tiffin
Subject: Re: GREAT David Update

Mary,

This news made my day! Praise God for miracles. I continue to pray for David this weekend and hope you have a special time together. We are safely in North Carolina and so happy to see the kids. Keep us posted.

WE BELIEVE.

XO,

D

From: Jyummie
Sent: Friday, February 7, 2003 7:25 PM
To: Mary M. Tiffin
Subject: Re: Reality Check

Hi, my Mary Mary.

Yes, it is very sad, and I have tears in my eyes. We are truly blessed that we can keep telling family and friends about how well David is doing. We had a snow day off from school today. It was pretty relaxing until Catherine decided she "had" to get to work. I wouldn't let her drive, and of course she was upset with me. Charlie will pick her up later tonight. Every time I tell Alex about David, he gets this sweet smile on his face. He is so happy to hear good news.

David has prompted Charlie to get a complete physical. All is well, I am grateful to report. My mother has finally decided to go to the doctor! Of all days, she's going on the thirteenth.

I love you and now feel in my heart that things are going to be okay. Please tell David we love him. He is truly an inspiration and a life changer for us all.

XXXXOOOOOOOOXXXXX.

BELIEVE.

Johannie

From: Jake G. Ravern
Sent: Friday, February 7, 2003 9:47 PM
To: Mary M. Tiffin
Subject: Re: Reality Check

Dear Mary and David,

We continue to "storm the gates of Heaven" in prayer for your continued strength, protection, and blessing.

Love to you both.

Robbie & Jake

From: Probst
Sent: Friday, February 7, 2003 10:42 PM
To: Mary M. Tiffin
Subject: Re: GREAT David Update

Mary,

This is truly great news. I have been submitting David's name to my church's prayer group that meets every Wednesday. I will continue to submit and pray for the two of you until David is home.

I will continue to BELIEVE.

Yours,

Paul

From: Mary Tiffin
Sent: Friday, February 7, 2003 6:11 PM
To: David's List
Subject: Reality Check

Okay, folks,

I think that I have mentioned before that this is indeed a scary floor.

Since we have been here, I would say about twelve people have gone to "the light." Please excuse the euphemism, but some words I cannot bear to write.

So when they bathe David, I generally leave the hospital and return to the apartment to do apartment stuff. It normally takes about two hours.

When I returned a few moments ago, someone was coding.

I am listening to the doctors and nurses attempt to resuscitate this patient.

The "All Clear" and the sound of the paddles is indeed a slap in the face and upsetting.

Up until today, all others left quietly or in the middle of the night.

Please pray for protection.

We can only BELIEVE!

XOXOXOXO,

Mary

From: Caitland Stewart
Sent: Friday, February 7, 2003 4:38 PM
To: Mary M. Tiffin
Subject: Re: Reality Check

Hi, my dear friend Mary.

This email rings with truth and love and sensitivity. I was "on call" the night before last, and indeed there was a "code" (would love to know the origin of that term) on Nelson, and as part of the "protocol" (yet another unfeeling term) the on-call chaplain is part of the responding team.

After forty-five minutes of physical, mental, and, I hope to add, spiritual work, the patient survived.

Thank you for reaching out to pray for others in your time of need. You, indeed, are a special child of God, and it continues to be a privilege to be a part of your journey. I am leading the Protestant service on Sunday, so I will come up after the service and just offer a hug, prayer, or sense of presence, and stand ready to do some practical things for you, if needed.

A mediation tonight for all of us:

"The light of God surrounds me.

The love of God enfolds me.

The power of God protects me.

The presence of God watches over me.

Wherever I am, God is."

Amen with grace,

Caitland

From: Jody Hutchinson
Sent: Saturday, February 8, 2003 4:20 PM
To: Mary M. Tiffin
Subject: Re: Reality Check

We are here, praying like mad, every day—for David, for Mark, for the others, and also for your mom and dad, the boys, and you. You have touched the hearts of countless people with your wonderful fortitude and spirit. When this is all over and David is back home and strong, we are so looking forward to meeting him (although I feel like we know him well). And boy, are we going to party!!!

We BELIEVE!

Love,

Jody

From: Mary Tiffin
Sent: Saturday, February 8, 2003 4:22 PM
To: David's List
Subject: David Update

Hi, all.

Saturday used to be my favorite day, but the last couple of them (today included) haven't been days to write home about. So why am I writing, you ask? Because things have turned around again (I am getting so dizzy).

Rounds started this morning with concern about David's blood gasses. He was too alkaline (which is not a good thing) and his pulse was also really low, like upper 40s to mid 50s (which is another bad thing—the gasses being low). There is a name for it, but who knows what it is? So they were concerned about that.

Then, like most things (fortunately), David did another about-face and is back again to where he was when I left him last night.

The doctors think that perhaps they were a little aggressive attempting to wake him by reducing his sedatives so significantly. So the awakening will be a little delayed or perhaps slower that I had hoped.

God is still working with me in that lesson in patience. Boy, do I need help in that area.

So that is our story.

The prayer Rx for tonight again is for protection from infection and a safe awakening.

Now, for all of you dear friends who have asked, Mark is on a new expanded radiation schedule. He is walking and talking and receiving symptom relief from the radiation. Hallelujah! He and Debby are now in North Carolina with their children, enjoying the weekend with them—the best medicine there is. So please remember them in your prayers. We are praying for a full recovery and a miracle.

Well, thanks, everyone.

BELIEVE.

XOXOXO,

Mary

From: Caitland Stewart
Sent: Saturday, February 8, 2003 6:21 PM
To: Mary M. Tiffin

Mary, my "dizzy" friend,

Oh, dear... patience? This is what you need? I may need to refer you, as that is not my strong suit, I will tell you.

So, in full denial of my limitations, I shall change the subject and offer the following:

"At times I feel the winds of illness have made a barren landscape of my life.

I can no longer see mountains to be climbed in the distance.

But then I look around me and I realize that I am soaring above the mountains.

They look so small from my new perspective." —Scott Shephard

Will check in with you tomorrow. Blessed hugs for you being you.

Cait

From: Mary Tiffin
Sent: Sunday, February 9, 2003 12:22 PM
To: David's List
Subject: David Update

Okay, so David is not Superman, as I was feeling a couple of days ago.

This is a quick email to ask you to start praying when you get this email for David's temperature to return to a normal number. He is currently at 93.7, which is very, very low. Hypothermically low. Sometimes an extremely or unusually low temperature can also be a sign of infection.

They are culturing again for everything, and we will see what happens.

Everything else is okay, but David always gives us something to worry about on the weekends.

Please pray hard and BELIEVE.

XOXOXO,

Mary

From: Mary Tiffin
Sent: Tuesday, February 11, 2003 11:15 AM
To: David's List
Subject: Baltimore Miracles

Please note that this e-mail contains information indelicate in nature.

Read at your own discretion.

Dear all,

I really wish that you were here with me to experience this journey because, quite frankly, I am having problems believing my own eyes. I'd like someone to witness the astonishment in the faces of the doctors and nurses.

Even though Baltimore is rated No. 2 in the country as far as violent crime is concerned, I really love this city and what we are experiencing here.

Here are a couple of "true cool conversion" stories.

Story No. 1

In a recent conversation with one of my favorite nurses, Kathy, she related that it has been a while (years) since she has been to church. Kathy was our nurse on the night they called me in to say goodbye to David. While discussing that painful night, and David's miraculous improvement, Kathy said what she saw in that room was sending her back to church.

Story No. 2

I had a conversation with our pulmonary doctors (a group of doctors who see these patients only while they are on ventilators and asleep—obviously not a group vitally dependent on social interactions). Anyway, while talking to Dr. W, I asked what she attributed David's great recovery to. I told her I knew.

She said that she knew also.

After several "you go firsts" ("You go first." "No, you go first." "No, you go first" —you get the picture), she said she thought it was "your prayers, a little fairy dust, and good medicine."

I agreed with her about the prayers; forget the fairy dust and great science. If you knew this woman, you would understand how big this was.

Story No. 3

Now here is the indelicate part.

Remember when I asked you to pray for David's GI (gastrointestinal) tract? That was our prayer prescription from Dr. Avi Levinson. When Dr. L started giving me prayer prescriptions, he had already witnessed several improvements in David's health following prayer. After he made this request, he said, "If David poops, I'm converting!"

Great stories.

So where are we today? David is still not awake, but they are lightening the sedation. He is doing fantastic as far as his lungs go, but he still has a problem with this third-space leaking. They are going to put a tube into his intestines to feed him and bypass the stomach.

His hypothermia (read "freezing cold"; everyone questioned whether that was a typo) is gone and he has a regular-ish temperature. No one has an explanation for that, either.

Again, we cherish your prayers as much as we cherish your friendship. Your prayers are saving David. BELIEVE that. I thank you.

Now, if you cherish your friendship with me, please delete this email, because David would be mortified if he heard I was talking about his poop.

BELIEVE and God bless you.

XOXOXO,

Mary

From: Shelby.lammerdorf
Sent: Tuesday, February 11, 2003 12:41 PM
To: Mary M. Tiffin
Subject: Re: Fwd: Baltimore Miracles

Mary,

David's miracle has touched and converted many of us. I especially share with Sasha, who, at this teenage stage, does not believe David's recovery could work with prayers. She prays together with us, but thinks it is some other form of power that is making David well.

I wish we could be there with you to see and feel this miracle. I so admire your strength, and feel your joy, and give thanks, and pray each day for his health.

We love you guys.

From: Bernie and Debbie Miller
Sent: Tuesday, February 11, 2003 1:42 PM
To: Mary M. Tiffin
Subject: Prayer

We are getting to know God as a very close friend these days. Thank you, David. You have worked some divine miracles, too.

Please forgive us for not making it to the dance. We had our tickets and were dressed and ready to go. Boyd came home from work unfit for a night out. His secretary had been sick last week and may have shared. We were thinking of you, nonetheless.

We continue to pray.

Bernie and Debbie

From: Carole Franski
Sent: Tuesday, February 11, 2003 8:05 PM
To: Mary M. Tiffin
Subject: Re: I Agree – Great Idea!

Dear Mary,

By the way, I got your letter yesterday and enjoyed reading it. It is amazing how circumstances do bring people together and you feel that you have known someone for years. I'm sure this is what God intended. People bond together quickly when they are going through very similar situations, because each is able to understand what the other person is feeling.

Our prayers will always be with David, and he will soon, like my daughter, put this all behind him and look forward to a new life.

I was so happy that you finally got to talk to my daughter, and, hopefully, soon you can meet her in person. She was happy to speak with you, and if you ever need to ask her anything, please do not hesitate. She is very open to any questions about her transplant.

Well, Mary, take care of yourself, and God bless David. I just know he is going to be up and about before you know it.

I will always BELIEVE.

XO,

Carole

From: Paula Hunt
Sent: Tuesday, February 11, 2003 8:15 PM
To: Mary M. Tiffin
Subject: Re: GREAT David Update

Praise God!!!!!!

I hope to stop by to see you tomorrow. I wanted you to know how often I have thought about you and prayed for both David and you. I put David on the prayer list at my church. I am so glad to hear of his improvement.

Happy eyes are definitely better than "those" eyes.

God bless.

In Christ,

Paula

From: Mary Tiffin
Sent: Wednesday, February 12, 2003 12:57 PM
To: David's List
Subject: DAVID Update

Hi, all.

So here is the David update for today. David is again rock stable; nothing new to report.

The weaning is going very, very slowly. David is liking the narcotics a little too much and having a little problem getting off the drugs. He is going through some withdrawal and is getting agitated.

So please pray for a safe awakening and continuing the road to recovery. This is a blasé day.

Thanks, guys,

XOXOXO.

BELIEVE.

Mary

From: Norman Donaldson
Sent: Wednesday, February 12, 2003 1:57 PM
To: Mary M. Tiffin
Subject: Re: DAVID Update

Mary,

Thanks for visiting with Paula today. She is seriously seeking God's will for her new life and feels that being a supportive presence among survivors might be part of her mission.

You and David just continue to help us all stretch and grow. Be good to yourself on this blasé day, okay?

YBIC,

Norm

From: Christine Gordon
Sent: Wednesday, February 12, 2003 5:34 PM
To: Mary M. Tiffin
Subject: Re: Fwd: DAVID Update

Hey! Remember that blasé (first I typed "balsee"—it might be more accurate!) is a good thing considering the alternative. Take a break and get some rest. "West Wing" is on tonight—have a glass of wine and relax!

We are thinking of you always.

Chris

From: Mary Tiffin
Sent: Wednesday, February 12, 2003 6:36 PM
To: David's List
Subject: Special Prayer Request

Hi, all.

I have a special favor to ask tonight when you get this email, or at the nine p.m. prayer time—could you please say a special prayer?

If you could, please pray for David's NG tube to find its way to his intestines so they will be able to start the tube feeds. If you could, also pray the red urine ends (again).

Thanks, I appreciate it so much.

XOXOXO.

BELIEVE.

Mary

From: Lynette Mitchell
Sent: Thursday, February 13, 2003 11:08 AM
To: Mary M. Tiffin
Subject: EMAIL from LANA in Allentown

Dear Mary,

Thanks for the continuing updates on David's condition. It is truly amazing with all the peaks and valleys that he has gone through. As you have said over and over again, miracles have been witnessed. How wonderful and great.

Mary, YOU are truly amazing also—yes, you are. I know you would dispute that, but you keep such a positive attitude through all the trials and tribulations. So many other people would have given up by now. Your emails carry your cheery personality, which is wonderful at a time like this.

We are all continuing to pray for David and your family, and look forward to the day we can visit him. We really want to see David, and I would love to see the hospital complex that has been so helpful to him and you. They sound like my kind of doctors and nurses. Just let us know when a good time would be in the future.

We will keep them in our prayers. Take care, and when David is fully awake, let him know we care.

Love,

Lana and Richard

Wake Up, Big Valentine

With all of this time on my hands, I had countless hours to think about stuff. Christmas, New Years, and now Valentine's Day—that's three holidays that we "celebrated" here. Jeez, I hoped that David would be awake enough for St. Patrick's Day.

From: Mary Tiffin
Sent: Thursday, February 13, 2003 12:04 PM
To: David's List
Subject: Valentines' Eve David Update

Hi, all.

So here is where we are.

David is liking those narcotics a little too much. The doctors indicated that he was having withdrawals from the sedation, so we are having to go even slower than before on trying to wake him. He gets very agitated and hyper-tensive when they reduce some of his meds. So the awakening will take a little longer than I had hoped. But of course, this is a lesson in patience and it appears that I STILL HAVEN'T GOT IT!

Otherwise, he is rock stable again. He is on a weaning trial using a T-piece for the vent. This means he is pulling oxygen from the air. The machine is off (hallelujah) and he's doing okay on it. It is just a test and we are not ready to make the full advance to room air.

The red urine is still a concern, so please keep praying about that. Also, please pray that he will wake comfortably.

I am going home this afternoon to spend Valentine's Day with my three other valentines. David's mom is coming down, and I will be returning Sunday to be with my big Valentine!

David looks fantastic and very much more like himself. He is still pretty puffy (edema), and if you could pray about those GI tract feeds, that will help the puffiness.

So, to condense our prayers, please pray for the red urine, that it goes away; the comfortable awakening; and the GI feeds. I will once again be prayer-in-debted to you.

Thanks, guys, and happy Valentine's Day in advance.

You gotta BELIEVE!

XOXOXO,

Mary

From: Norman Donaldson
Sent: Thursday, February 13, 2003 3:12 PM
To: Mary M. Tiffin
Subject: Re: Valentines Eve David Update

Mary,

You're doing an awesome job at keeping all the balls in the air, right down to these daily updates. Be safe getting home, enjoy the kids, and we'll see you next week!

Love in Him,

Norm

From: Mary Tiffin
Sent: Thursday, January 13, 2003 10:05 PM
To: David's List
Subject: David Update

Dear friends,

Thank you for your prayers. Boy, we are really making nice strides now.

Listen to this:

David was totally off the ventilator for seven-and-a-half hours. They thought it would be a couple-hour trial, but David kept going. Yay!! Go, David!!! Go, David!!! Go, David!!!

The endoscopy team came to correctly place the NG (nasogastric) feeding tube. He will now be able to receive tube feedings, and we won't have to worry about his poor nutritional status (read "malnourished").

He still has the red urine stuff, so if you could pray for that I would appreciate it. This is just a quick note because I was so excited about the breathing. Pray that he will be extubated soon.

I am at home with the boys now. Hope you all have a good Valentine's Day.

BELIEVE.

XOXOXOXO,

Mary

From: Hugh Keegans
Sent: Sunday, February 16, 2003 2:22 PM
To: Mary M. Tiffin
Subject: Our Travel

Dear Mary,

Thank you so much for sending on the continuing good news of David. The Lord is hearing all our prayers, and we do believe!

We are going to our Mary's in Aurora, Ohio, for a few days. Then on Thursday of this week, we are scheduled to fly to Phoenix, Arizona.

You are an inspiration to us all, Mary. May God love and bless you, David, and your three boys.

Love,

Joan Keegans

From: Mary Tiffin
Sent: Tuesday, February 18, 2003 9:08 AM
To: David's List
Subject: David Update and Special Prayer Request

Hi, everyone.

I am writing to you from Pennsylvania, where I am nursing our three children back to health. All three little ones contracted a stomach virus, but we are on the mend.

I just got off the phone with David's nurse—actually my favorite at Hopkins. I have a special prayer request for David.

Remember when I mentioned that David was liking the sedation a little too much because he was having trouble coming out of it? There is now a concern about his neurological abilities. There is some concern that perhaps with his low platelets and the volume of heparin that he has been on, there could have been a bleed in his brain.

So I ask that you pray that God will protect him once again and let the brain be clear in the CT scan. If you could do that when you get this email, I would really appreciate it. If you could please also remember that at the nine p.m. prayer time, I would be grateful for that as well.

I'll keep you posted.

BELIEVE.

XOXOXO,

Mary

From: Mary Tiffin
Sent: Tuesday, February 18, 2003 1:10 PM
To: David's List
Subject: David FLASH

Okay, folks,

I just got off the phone with Dr. Rick Johnson, director of the Bone Marrow Department.

He feels, after examining David, that David is fine, and at this point they have decided not to do a CT scan.

He indicated that the fact that David has been on so many narcotics for so long is why he is having trouble waking. The doctor reiterated that it is a very long process.

So that is our minute-by-minute update.

If I haven't mentioned to you before, in transplant, we live moment by moment, as opposed to longer chunks of time (like day by day).

Please keep praying that "Rip" (Van Winkle), will hurry up and wake. His wife is starting to lose her patience—it's going the route of her mind.

BELIEVE.

XOXOXO,

Mary

From: Cale, Lisa H.
Sent: Tuesday, February 18, 2003 1:24 PM
To: Mary M. Tiffin
Subject: Re: David FLASH

You are very brave and definitely so strong. I am very proud of you, as well as David, for being so brave.

Luv U,

Lisa

From: Mary Tiffin
Sent: Thursday, February 20, 2003 1:03 PM
To: David's List
Subject: HIP HIP HOORAY David Update

Hi, all.

I am still writing from Pennsylvania, and Baby Stephen is the last to shake the bug, but he is doing better now.

Here is some exciting news regarding David. He is totally off all of the sedatives and is tolerating it very well. David is more aware.

Occupational Therapy is working with him to start getting him moving.

David is now on a trach collar as opposed to the pipe. This collar brings us closer and closer to him being able to breathe on his own.

All of his numbers are in the perfect range, with the exception of his albumin (which is an indication of his poor nutritional state), but that is not a huge problem. The doctors are still working on tube feeding.

I wanted to also tell you that when I spoke to Dr. Rick Johnson (head of BMT) the other day, I wanted to thank them for their care of David and expressed how pleased I have been with the staff. His response was they are only doctors and there were "other forces at play."

Thank you for your prayers and helping with the other forces.

Okay, guys, that is what I can say for now.

BELIEVE.

XOXOXO,

Mary

From: Mary Tiffin
Sent: Thursday, February 20, 2003 1:42 PM
To: David's List
Subject: ANOTHER David Update

Hi, guys.

I think I mentioned before that things at Hopkins change at lightning speed.

I just got off the phone with one of David's doctors, Dr. Thudd (yes, it is his real name) and here's a newer update.

Dr. Thudd mentioned they're going to want to put a tube directly into his stomach (called a PEG tube) for feeding. Dr. Thudd does not anticipate David taking food for the next month or so, and we need something better than the ones in his nose and mouth.

Here is the other point that I'm somewhat distressed about. They're talking about sending David to a rehabilitation hospital in the "near future" (timetables escape definition at Hopkins) and leaving Hopkins. He's making such good progress now that they are thinking about the next step.

The next step scares me. I don't know where this hospital will be, and, more importantly, I am afraid to leave Hopkins. I expressed my concern to Dr. Thudd, but will have a conversation with Rick Johnson. There are still too many areas that I am concerned about. Primarily (and this is no surprise for anyone who knows me) germs!!!! There are other things as well.

If you could, pray that David will once again surprise them, so he'll need just a little rehab, and that can be accomplished at Hopkins so they won't have to ship him to who knows where. Also pray that when he goes into surgery, the PEG tube will go okay.

Thanks in advance. I will keep you posted.

BELIEVE.

XOXOXO,

Mary

From: Diane Mail
Sent: Thursday, February 20, 2003 7:09 PM
To: Mary M. Tiffin
Subject: Re: ANOTHER David Update

Mary,

This scares me a little and reminds me of the Hopkins Mark Maul plan—that is, "We're done with you, there's nothing more we can do, so bye-bye." Please let me know what is up. I am so concerned about you and David. When will you come back here?

We had Rick Johnson on one of our inpatient stays and found him to at least be a decent human. I hope he is treating you well.

Praying for more miracles,

D

From: Mary Tiffin
Sent: Thursday, February 20, 2003 8:19 AM
To: Diane Maul
Subject: Re: ANOTHER David Update

Hi, Diane.

I am sorry that I haven't responded earlier to your emails, but I had dueling vomiters and it became very difficult to type while trying to catch vomit (ooh, sometimes I am way too graphic).

A couple of things before I get into the body of your last email. I am so glad Lauren is with you. I am sure you must be enjoying her sweet presence.

The baby was the last to finish his virus and we are doing much better. After talking with Rick Johnson and Jim Thudd, it was determined that Monday would be a good return time. What is your schedule like?

Now to answer your most recent email. I spoke to Jim Thudd and Liz Costus, and certainly made my concerns known regarding rehab. My hope is that Hopkins will reverse themselves one more time. The bottom line is; I will handcuff my husband to the radiator (are there radiators in that room) before I let David leave Hopkins.

It is more than just a comfort zone. We entered with a plan of the preparatory regime, transplant, IPOP treatments, and then (and only then) will we return to our home. So I am digging in on this issue and it will be very hard for me to relent on this. I am not (and here is the germaphobe part) going to let my husband leave the controlled environment on the BMT unit, to enter into a less impressive Rehab Center. My fear of course is that he'll contract a virus and get so sick.

Again, I will crazy glue his butt to the floor before we leave.

He'll be rehabbed at Hopkins and I will assist with that. Now, I am not an occupational therapist, but I can get him to do the work, or we can have someone come to the apartment and work with us there. David is smiling now and nodding and shaking his head and he has lifted his leg, so God will assist us with this as well.

Well, that's my story. I gotta scram. Michael is in front of "Sesame Street" and I feel bad that the TV is babysitting him. I gave Heidi time off.

Blessings to you, my friend.

XOXOXO,

Mary

Focused and Directed

Yay!! It felt so good to be home with our boys! How I missed their little faces. Being at home, doing mommy things, felt so good. Even cleaning the house, doing laundry, washing the boys' dishes made me feel energized. Who would have thought that folding towels and sheets could have such a benefit?

From: Mary Tiffin
Sent: Friday, February 21, 2003 9:28 PM
To: David's List
Subject: DAVID Update

Hi, all.

Again, I'm writing to you from the home front. Mom and Dad are on the "David front," and how I wish I were there, too.

But I need to be here.

I am having a marvelous time with our boys, but David's awakening has the excitement akin to the births of our little fellas. I wouldn't have missed those either. Well, technically (or at the very least, anatomically), I couldn't, but I hope you get my drift.

Now more than ever, I feel the desperate need to be in two places at the same time. That, coupled with the anxiety regarding the "rehab issue," is making me more than a tiny bit cranky.

Here is the important stuff. David is nodding, shaking his head, laughing (not gut busters, but small laughs), and smiling. He has been trying to form words. He is lifting and turning his head and making a few spontaneous movements in his extremities.

He had his PEG tube placed in his stomach today and it went very well. So that means no more lines in his nose and mouth, and he will be able to receive nutrition through his stomach.

So here is the new prayer request. Please pray that David will not need rehab other than that provided by Hopkins. Please also pray that David will have his body move on his own and that he will continue to make great strides in his full recovery. Sounds kind of simple, but it is big.

Thank you. BELIEVE.

XOXOXO,

Mary

Awake at Last

It seemed so long in coming, I almost could not believe my eyes, but once again, I saw my husband's beautiful blue and sometimes green eyes. Two months after his transplant, despite all that he endured, God had blessed us again.

From: Mary Tiffin
Sent: Tuesday, February 25, 2003 2:58 PM
To: David's List
Subject: HE'S AWAKE !!!!!!!

Hi, all.

It is with unbridled joy that I tell you that DAVID IS AWAKE!!!!!!! DAVID IS AWAKE!!!!

Praise God, he is with us.

David is his precious self and has been "talking" (mouthing words) to me.

We have been blessed again (can you believe this????). For many of you logistically close to me, you know that the hearing loss that I experienced in my pregnancy with Baby Stephen never improved. As a result, I have been a somewhat proficient lip reader. It has come in very handy today. David has been able to communicate with me. You know, I thought it odd that my hearing never improved these past nine months, but now I know. It's funny how everything is eventually revealed—you just have to wait.

David has a lot of questions about stuff, and I've answered, sparing him much of the details.

His sense of humor is intact, and that has been revealed as well.

We had some good physical therapy. He is moving his legs nicely, doing the "Funky Chicken," and David continues to ooh and aah the people around here.

So again, thank you, dear ones, for your beautiful prayers. Here is our prayer prescription. Please pray that David will continue to show improvements in his physical strength. It is my goal to have him able to sit up next week and that God will keep the leukemia away forever.

God bless you all.

BELIEVE.

XOXOXO,

Mary

From: Mary Tiffin
Sent: Wednesday, February 26, 2003 4:20 PM
To: David's List
Subject: David Update

Dear ones,

So we have our great days and our not-so-great days. Yesterday was the former, today is the latter. The not-so-great days tend to follow the great days.

But this is progress. I used to measure by hours instead of entire days. So this is good—I'll take it.

When I spoke to Rick Johnson (as in Dr. Rick Johnson, head of the BMT Department at Hopkins), he said that sometimes people overuse the expression, but that David *is* really a miracle.

That was beautiful, and, at the same time, so scary. You would think that I'd be used to boo-scary by now. I don't spend a lot of time reviewing from where we have come, but focus more on the present and where we have to go.

So David, although wide awake, is very quiet today. I think that he is realizing a few things.

They put him back on the ventilator this a.m. (did I mention that he was off yesterday? It's so nice to see equipment disconnected). Anyway, he was struggling for his breath, so they decided to give him some help. He didn't sleep all night, so he was just so tired.

Christopher played Simon Says with David on the phone, and David played along very nicely. Simon Says lift your right arm...Simon Says turn your head...Open your mouth...He is moving his body parts, and I anticipate him working harder tomorrow.

I am giving him a mental health day because he needs it. Actually, he will probably need many (or at least some time to process what's happening).

So if you could, please pray for a couple of things. Pray his lungs will get the much-needed strength and his body will continue to respond to the therapy. Here is the biggie: that God keeps the leukemia away forever. That is the big prayer.

Well, guys, thanks again. Blessings on you today.

BELIEVE.

XOXOXO,

Mary

Always Lurking Around the Corner

I clicked on "Send" and leaned back in my chair, partly afraid to exhale. Our sense of well-being always seemed so fleeting. When will it return and how long will we be able to hang onto it again? We'd been taught by this experience that something hazardous or life-threatening is always lurking around the corner. Did I jinx us by talking about David's good day? I'd become so superstitious, never wanting to push our luck.

I haven't had a chance to relax in the calm periods. Since we started this journey, we haven't had any time to review and reflect on how we got to this point in dealing with David's disease. Since the previous August, we had spent every moment consumed by the thought of and mission to win against this cancer. Acute Leukemias can be like this, so very all-consuming, striking the patient with emergency after emergency, keeping them off-balance and unable to regroup and catch their breath. And when you think you have hit rock bottom, you realize that the bottom is farther away than you initially thought, or could even envision.

From: Mary Tiffin
Sent: Thursday, February 27, 2003 11:46 AM
To: David's List
Subject: David Update

Dear ones,

So a good day follows the bad ones and today is a good day.

The doctors on rounds decided to get David sitting up today. Occupational Therapy is here now and will return later with Physical Therapy to accomplish that goal.

David is responding very well to the OT.

Many of you have remarked in your return emails that this is a roller coaster for you. My response to that is, although there are still a lot of rises and precipitous and precarious falls, the time in between them is longer and I'm not falling out of the car, yet. My seat belt is tight.

We are having a little problem with amnesia, but I keep trying to orient him. Some of what I say he retains and other stuff requires more review.

I ask for you to continue to pray for his continued physical and mental strength and that we keep the leukemia away. Let's pray David is in the 30-percent survival category. Let's pray heavy duty for that one, please—oh, please.

Okay, guys, I gotta go visit with my husband.

BELIEVE.

XOXOXO,

Mary

From: Mary Tiffin
Sent: Thursday, February 27, 2003 6:06 PM
To: David's List
Subject: Kind Of Tough

Hi, guys.

This was a hard afternoon.

David asked me every five minutes or so to take him home.

He also knew that I was his wife but didn't know my name. He thinks we have four children, and has problems remembering Michael and baby Stephen.

David has had a lot of amnesia and is a little on the paranoid side, but the paranoia is getting better. The doctors said this is all normal considering what we have been through.

With his emotions all over the place, I am finding it harder now than when he was so close to the light.

One of my friends, Patty, came to visit me today. She is a cancer survivor (and also had a few altered states). She told me how to speak to David, what to say, and I found that to be very helpful, although David wasn't real responsive.

So I ask once again for prayer that we will work through this stuff and David will be David again. The doctors have assured me that it will happen. It's just upsetting.

Please BELIEVE.

XOXOXO,

Mary

Fragile States

"Hello, Mary." I recognized my father-in-law's voice immediately.

"Well, hello, Pa."

"Goo Goo and I are on our way down. We'll be down early today."

"Oh, great."

"So how is David today?"

"Well, physically he appears to be getting stronger, but he's become pretty forgetful," I said, wondering if the leukemia cells had infiltrated his spinal fluid.

"Yes, we noticed that, too, but I believe they gave it a name, right? 'Sundowning'?" my father-in-law asked.

"Yeah, that's what they call it," I responded, still with the niggling doubt lurking in the back of my mind.

I learned that sundowning or ICU Psychosis is the name of a condition where Intensive Care patients experience confusion, amnesia, or heightened states of anxiety or arousal. Although it can happen at any time of day, it commonly occurs at sundown, hence the name sundowning. For all the leaps and bounds that he was making, David was not immune to sundowning. And when it came on, it was sudden and disorienting for all of us.

"Well, I have a favor to ask of you."

"Sure. Shoot."

"Do you think you could delay your return to Winfield to visit with us? For just a little while?"

I was really anxious to get home to the boys, but I knew that my in-laws wouldn't ask unless they really needed me to stay. As if my father-in-law was reading my mind, he offered, "There have been so many changes in David since his waking."

I knew what he meant. David was not the same. There were marked changes, both physical and emotional. For starters, he was seventy-five pounds lighter. The coma had left him without much muscle tone, he'd atrophied and couldn't hold up this new thinner body, he could not speak because of a tracheostomy, his short-term memory was gone, and he was noticeably impatient. The impatience was very unusual for David. And he seemed quieter. I couldn't figure out if he was quiet or maybe I needed him to be chattier since he had been so silent for so long. Not that I expected him to fill me in on every moment of his sleep, but he simply had nothing to say about his slumber. When I persisted in my questions about what he experienced while he was napping, he responded that it was sleep, just sleep.

"He's David, but he's not David. He seems so much more fragile."

"Well, that is because he is," I said, immediately wishing that I hadn't. I tried to repair the hurt by adding, "He'll be better; it will just take time."

"Yes, we know. But Goo and I have noticed that David seems more alert, maybe more connected and grounded, when you are here. He seems healthier when you are here."

At that moment, I felt the fear that my in-laws were feeling. It was palpable and saddening. The feeling had been a constant and most unwanted companion for the past five months. I tried to carry this burden and save others from it, but I realized that I could not. While David was my husband, he was, first, their son.

"Yes, Pa, I can delay my trip home and visit. That sounds like a really nice idea."

"Thank you, Mary," Pa said, sounding relieved.

"Please don't thank me. I have so much to be thankful to you for. You both travel safe and I'll see you soon."

I hung up the phone and announced to David, "Honey, looks like we're gonna have a Tiffin shindig. Your parents are on the way. It's Friday, and I think I just might hang with Goo Goo and Pa and fill them in on this exciting week. Won't that be great?"

David looked at me and nodded.

The Tiffin's home in Elkton was an hour from Baltimore, so I expected them within the hour. When they arrived some 50 minutes later, David had been visited by Physical Therapy and had had a difficult workout. It exhausted him and he'd fallen asleep. Goo Goo and Pa, gowned and gloved, entered the room smiling.

"So how is our patient today?" my mother-in-law asked sweetly.

"Oh, Goo Goo, you should have seen the good work he did with PT—he's really working on his control. I think he is getting stronger."

"Oh, that's good. Hello, David," Goo Goo said to her sleeping son.

"He's asleep now?" Pa asked, worried.

"Pa, it was a short but strenuous workout and he was pretty tired. He really tried to stay awake, but it took a lot out of him. I don't expect that he'll sleep the afternoon away."

"Oh, okay." My in-laws took seats around the bed.

Sensing worry in my in-laws, I said, "You know, I think that our bodies repair themselves in their sleep. Just think of all the good work David's body did fighting leukemia. I think sleep is good."

"Yes, sleep is good," my father-in-law echoed.

"You know, Mary, when David was between his junior and senior years at Sanford, he slept the entire summer. On the couch in the family room, with Freckles by his side. The entire summer. He started that summer at five-foot-six and ended the summer at six-foot-two."

"Are you serious?"

"Yes. Remember, Jim?"

"I do," my father-in-law confirmed. "David on the couch the entire summer with Freckles, right beside him. That dog loved David." I saw my father in law drift off into memory land.

"So what is that, like six inches in a summer?" I asked, trying to do quick math.

"Well, actually, it's closer to seven," Pa gently corrected me.

"Oh, yeah." And we giggled, as we all know quick (or not-so-quick) math has never been a strength for me.

"So this will be like that summer of great growth. I am okay with him sleeping. He's getting better," I said, for myself as much as for them.

"David has always liked sleep," Goo Goo added.

"And Freckles." My father-in-law added, back to the family's sweet cocker spaniel.

We talked for another half hour, and I found myself working really hard at conveying the upside for David's parents. I thought that this must be so frightening, for them to see their son this way. I really did not want them to lose hope. I was convinced (on most days) that David would make a full recovery and we could all return to our happy, scheduled lives.

David woke when the nurse's aide came in to check his vitals.

"Well, hello, David," Pa said, happy to see his son awake.

"Hi, Dad," David mouthed. "Hi, Mom." And then he looked over to me. "Hi, honey."

"Hi, David!!" I sprang out of my chair and covered his face with kisses. I still could barely contain my happiness when this man woke up. I made a mental note to get that under control.

David smiled.

Goo Goo kissed him hello and asked, "How ya' doin', sweetie?"

"Good," David mouthed.

David's waking, his talking, were so big for us. We gathered around his bed and marveled at his every word, eagerly anticipating what he would say next. But instead, he looked at Goo Goo, Pa, and me with an expression of, "Why are you looking at me?" He shrugged his shoulders and mouthed, "Love you," and looked past us to the TV—he wanted to see what was on "Sports Center." This, of course, we also delighted in, because David was normal again. Goo Goo and David had always watched sports together. She turned her chair to face the TV, took the bedside control, and started scrolling for ESPN.

"What do you want to watch, David?" Goo Goo asked her son.

"Basketball?" David responded, and looked toward his mom.

"Well, Mary, I think those boys are probably really looking forward to seeing you this afternoon," Pa said to me.

Taking my cue and sensing their increased comfort, I said, "Yes, Pa."

To David, "Honey, I think I'm going to skedaddle now. Gotta run home to relieve Heidi and Mom and Dad. I'll see you Sunday night. Love you." I kissed him again, hugged and thanked my in-laws, and was out the door headed home.

From: Mary Tiffin
Sent: Friday, February 28, 2003 12:31 PM
To: lburley, lauriebc
Subject: David

Hi, Lude and Laur.

To follow our conversations, I spoke to the doctor on rounds today, and David does indeed have some ICU psychosis actions happening. Laur, do you know where I could find information on that?

I have decided the occupational therapy is something that I could consider once David is better, and I would be able to go to school on the weekends. I think the shots would get to me for critical care.

He sat up at the edge of the bed today, was wobbly and couldn't hold himself up. I now see what they mean when they say he will need rehab.

Gotta scram.

BELIEVE.

XOXOXO,

Mary

From: Mary Tiffin
Sent: Friday, February 28, 2003 9:45 PM
To: David's List
Subject: David Update

Hi, all.

I'm writing from Pennsylvania. So here is the deal. David is awake and is really struggling in his attempt to make sense of his environment after being in a medically induced coma for almost two months. He has asked repeated questions about the ventilator and the rest of equipment surrounding his bed. His short-term memory is gone, so he doesn't remember the answers.

He is also experiencing considerable frustration because I haven't been able to read his lips as clearly as before.

The physical and occupational therapies are working nicely, but very slowly. His extremities show severe atrophy. Several members of the OT and PT teams were able to get him to sit up in bed today. They said that he had good head control, but there is still a lot of work to do. I understand what they mean now when they say David will require rehab. Hopkins has two different rehab centers. I don't want him to go anywhere but a Hopkins rehab.

I am home tomorrow with the boys. I am feeling comfortable enough to leave him and I have come to the realization that he will not be able to miraculously jump out of bed and razzle dazzle all of the staff here. He's going to need help. Even though everyone thinks he is Superman, even Superman has his kryptonite.

I had a conversation with one of the nurses on the floor. Her name is also Mary and she has been in this department for twenty-plus years. She was remarking about what a miracle David is. Mary went on to say that she always believed in God, but it was so wonderful to see him work through David and be so present with us.

Everyone is in awe of this wonderful man—and I am at the head of the line.

Okay, guys, so here is our prayer prescription. Please pray that David will continue to gain strength, both mental and physical; that he will be free of infection; and—here is the major one—the leukemia will stay away forever (or I'll take at least until age seventy).

Thanks in advance, and I appreciate your BELIEVING.

XOXOXOXO,

Mary

From: Mary Tiffin
Sent: Sunday, March 2, 2003 10:11 AM
To: David's List
Subject: Special DAVID Prayer Request

Okay, all,

I am writing to you from Pennsylvania. I am planning on going to work tomorrow for a couple of days to try and get back into the swing of things. The boys are wonderful and we are having a super time.

Just when you think that everything is perfect, or at least manageable, there is always a catch.

Some David facts. He has lost at least seventy pounds since we have been at Hopkins. We anticipated a weight loss, but I was thinking more like forty pounds. I was a little concerned when I saw his weight in the 165-pound range at six-foot-three. I guess bulking him up was a really good idea after all.

His ICU psychosis (quite normal for patients like him) is improving with Haldol. Of course, he's not crazy anymore, since I am away. I guess that I get to see him when he doesn't know who I am.

"Hello. Nice to meet you. I'm your wife."

I hope he doesn't decide now that gentlemen prefer blondes!

It's quite apparent to me now that David will indeed need intensive rehab. My once very strong husband has very little muscle tone, almost like he was paralyzed. It's hard to see.

They are going to get a trach voice box so he will be able to speak. I have spent a considerable amount of time reading from his lips, but he is still getting frustrated.

When I spoke to Rick Johnson, I asked him when I could stop worrying about leukemia. He gave me a two-year timeline.

But I am already worried.

All of David's blood counts took a drop last night. The red blood and platelets have been fluctuating, and his white blood also took a dip of 1,000 points.

He also had a temperature last night. I am hoping his white blood cells are working at the point of infection. (My prayer is they are busy and not available in the peripheral.)

So here is my desperate prayer. Please pray that David will continue to gain clarity and strength, and his blood is just "busy." Please pray, pray hard, the leukemia will stay away for at least thirty years.

It would be the worst of both worlds to have gone through all of this to have the leukemia return. I can't imagine that God will have carried us this far to drop us, especially now that we are both lighter.

I know God can help us with this as He has so much in the past. Please pray now and at nine p.m., if you would.

Much love to you all.

BELIEVE.

XOXOXO,

Mary

From: Mary Tiffin
Sent: Tuesday, March 4, 2003 1:45 PM
To: David's List
Subject: Another SPECIAL Prayer Request

Hi, all.

So here are some happenings on the David front.

Yesterday and today, David has been sitting (strapped) in a chair. The occupational therapist has remarked that he is participating in his therapy. This is great! Hip, hip, hooray, let's have a party!

Another reason for a party is, I actually heard David's voice the other night when I called. He said (as in spoke out loud) four sentences to me on the phone. I was jumping for joy.

Very concerned about hearing his voice with the trach, I checked with the nurses and respiratory therapist concerned about the airflow. He's fine. No one can figure out how we heard David's voice with a trach in (there is no voice box on the collar yet).

But I guess it's just another David story.

Now for all of you who are worried I have fallen over the edge (which, I must say, surely seems like a real concern): my mother-in-law (Goo Goo) heard him speak to me as well, and the nurse heard him grumbling earlier in the day also. Unless we all have some collective mass hysteria, that boy was talkin'! I was just telling Denise how much I missed hearing his voice.

The speaking has stopped and he is back to mouthing words. David has been talking to me on the phone. He has been mouthing words, and my mother-in-law has been interpreting his replies.

David has been blowing kisses to the boys and me over the phone. This is nice but, hopefully, he stopped kissing the nurses as well. I do feel special!

SO ALL THAT STUFF IS JUST MARVELOUS.

So here is what I ask earnestly for your prayers. Do you remember in an earlier email I mentioned his falling white blood counts? Well, they steadied for a day or two, but they just took another drop (2,800).

I am praying that it could be one of several things:

David is having what is called the "sixty-day slump." Yes, we are, so far, past sixty days, but we have done everything else on a slower schedule.

His white blood cells could be very busy with the infection that is now past. The temperature is gone.

Lab error.

Could you please pray that David's white blood counts will rise to a normal range—4,500s, or I'll take higher. Thanks in advance, guys. I know we can work through this as well. Thanks for joining me on the roller coaster trip. Until next time.

BELIEVE.

XOXOXO,

Mary

From: Mary Tiffin
Sent: Wednesday, March 5, 2003 10:08 AM
To: David's List
Subject: David Counts

Hi, all.

I just spoke to David's nurse, and his white blood count is down to 2,100. This is not the news I was hoping for.

Please pray hard these numbers will rise.

Thank you.

BELIEVE.

XOXOXO,

Mary

From: Mary Tiffin
Sent: Friday, March 7, 2003 1:56 PM
To: David's List
Subject: David Update

Okay, guys,

Please remember David right now and tonight at nine p.m.

David's temperature is spiking again, and, to make matters worse, he has the rash again.

And to add insult to new injury, David is not lucid. (Actually, that may be a mercy for him, at least.) There is a new doctor group on the service, and, of course, there are new theories on this stuff.

They have done another skin biopsy, and I am once again asking about the drug reaction to the vancomycin—and, with transplant, there is always talk of graft-versus-host (GVHD).

So, as in all things transplant, we take two steps forward and twelve steps backward.

I am distressed because when I left, I was comfortable enough to leave. Now I am once again worried about my dear husband.

Please pray hard his temperature and rash go away. They are also going to take fluid off his lungs today. Please pray all these things go well.

Well, that is it, guys. I have faith our prayers can be answered.

Please BELIEVE.

XOXOXO,

Mary

Two Steps Forward...

I had come to realize that transplant is a dance, with the patient constantly moving; a state of flux. The challenge for the clinical staff is to balance all of the patient's systems during the precarious periods of the transplant, those times without counts. With good care, medications, and prayers, the patient needs to achieve a temporary homeostasis until the body can take over and help itself. What a lesson this was for David and me.

From: Mary Tiffin
Sent: Sunday, March 9, 2003 11:38 AM
To: David's List
Subject: David

Hi, all.

So, it's Sunday morning and here is where we are. David has a low-grade temperature, he is pretty lucid, and the skin condition is about the same, if not better.

He is now on the trach collar and breathing on his own. Once again, we will start the vent weaning. Remember, two steps forward, fifteen steps back.

David has a lot of spontaneous movement in his legs and is really working on his upper body.

Dr. Levinson thought it might be a good idea for everyone to see a little of Christopher (he advised me to talk to the psych group to get their take). Both David and Chris were thrilled with that idea. So I mentioned to him that when Christopher comes to visit, he is going to expect a hug—so we have been working on his hugging muscles.

David is really thirsty and has been asking for stuff to drink. I am hoping to get the speech and swallowing people in here to evaluate those areas.

As much as I love Hopkins, I really want to get him out of here. I want so much to resume normal life, and so do our boys.

Christopher was sad the other day because he said he didn't have a family like everyone else's. I indicated that yes, this is true, we are not like other people. I added that Christopher was so incredibly lucky and he is surrounded by the love of so many people. He has people like Heidi, Grandmother, and Poppy around every day to help him. But the part he was most excited about (sorry, Mom and Dad) is the fact the doctors think his daddy is Superman. Chris thought that was very cool. None of his friends have dads who are Superman.

So, guys, here is the fervent prayer. Pray that David's recovery is stable, the skin improves, and the leukemia stays away forever (or at least until he is seventy-five-ish). Thank you.

BELIEVE.

XOXOXO,

Mary

From: Mary Tiffin
Sent: Tuesday, March 11, 2003 10:22 AM
To: David's List
Subject: David Update

Dear ones,

Here is where we are today.

Actually, I am writing from home. I plan on working through Thursday and, of course, I love the time with our little tigers.

It's really nice to resume at least part of our former lives.

David spends time daily with occupational and physical therapy. The therapists said the work David is doing is awesome. He is making wide general movements in his extremities. No real fine motor skills yet, but he's working on it. David is really working hard toward giving Christopher that hug.

I am anxious for Speech Therapy to come in to do the speaking/swallowing test so he will be able to get his speech valve. I can't wait for that, 'cuz, you know, we Tiffins love to talk and talk and talk.

David is fever-free (thank you for those prayers; they worked) and he is much more lucid (thanks again). He knows who I am and the accurate number of children we have and the boys' names. He also knows my correct age (drats—I should have used the opportunity to let him think I was thirty-one instead of feeling ninety-one).

But the rash is still a very big concern, particularly when the doctor mentioned on Saturday that David's rash scared him to death. Not exactly music to my ears. This is a big concern for us.

Also on Friday, the talk of sepsis is once again history (thank God). His heart rate was way up, blood pressure way low (supported by vasopressors), and temperature very high.

Yuck. Not again!

As in the past, I assumed the role of telling the young interns not to worry, that everything will be okay, and we just do this from time to time. That tomorrow will be miraculously better (and Saturday was).

But I am still waiting for the news on the skin biopsy and the blood test.

We are back to a slow wean off the vent.

You know that I have to realize that everything in life happens the way it is supposed to.

For the longest time, we've been talking about doing something other than UPS. Not only is the work physically hard, but the hours are hard on the family. If David had left UPS earlier, there is no saying what kind of shape he would have been in. I mean, we have three kids. Who gets to work out daily if not at your job? My treasured daily runs disappeared with Michael.

The job kept David in good shape. The doctors have remarked, with amazement, at how much his body could take.

We had a surprise visit from two dear angels the other day. Jill and Angie. They came up with this great idea to mention in my emails: If every time you saw a UPS truck, if you could please say a prayer for David. That would be great. Do you think you could do that? We will be surrounding him with prayer. Those trucks are everywhere! It doesn't have to be a Novena or anything elaborate, just something like, "Please God, give David total earthly healing." Thanks, Jill and Ang.

Now, tonight's prayer prescription is a little more (if you don't mind).

Please pray for David's total healing, his counts to rise, his skin to clear, and that God will keep the leukemia away forever. Phew—I know that's a lot. Thanks.

BELIEVE.

XOXOXOXO,

Mary

P.S. He also mentioned last night he wanted to go for a bike ride.

From: Mary Tiffin
Sent: Friday, March 14, 2003 2:29 PM
To: David's List
Subject: David Update

I apologize to everyone for not getting out an email earlier, but I wanted to let you know what was happening first-hand. I was really busy with our boys and work. Thank you for your calls and emails regarding the lapse in David updates.

Dear ones,

I returned to Hopkins earlier today, and it is with great joy to let you know that David and I had a wonderful conversation. This time without me reading his lips; he was SPEAKING!!!

I love that speech valve, and it works wonderfully.

There have been so many nights these past several months when I really missed the simple things of our lives, like just hearing David's voice.

Now that I am back at Hopkins, I am thrilled to see my husband, but now also miss the boys fiercely. As far as our children are concerned, in the early days of our transplant, I played head games with myself to help get over my sadness at missing them. For the first two months or so, I pretended I was still in college and didn't have kids. It was the only way I could deal with being away from my babies. Of course, some twenty years later, it's obvious I am not in college, so that mind game ended rather quickly. I miss the boys very much right now. This would be my only argument for cloning.

But onto my darling husband. He is a little confused, not knowing exactly where we are and what has happened, but again, at least he knows who I am. I continue trying to orient him.

No fevers, and his kidneys—which were a little worrisome—are better now. But those counts keep dropping.

The prayer Rx for tonight is to please pray that David's white blood counts will rise and the leukemia will stay away forever. Please pray hard for that. Thank you.

BELIEVE.

XOXOXO,

Mary

From: Mary Tiffin
Sent: Friday, March 14, 2003 3:52 PM
To: David's List
Subject: Skin Biopsy

Hi, all.

I forgot to mention in my earlier email that David's skin biopsy indicated it was a drug reaction and not graft-versus-host disease. This is a big weight off my shoulders. Just an FYI.

BELIEVE.

XOXO,

Mary

From: Mary Tiffin
Sent: Saturday, March 15, 2003 11:36 AM
To: David's List
Subject: Musings

Dear ones,

In a recent conversation with our new and very dear friend, Debbie M, we discussed living on the precipice of life.

Families of critically ill patients try to balance so precariously on this edge. With the prolonged "teeter," you develop a familiar, though never comfortable, view. And, like with all other experiences that have been so hard here, there have been real benefits — with pain comes gain.

Balancing on this cutting edge while your feet are bleeding has provided wonderful insight on the power and beauty of God. He has converted this edge to a ledge (with handles, too!).

Here are my "Lessons from the Ledge."

God provides all things for those who BELIEVE. No explanation needed if you have read my other emails.

The moment is the most important. We need to live now. A natural-born planner (What's that? You have a special event—birthday, anniversary, wedding—coming up? Let me help you), this has been particularly difficult for me. Hard as we try, life can't be planned, but we must know there is a plan for us. We need to be patient and it will be revealed.

This next one I am so appreciative of learning:

Kids have only one visit to childhood. Every day, I try to keep in mind that this is our babies' one trip. Also, it is so important they are only caught up in the moment, so it's okay to stay there with them. Never once have I heard my boys ponder where they will go to college (Duke or Cornell—where to go?).

In a precarious position like ours, news from a clinician does not always sounds good, but that doesn't necessarily mean that it's bad either. As the recipient of repeated unfortunate news, I have learned to listen and then reframe it. The news you are given provides you with a new starting point from which you can always pray for improvement.

God continues to reveal Himself to us, and that has been so beautiful. We continue to see the beauty in people, and God working through them. What a glorious gift.

We are most limited by our minds. I am so thankful David was so somnolent in the earlier part of our transplant. Luckily, his worries were temporarily abated by his dreams. I fear it would have been much more difficult, had he been more conscious.

From: Mary Tiffin
Sent: Saturday, March 15, 2003 12:54 PM
To: David's List
Subject: More Musings – A Continuation

Sorry, guys, but I was having Internet problems, so I sent my last email before concluding.

So here are my concluding thoughts.

I must respond to the words and remarks many have made about my strength. Although it was nice to hear, I cannot accept any accolades, but say that it is God. He has given our family the strength needed to get through this. He has also given strength to my parents as they continue to take care of the three tigers at home.

You know, it can be very terrifying to see the absolute love of your life, the man of your dreams, in this type of fight.

And it's certainly scary to think about the three boys we have at home and raising them. Boys, for heaven's sake! We need my husband.

With that said, I feel a sense of peace and calm.

Many families on this floor ask why this has happened to them. David has never asked that question, although I must admit it has entered my mind a time or two. I know now we were chosen. Particularly because David is so loved, many are motivated to pray (and thank you, thank you, thank you).

This, of course, makes the world a better place.

Please continue to pray for David's total earthly healing and that the leukemia will stay away forever.

God bless you all, for He has blessed us with you.

BELIEVE.

XOXOXO,

Mary

From: Mary Tiffin
Sent: Sunday, March 16, 2003 6:12 PM
To: David's List
Subject: David Update

Dear ones,

So here is the David update for the eve of St. Patrick's Day.

David's counts are still all over the place. They are planning a bone marrow biopsy this week (no date yet). All the vitals are good, although he had a cardiac episode last night (jeeze). It resolved itself.

He is lucid and has been discussing some real detailed and specific stuff just like he used to. So this is wonderful!!!! Just wonderful!!!

On Friday, he was convinced he'd had a motorcycle accident and was a paraplegic. Now he understands, I think, what happened.

He has also been taking speech therapy to improve his ability. He took a video fluoroscopy test to measure his swallowing capabilities, and he flunked. This disappointed him because he is dying to have ice chips over water. We have been doing exercises to assist him so he will be allowed to eat or drink.

David wowed the doctors today with his demonstration of lifting his hand upward to his chest. Then, because we are show offs, he did a couple of leg lifts and a couple of mini crunches. Dr. Mattsui said it was awesome.

Okay, so here is the prayer Rx. We want you to pray that David's counts rise. We also want to pray the bone marrow biopsy comes as Missa, and the leukemia stays away forever.

Well, thanks, guys.

BELIEVE.

XOXOXO,

Mary

Looking Up

Holiday number four. What's another holiday? Okay, so luckily we are not tremendous fans of St. Patrick's Day. We are finally inching closer to being free of leukemia, getting discharged from Hopkins, and free to live our lives again. Who cares if we have to miss St. Patrick's Day. I'm feeling more confident now that he will be out to celebrate Easter.

From: Mary Tiffin
Sent: Monday, March 17, 2003 7:08 PM
To: David's List
Subject: David Update

Dear ones,

So here is the David update for St. Paddy's Day. I have some excellent news.

Do you remember they did a RFLP (FSH) test last Monday? This is the DNA test on the blood that decided who the cells belong to. The doctor came in today and said the blood is 100-percent donor (Melissa). Hip hip hooray!!!!! I am doing a happy dance. Please don't visualize it (the happy dance); I'm sure it can be very disturbing.

The other excellent news is David is making great strides in his occupational/ physical therapy. He sat up in bed for fifteen minutes—which is a record— and he is able to lift his arms to wave, and has been moving his legs. They are talking now about getting him to stand up this week. Won't that be in-credible!!!!!! Thank God.

He's pretty tired from the workout today, but we are definitely gaining momentum.

We are also working on his speech therapy, and that, of course, is going easily because, you know, we love to chat.

The only bit of not-perfect news is, he has been running a temperature for about the last twenty hours. They are doing all of these tests to determine what is going on.

Okay, guys, that is our happy story. Please keep praying those prayers, as they have been, in the past, working. It is such joy.

I ask you pray for his counts to rise, and the temperature, along with the leukemia, to go away forever. And be on the lookout for those UPS trucks.

BELIEVE.

XOXOXO,

Mary

From: Christian Bartlett
Sent: Tuesday, March 18, 2003
To: Mary M. Tiffin
Subject: About Your E-Mails

Hi, Mary.

I get your emails forwarded to me from Brenda Patterson, as does our whole little church, so I am one of the many prayer warriors coming alongside of you in your petitions for David.

I just wanted to tell you what a blessing it is to receive your emails. At first, because I was praying, I was interested in reading them just to see how David was doing. Of course, I still am interested in that; the fact is, I feel so close to you and your family because of all the prayer!

Please just keep doing what you're doing as far as the emails are concerned— don't change a thing. God is really using you.

Lastly, I just want to thank you for always giving all the glory to God. When we are weak, He is strong! May He continue to bless you. You are in my constant prayers.

In His love,

Jan Bartlett

From: Mary Tiffin
Sent: Thursday, March 20, 2003 4:06 PM
To: David's List
Subject: David Update

Dear ones,

Sorry, everyone, that I didn't write yesterday, but all of a sudden things have gotten very busy.

Not only with David, plus now I have returned to work, and I am starting to get really busy with that and the fact that David is now awake and wants to visit.

So here is where we are today.

We have had a lot of activity in the last day or two. David has had some pretty high temperatures, and the doctors are trying to determine from where they are originating.

He has had a bronchoscopy (cleaning and fluid aspiration, kind of) of his lungs, an ultrasound of his extremities to look for clots, visits with the speech therapist and occupational therapist, and a few moments ago he had a bone marrow biopsy.

The good stuff: Speech Therapy was impressed by his speech work, so that was great!

Occupational Therapy was very impressed by his muscle work. He sat up in bed relatively unassisted for fifteen minutes. He is very motivated to make it to our Christopher's birthday party. We may have it here. Today, they said they want to take David to the BMT's rehab gym next week. He was pretty excited about that. I was excited about how it sounded—out of bed, out of this room, and moving down the hall. So, yet another great thing.

We are waiting for the cultures of the lung washing (bronchoscopy), the results of the ultrasound, and, of course, praying hard for the bone marrow biopsy to be 100-percent Melissa in the new "baby, teenage, and mature" cells. The RFLP indicated his blood was 100-percent Melissa; now, we just have to check the marrow.

Mentally, he is very loopy today. To do the bronchoscopy yesterday, they gave him fentanyl and Versed, and today, for his biopsy, he got a little Ativan. He is a little whacky, but he has moments of great clarity and understands he is a little off, and jokes about it.

So, here is the prayer prescription for tonight. Please pray hard for the bone marrow biopsy to come out great and be free of leukemia and to have Melissa's combo cells.

Thank you all.

BELIEVE.

XOXOXO,

Mary

From: Mary Tiffin
Sent: Friday, March 21, 2003 10:11 AM
To: David's List
Subject: Special David Prayer Request

Hi, all.

I ask that you say a special prayer for David now. He had his bone marrow biopsy yesterday. It was very painful, but he was a trooper.

Please pray the results, which we should receive today, will be 100-percent Melissa's combo cells.

Also, pray that he loses this loopiness. He's so confused right now. Hoping it's all due to the drugs from the last two days of procedures.

All the cultures have come back negative (thank God), but he still has a temperature.

Sorry to keep prayer imposing on you, but your prayers have worked so well in the past.

Thank you.

BELIEVE.

XOXOXO,

Mary

From: Mary Tiffin
Sent: Sunday, March 23, 2003 8:19 PM
To: David's List
Subject: EXCITING DAVID News

Hi, everyone.

David's bone marrow biopsy came back today free of cancer!!!!!!

THANK GOD. THANK GOD. THANK GOD a million times.

I spoke to Dr. Mattsui, and he said that we'll have to get him checked every six months, but for now (and, prayerfully, forever), he's cancer-free. God is good.

So thank you for your prayers.

BELIEVE.

XOXOXO,

Mary

From: Mary Tiffin
Sent: Sunday, March 23, 2003 9:24 PM
To: David's List
Subject: Levity from the Ledge

Dear ones,

So not every moment is life-and-death stuff from the BMT floor. I thought you might enjoy a break from the recurrent heavy tone (theme) of my emails about David.

Here are some of our more fun moments:

The other day, when David was so loopy, he was talking to someone (read "hallucinating") in the room. When I asked him with whom he was speaking, he told me, "Mary."

I asked, "Mary who?"

"Mary my wife," was the reply.

I thought, "*Oh.*"

I asked him to tell me about Mary. He said, "Her name is Mary Mathilde Margaret Santucci."

I asked, "Is there a 'Tiffin' at the end of that?"

He nodded.

Understand that I am standing by his bed trying to help him out with this next question.

"What does she look like?" I asked.

He replied, "Oh, she's beautiful. She has brownish-black hair, brown eyes, and she's five-foot-seven—and three-quarters."

Again, I thought, "*Oh,*" and I made a note about having his eyes checked.

At this point, I must say I was relieved he said I was a brunette.

To jolt him into reality, I pulled down my mask, got really close to him, and asked, "Does she look like me?"

"Oh, no!!!!" he replied emphatically, and I must add that I think I detected a hint of repulsion in his answer.

Oh, well, from the mouths of babes (you know his new birth date is December twentieth, so he is still kind of a babe).

Another funny story related to that, a couple of days pre-full-loopy:

When I arrived one morning, David was really excited because he had decided what he was going to get me for our upcoming tenth wedding anniversary.

He said he was watching an infomercial the night before and found this wonderful facial cream for me and it was only $275!!!! He was delighted.

He then said he was going to get me some of the stuff that I'd been asking every doctor for. "That B stuff," he said.

"B stuff?" I asked.

His reply: "You know, the B stuff for your wrinkles."

"Botox," I said.

"Yeah, yeah, I am going to get you Botox."

I told him I was kind of joking about that. Kind of joking. But you know, with my luck, I'll tell the doctor brow line and he'll think I said lip line; he'll slip; accidentally shoot me in the tongue and I'll die of food poisoning.

Lastly, I was talking to a new pulmonary doctor the other day about changes in David's care. Halfway through the conversation, he asked me if I was a medical professional. I told him that I wasn't, but I do play one on television. It took him awhile to get that. Then David spent the next twenty minutes talking about how I should play a doctor on a soap opera (this was right after the loopy and well into wacky). David said he would love to watch me on TV (remember, I said we are wacky now). I ended the discussion by telling him that I would go to the next "Guiding Light" cattle call in Winfield.

So we have had some fun.

The David update for today is, after three somnolent days, sleeping beauty is awake and has all of his faculties intact (a real concern with his unresponsiveness). He is once again himself, and I say, "Just say no to Fentanyl and Versed."

I am at home with the boys this week. I have appointments and a project to take care of. I am glad to be home. I always feel like I am on vacation when I am with our wonderful kids and they are doing okay. Christopher is, naturally, feeling David's absence more than Michael and the baby, but we are working on that.

God bless you all, and thank you so much for your prayers.

BELIEVE.

XOXOXO,

Mary

The Most Beautiful Rainbow

We are settling into a reserved confidence with our new wellness. We are feeling so grateful that God has really come through. I see more and more of David coming through, and that has been a relief. But, as things go with this disease, there always seems to be a catch. My relief tends to be short-lived.

From: Mary Tiffin
Sent: Tuesday, March 25, 2003 12:20 PM
To: David's List
Subject: Lung Trouble

Dear ones,

So the way this appears to work is one thing gets fixed, then something else falls apart. Kind of like too many items in the grocery bag—you try to catch the escaped orange, and the watermelon falls out.

So we had that super news about the bone marrow biopsy. Well, my jubilation lasted about twelve hours. I don't get to have the Mardi Gras-length "joy parties," but spurts of short-lived glee.

I just got off the phone with David's nurse, and they had to increase the ventilator setting for David to get more oxygen. They also detected a new infiltrate in his lungs, the right lower lobe. They are treating this with a new antibiotic, and David was pretty agitated today.

And, of course, as my luck would have it, I am writing from Pennsylvania. I have work appointments today in addition to my mothering duties in the evening. One of my biggest challenges is in my feeling comfortable where I am. This is a strange way to put it, because I am never comfortable wherever I find myself (PA or MD? MD or PA?) these days.

My parents are on their way down as I need to be here this week.

So please, please, pray that David's lungs will clear and we can escape another visit to pneumonia. Please also pray that his counts will rise and the temperature will go away.

Please pray for total earthly healing.

Thank you so very much.

I BELIEVE that we didn't come this far to fail.

XOXOXO,

Mary

From: Mary Tiffin
Sent: Tuesday, March 25, 2003 5:47 PM
To: David's List
Subject: URGENT Prayer Request

Dear ones,

Please pray right now that David's lungs are healed. He is having very bad problems with his lungs.

He has a high temperature, and they think he has pneumonia. Once again, he is struggling.

Please pray, and hard.

BELIEVE.

XOXOXO,

Mary

From: Mary Tiffin
Sent: Wednesday, March 26, 2003 6:29 AM
To: David's List
Subject: PNEUMONIA

Dear ones,

So last night, let's say six-ish, I spoke with Dr. Matsui (attending doctor, and on my short list of favorites), and he indicated that he believes David's progressing illness was aspergillus pneumonia. Yikes!

They had to put the arterial line (A-line) back in, put him back on the vasopressors, provide full vent support, and give him morphine. None of those are good. The biggest downer for me was the A-line, because I had been thrilled to see him not connected to so much.

Dr. Mattsui was hoping they wouldn't have to call me in last night. I read between the lines, and I quickly tried to get everything in place, should I need to drive to Baltimore around four forty-four. You may recall, this is our most critical time.

I went into Mary Critical Care mode and did what I do best: made my prayer-beg calls.

I knew that, at least for last night, rest would not come, so I begged and prepared for a quick departure south.

The upside, and there always is an upside, is that I'm writing to you from Winfield, so David made it through the night. Thank God again.

I called the nurse several times during the course of the evening, but most recently at six a.m., to find that David is working hard to fight this raging infection. He still has a high temperature; his platelets and white blood counts are very low... What can I say about that?

So I ask you again to please pray the pneumonia will clear, his counts will rise, and that God will give him total earthly healing. Also remember to look for those UPS trucks ☺.

BELIEVE.

XOXOXO,

Mary

From: Mary Tiffin
Sent: Wednesday, March 26, 2003 3:19 PM
To: Norman Donaldson
Subject: Intensive Prayer Request

Hi, Norm.

I am back in PA now and will be returning to MD probably on Friday, if David is okay.

But as you know, he is having problems once again. Could you please put in an intensive prayer update for me so we can get started right away on those prayers?

I am trying to work (need those benefits), but my heart is heavy. Must get back to work.

YSIC,

Mary

From: Norman Donaldson
Sent: Wednesday, March 26, 2003 3:33 PM
To: Mary Tiffin
Subject: Intensive Prayer Request

Mary,

I know it's hard to know what to do when you're so far away and this is the umpteenth crisis to date. I will re-up the request through some great people. See you when you get here!

Norm

From: Karen Barlett
Sent: Wednesday, March 26, 2003 2:26 PM
To: Mary Tiffin
Subject: Re: Fwd: PNEUMONIA

Hi, Mary.

I am praying and praying and praying . . .

I will make an appointment here locally to donate platelets and tell them they are a direct donation for David Tiffin at Johns Hopkins. Hopefully, my platelets and my prayers and my love will make their way there for you both. I have been donating platelets for years, since my good friend was diagnosed with leukemia. I so understand the importance of it.

I'll let you know after I have donated.

Keep the faith!

Karen

From: Mary Tiffin

Sent: Saturday, March 29, 2003 11:18 AM

To: David's List

Subject: PLEASE PRAY NOW

Hi, all.

So I do believe this is the sickest we have been, and I am so upset I can barely type, but I do need to get this request out to you.

PLEASE, I beg you to please pray now for God to carry David to wellness.

Thank you.

BELIEVE.

Mary

From: Mary Tiffin
Sent: Sunday, March 30, 2003 5:25 PM
To: David's List
Subject: Final David Update

"I asked God for things, that I may enjoy life. God gave me life so that I might enjoy things." —paraphrased from the poem "And God Said No" by Claudia Minden Weisz

Dearest ones,

David became God's newest angel this Saturday, March twenty-ninth, at two-thirty in the afternoon. I passed him to God surrounded in love, and God welcomed him with open arms.

He entered heaven with the same beauty, dignity, and grace that he lived his life. As you know, I have always been proud of him, but that was my proudest moment!

My much-beloved husband has taught me so much in these past four months, and, so like David, he didn't need to say a word. He was beauty, strength, kindness, and pure love in his silence.

I will do my best to help our sons live by his example. I will try to make him proud of me. Before David left us, I told him I will continue to defer to his judgment in matters regarding the boys. I know I will hear his answers in my silence.

Although we have had some excruciatingly painful times in these last twenty-eight hours, I can't be too sad. He was the perfect husband, and I was so incredibly lucky—so abundantly blessed to be married to him. We were approaching our ten-year wedding anniversary, and not one day went by that I didn't thank God for David.

If you knew David well, you knew David always put others before himself, but his greatest gift to me is our sons and his absolute unconditional love for us. David always knew it wasn't about the "things," but about love. With all these beautiful gifts, how can I feel sorry for myself?

My parents, Billy and Christopher were on route to Baltimore when David left us. At precisely two-thirty p.m., Billy called everyone's attention to the most beautiful rainbow—perfect—that they all saw in the eastern sky. That was David's path to heaven.

So, it's still a beautiful story—not with the ending of my choosing, but the ending I was given.

May God bless you all, for he has blessed me with my beautiful husband and our sons.

I still BELIEVE.

XOXOXO,

Mary

From: Melissawit
Sent: Sunday, March 30, 2003 9:31 PM
To: Mary M. Tiffin
Subject: Re: Final David Update

Mary,

David was always telling me what a beautiful and wonderful wife he had. I used to worry about him being sad or lonely when everyone in the family moved back down here from Lewisburg. Then he met you and he was happy. I knew I wouldn't have to worry anymore. I'm so sad that we don't have him here, but I'm so thankful that he married you and brought three beautiful children into the world. Take care, and let me know if I can help you.

See you soon.

Melissa

From: Mary Kikki
Sent: Sunday, March 30, 2003 6:13 PM
To: Mary M. Tiffin
Subject: Re: Final David Update

Dear Mary,

I know that you might not see this for days or even weeks, but I want you to know how much you are loved. Your strength has been something at which we all marveled. I know you believe and have taught so many more of us to believe. But not to believe there was a miracle cure; to believe there is a reason for everything that happens to each of us, and to believe that God will provide us with the answers in due time. To believe that, even in pain, there is always love, strength, understanding, and hope. To believe that it is God's will, not our own, that in the end will come to pass.

I believe that God is there right now in your home, in your heart, and will forever be there as a source of guidance for you. There are so many who never get the chance to be there to say goodbye. I know it's your unshaken faith that allowed this miracle to happen for you.

You have never shown pity for yourself in front of anyone, which is another thing you taught us all. But keep in mind, grief is not pity. Allow yourself time to grieve. There are so many people out there just waiting to give you a hug, and offer anything they can, to help ease the pain. I was in your home as you wrote your final email. I hope you know I did not mean to impose or interfere. I just wanted to let you know how much you are loved, and if there is anything I can do for you, at any time, please let me know.

Thank you for your faith.

I will miss David.

XOXOXOXO,

Mar, and Bronson too

From: Denise Kellcher
Sent: Sunday, March 30, 2003 10:04 PM
To: Mary M. Tiffin
Subject: My Dear, Dear Friend

My dear friend, Mrs. Tiffin,

How sad I am tonight. No words can express it.

The saints in heaven are rejoicing, for they have another angel in their midst, one we will miss terribly here.

My prayers are with you, Mar, and especially Chris, Michael, and Stephen. I'm glad you have Chris with you tonight, for you will be able to draw strength for, and from, him.

Our Rosary group will be meeting tomorrow (Sunday) to pray for David, you, and the boys.

I know how overwhelmed you will be over the course of the coming weeks. Please know I am here for you to listen, laugh, cry, scream, pray, or just to sit with—anytime, day or night.

I love you, Mary.

God's peace be with you.

XOXOXO,

Denise

From: Lisa Kahler
Sent: Monday, March 31, 2003 7:59 AM
To: Mary M. Tiffin
Subject: Re: Final David Update

Mary,

I just got to work and saw your email. I am at a loss for words. I am thinking of you every single second and will call you, I promise. I know you probably just need some alone time right now and have a lot on your mind.

David fought so hard.

I am so sorry.

Love,

Lisa

From: Caitland Stewart
Sent: Sunday, March 30, 2003 4:06 PM
To: Mary M. Tiffin
Subject: Fwd: Mary Tiffin

Mary,

As I have referenced more than once, the pebbles of faith that you and David offered to so, so many have ripples that you will never know of, and below is just one. Sarah is a deacon in the Episcopal Church and a chaplain adjunct at Hopkins as well as an extraordinary woman of faith and compassion. She has come to know your story through our ministry together. As you can see, she asked that I forward the below to you.

As an aside, she is the source of the wooden cross I brought you yesterday. It is made of olive wood from Jerusalem.

The following brought you to mind:

"There is a force within you that gives you life....Seek that.

In your body, there lies a priceless jewel....Seek that.

Look within and Seek that...

....and THAT is God....

Amen" (from the 13th Century Persian Poet, Mewlana Jalaluddin Rumi)

Love and support continue.

Cait

From: Mary K. LaRue
Sent: Monday, March 31, 2003 8:30 AM
To: Mary M. Tiffin
Subject: David

Dear Mary,

I am very sorry to hear about David. He is with you.

Brenda, Scott, Scottie, and Andrew are my dearest friends—actually family. I have never personally met you and your wonderful family; however, I know you so much through Brenda and Scott.

My twelve-year-old twin daughters, Sarah and Katherine, and I have been praying very hard for David, you, and your family. We helped Brenda and Scott with David's fundraiser. We have followed your emails that Brenda has forwarded. I asked our parish priest, parishioners, and many friends to pray for David.

I just read your beautiful message about Saturday. Your deep faith is precious. I was on the phone with Brenda several times on Saturday, one of them around two-thirty p.m., making plans for her to go to the hospital with Scott.

My daughters and I were in the car together and we saw the most beautiful, vivid, colorful rainbow, with the deepest hue of color we have ever seen. What meaning that had.

I admire your strength and your strong love for God, David, and your family.

My daughters and I continue to pray for David, you, and your family.

May God and our Blessed Mother comfort you and yours.

Bless you.

Mary K. LaRue

From: Linda Paul
Sent: Monday, March 31, 2003 8:44 AM
To: Mary M. Tiffin
Subject: Re: Final David Update

Hi, sweetheart.

I am so sorry to hear of David's passing, but I know that he is looking down on you and your family and swelling with pride to know how much love you have for him. You are a wonderful wife, mother, and friend, and you are blessed to know love in ways that many people only dream of. I know that it must be difficult to feel blessed right now, but know that you have friends and family around you, who love you and are here to support you in the same manner in which you have supported David.

Love always!

Linda

From: Barlett, Karen
Sent: Monday, March 31, 2003 8:59 AM
To: Mary M. Tiffin
Subject: Fwd: Final David Update

Dear Mary,

Thank you for allowing me to share your and David's journey. I feel honored to have been able to add your family to my prayers. I will continue to hold you in the light.

I attended a wonderful interfaith memorial service yesterday for a friend of mine who was hit and killed by a car last week. The outpouring of love was amazing. That love is what we are here to give and to leave behind.

David's love lives in all the people he touched along his way.

Take care.

Karen

From: Jody Hutchinson
Sent: Sunday, April 6, 2003 2:24 PM
To: Mary M. Tiffin
Subject: David & Mary

Dear Mary,

I hope you don't mind my writing to you so soon. I wanted you to know we are continuing to pray for you. David and I start each day with a prayer for David, you, and the boys, and throughout the day, the hundreds of times our thoughts go to you, we send our love and prayers.

I also hope it's okay that I am sending you this copy of an email I sent to all of those people I copied whenever I got a message from you. Being a part of our prayer group, I wanted to share a little of what we experienced last week.

I will be in touch very often, my sweet cousin. I am so very proud that I not only know you, but we even share some of that crazy Montani blood!

Love you.

Jody

From: Jody Hutchinson
Sent: Friday, April 4, 2003 10:23 AM
To: All My Prayer Request Friends
Subject: David & Mary

My sister Darlene, David, and our dad returned last night from David Tiffin's funeral, and I wanted to share our thoughts and feelings with all of you who have been a part of this incredible experience. I know it was hard for all of us who prayed and prayed, so we need to share this because you will know that it was not in vain. Get ready for all the miracles!!

The wake was both Tuesday and Wednesday, with hours in the afternoon and evening. We arrived Wednesday just after the evening session started. On the trip from the hotel to the funeral home, we saw the most incredible cloud formation any of us has ever seen. The sky was so blue, the sun was setting, and there were no clouds except for one shaped exactly like a huge angel. It never moved, and stayed with us the entire way in its original vivid form. Even my dad, who "doesn't believe any of that stuff," was inspired.

The line to get into the funeral home was enormous. We did not get into the line because we could see there was not anyone at the coffin. It was Mary holding up the line because she was greeting and spending time with each and every person. She did not rush anyone along, but was talking about David to all. She looked so beautiful and even radiant at times. She did this for three hours without even sitting down.

All three children were there, and they are so precious. The baby, Stephen, is ten months old. Michael, the comedian, is three, and I think Christopher is about six.

I've always disliked when, after a wake, people remark, "Didn't he look good?" I must share that I have never seen anyone look so happy and at peace. David was actually smiling. I did not feel sad when I looked at him.

As most of you know, I often plan funeral liturgies with family members of the deceased for my church. I have never been at one as beautiful and as comforting as this one. We felt as though there was a blanket of love around our shoulders throughout the service. Each and every song and psalm (ones I never heard before) that Mary chose were so beautiful in both lyric and melody. The priest was the same one who married Mary and David on April 24, 1993. He also worked with David as he went through RCIA a few years later. He was close to both Mary and David when David became ill.

At the end of his homily, he said, "I see David right now, standing at the Pearly Gates, and he says to St. Peter, 'I delivered packages for UPS for twenty-five years. What do you think I'll be doing now?' St. Peter answers, 'God told me, David, that you will be a Messenger of Love for eternity.'"

Wasn't that perfect? Isn't it so true?

Guess who gave the eulogy? You guessed it—Mary. Though her voice wavered once or twice, she was a pillar of strength. Testifying her gratitude and love for this wonderful man, for "the gift" of the last four months, for her children (Stephen was hamming it up through her entire talk, waving to us, fake laughing, and helping us all). Mary also expressed her gratitude and love for all of us—her family and friends and those of you whom she has never met. Her last gift to us was once again assuring us that her faith is as steadfast as it ever was. As the priest said, our best tribute to David will be to try to live our lives a little bit as he lived his—with faith and unconditional love. I'm really, really going to try.

I wanted you all to know, at the reception afterward we also met David's mom and dad (called Goo Goo and Pa). So sweet. His dad told us that once David had become conscious, he had been told about the 9 p.m. prayer group, far larger than any of us could imagine. He was so happy and thought it was the neatest thing!

Mary told Darlene, David, and me, as we were saying goodbye, that in his last moments, the doctors had explained that David would not be able to open his eyes, but as she lay next to him, right before he passed on, his eyes opened wide, and Mary is sure David was looking at Jesus.

As my sister Darlene said on the way home, God didn't give us what we asked for when we were praying, but the actual act of praying created all of this wonderful energy that cannot die.

David, the messenger of love—that is the real miracle.

Let's try to cherish every moment, not sweat the small stuff. It's going to be hard—we are human, after all—but we can always remember.

Love you all!!!

From: Mary Tiffin
Sent: Thursday, May 1, 2003
To: David's List
Subject: Update?

Warning, this is a long-winded email.

"Faith is telling a mountain to move and being shocked only when it doesn't."
Luke 7:9

Dear ones,

Sorry I have been so conspicuously silent these past several weeks, but there has been quite a bit to digest.

Also, I think it's time to let you in on a little-known fact about me. I type three words per minute (okay, the truth is out, it's seven words per minute when I cheat, but the sad truth is, I type three—not two, not four, but three).

Oh, you're saying that I am kidding, right? I wish I were. So my thoughts of returning to the keyboard without anything exciting or for a prayer beg, well, I was neither inspired nor motivated. Coming from my previously over-communicative self, you may feel left in the lurch. I apologize. But to say it's been hard is not quite right; it's also been confusing, unsettling, disturbing, bewildering, and unbalancing, all rolled into one.

Here are some of my personal reflections on this past month:

Yesterday was the one-month anniversary of David's death. The boys and I commemorated the day by going to the cemetery. The boys turned the visit into a game of tag. David would have loved that. It was fun for the boys; for me, it was another reminder that after all that work, our collective work, we still didn't make it. David didn't survive.

Rather than focus on that truth, Michael tagged me and I was 'it'...Boys can find joy in a paper bag. All they need is air, sunshine, and some brothers to chase. As I ran chasing my boys, I found joy in their glee, it was sweet. We took a horrible day and made it better. I realized that I need to start running again. It's fun, freeing, joyful. I'm committing to return to running, just as soon as I can get some organization to my new life.

Many of you asked how they boys are doing.

Chris is in Little League. His team is the Sand Gnats, and they had their first game the other night. I am going to talk to Pamela about resuming violin and also Tae Kwon Do. Chris and I have spent a considerable amount of time talking about Daddy. He now feels Daddy is always with him in his heart. Christopher turned seven the day after Easter, and we carried on as I think David would have wanted, with our family party and a class party at the skating rink. Too frequently, when I look at Chris, I am so painfully reminded that David is gone, and for my sons, it is very hard for me to bear.

Michael has had some sad times, but since he's not as verbal as Chris, I've been trying to go with the flow for him.

A blessing right now is Baby Stephen never got to know Daddy, and it is an emotional blessing for me.

It's actually a double-edged sword, because the more you knew David, the more you absolutely loved him, and in knowing you were so blessed, the pain is so much more intense. The same goes for our boys—while Chris will have the benefit of happy memories with David, he's experienced the most pain and feels his absence most fiercely.

As with all other things, we'll do our best.

In these past several weeks, I kept feeling the almost knee-jerk reaction to return to Baltimore to the Hopkins condo (also more commonly referred to as 5B room 12) and to return to the roles of caretaker and wife. I did make a solo trip to empty out our apartment and empty the emotional valise that I was dragging around. I wanted to also say goodbye and thank you to the dear friends and near family that I had at Hopkins. I still love the medical staff.

As I entered Charm City, I was struck by the dramatic change in seasons. I noticed the cherry blossoms and tulips were blooming, the weather was warm, and the days longer. This was a stark contrast to the snow that we left almost three weeks earlier. I was visually reminded that life goes on—not the way I wanted, but it does go on.

I love Baltimore. How could you not love it? I feel so connected to the city, and I desperately miss Hopkins. Look, it's been my second home for five months. I've had such lovely experiences in Baltimore. I know it sounds crazy, but I feel David alive in Baltimore.

To keep David's memory alive, I have decided to do several things. The first, which was quick and easy, was to organize the millions of photos we'd taken over the years.

If you have spent any time with me over the past thirteen years, you have probably heard, when talking about David at one time or another, that whenever I looked at him, it was if I were looking at him for the very first time.

I remarked about it because I never experienced that before with a person. I knew that this feeling was rare and special. It was never staid or boring, our marriage felt like a lifetime of really good first dates. I understood how lucky I was to feel this way, and I was grateful.

Upon reflection, I have figured out this is what happens when you look at an angel. I don't think, as a rule, that angels can't look like your regular "Joe Husband."

So, because I feel lucky and blessed, I try to not be mad or angry.

So, this is why I am not mad at God. You know, I was so relieved in thinking that we survived sooo much, and he was a walking miracle, and we were leaving Hopkins in an ambulatory way. I mean, let's look at what David survived:

No blood counts for forty-two days. HUGE miracle; his own flora should have gotten him.

A pulmonary embolism. The mortality rate of PE's on a ventilator is very high.

Toxic epidermal necrolysis—he lost all his skin. They thought this would surely off him.

Fungal pneumonia on a ventilator.

He had multiple organ failures.

David survived all of these assaults without a working immune system. The doctors could not understand why David survived all that he experienced; there was no explanation. I believed my husband was, as I knew all along, simply miraculous. God gave us the gift more precious than anything, and that was more time together.

At Dreams' End

David's illness wasn't all sadness and misery. We did have moments of happiness and even some levity. The happiest time of David's illness was his waking from his prolonged slumber. When he woke and his thoughts were clear, we talked about everything. His illness, his new hard-fought wellness, how strong he was, and how incredibly proud of him we all were.

He had questions—about time and dates, about the season he slept through, the machinery in his room, and his lack of strength. I gave him the "Spark Notes" version, sparing the jarring details. Like a soldier returning from battle, he was attempting to reintegrate into a world that he was absent from for months. We delighted in our catching up and were so grateful for having survived. Added to the feeling of thankfulness was the absolute, unequivocal joy that God listened, and that we had, indeed, been granted a miracle: David was free of leukemia and we were on the road to wellness.

We started planning our lives, the boys' lives, and our future, now renewed with great hope and purpose. David and I went right back to dreaming our dreams, talking about our family's future, and planning our lives. Surviving leukemia was monumental and a pivotal family experience. We felt compelled to do something with this experience. We had to. Our faith and the faith of so many who witnessed this ordeal was reinforced. We felt that, validated by this journey, there was indeed a God who listens and responds. I was relieved that God was definitely still in the business of creating and delivering miracles.

Forty-five years, five months, and seventeen days after he was born, he died. This larger-than-life, wonderful man and amazing human being with so much left to give the world, quietly slipped out of this world. He was here one day, gone the next. In a breath, his place was erased.

His death seemed like a hiccup, a surprise, an artifact on the monitor, a mistake.

As we sat around his bed, Goo Goo and I expected him to bounce back, rebound one more time. Even though he had stood on the precipice for so much of his treatment at Hopkins, these dalliances with death were common, but he always managed to come back from the brink. This time, there would be no recovery; David's death caught us by surprise.

With all of those close calls of the earlier months, many thought that shock was the last thing I would have felt, but still, I was stunned. And there I remained for a number of months following his death. I felt confused, disoriented, out of sync—probably much the same way David felt when he woke from his nap.

David fought. He did not want to die. He fought this disease with everything he had. His will to survive, good medicine, and copious prayers were the only explanations for his living through the unsurmountable challenges he faced during our nearly five-month Hopkins stay. My husband was a Superman, made by God, and made even stronger by the prayers of thousands. But yet, quickly and quietly—so quickly—he just slipped away.

As most parents feel, my first, single, and greatest concern after David's death was how this was going to affect our children. How would they grow up without their dad to guide them? How could I possibly assist them to grow up to be the men they were destined to be if David wasn't here to guide them? What would their new destiny look like? That question prompted many sleepless nights for me. Were we really at the dreams' end?

Still another question was about how to balance honoring the end of David's life while celebrating the boys' lives just starting, their dreams' beginning. I did not want David's death to become their lives, to define who they were or to overshadow any happiness. My dear friends Linda and Denise provided wisdom and insight. They shared gentle lessons that only a child who suffered the loss of a parent could know. While others offered ways around the pain, these two wise women helped navigate the treacherous waters of grief. Grief is like a bad storm on the ocean. The death tosses the griever out of the comfortable cruise ship that was her life, onto a small, ill-equipped lifeboat, her new existence. The waves of the storm are the waves of despair, and are unrelenting in the early days. They can hit from all directions and at any time. These waves are also an emotional assault; your energy is spent to keep the boat afloat. Some days, you are better at this than others. At times it is most difficult and the skies are dark, with little to help you focus on the horizon. But then you remember that you were given a life vest. This 'vest' represents your family, your friends, and your faith; it's hardly a coincidence that it covers your heart. You remain afloat as you cinch the vest tighter around you, more secure in the support.

After a while, you find that instead of the waves coming nonstop, you notice there is a break in the action. This surprises you, the griever, and it gives you the strength to move on to get your sea legs. There is no timetable as to when this happens, it just does.

I remember Denise helping me to get my first pair of sea legs. About a month after David died and I was feeling his loss very deeply, I asked her when the grief would go away, thinking that I could wait it out and just "wake up" when it was all over. Denise gently and sensitively indicated that it would never go away, it would just be different.

Her answer was crushing. But as difficult as it was to hear, it was equally helpful, because it motivated me to get my bearings to face my new reality. I could no longer avoid or hate this grief, my own bête noire; I would have to deal or partner with this pain, if not for me, then for our sons.

Over time, the more I felt comfortable with the sadness, the smaller the waves became. An occasional wave would come and knock me to the sand from time to time, but my sea legs got stronger and stronger. And I learned to view my grief as a natural expression of the love that I had for my love lost. I stopped putting a timetable on the process and understood that, when I felt better, I would feel better and this was just our reality. It was horrible at times, but, yes, it was our reality.

A few months after David died, my dad was helping me with my sons. We were driving on a short trip and the boys were strapped securely into their car seats in the back of the van. They were accustomed to falling asleep in the car, and this trip was no exception. My father turned around, looked at his grandsons whom he adored. My dad expressed his own bewilderment at why God would have taken David from the boys and me.

"I just can't understand how He let that happen," my dad said.

"I don't know why it had to be us, Dad, and I think a lot of people ask the question. I can't focus on that. As Father Nessel said, 'These are the things of life.' I choose instead to think of how incredibly lucky I was to have had him as a husband. He could have married anyone else. It was random that we met, and for that random act, I feel lucky. I was living the dream."

"I just don't get it," my dad went on to say.

"Me either, and I have thought about this seven ways to Sunday, and I don't know what we could have done differently. I have too much going on. I made a promise to David, and it's going to take all of my energy to keep my end of the promise."

Up until David was diagnosed, I thought life was very orderly. I believed that if you behaved in a certain way, you would either be rewarded or punished. The choice was up to you. David and I chose a life of good, clean living; eating well; not smoking and exercising like crazy. We assumed that if we followed the rules, we would live a long and happy life. But we learned that cancer plays with a different set of rules.

Disease does not discriminate. Leukemia is arbitrary in its choice of victims. It's a disease that lacks a moral compass—it chooses to live and grow in children, the elderly, the good of heart. Not a single socio-economic, ethnic, cultural, education, or religious group is spared the vile and destructive disease. It just grows like a weed in your otherwise nicely tended yard.

For us, leukemia was a randomly horrible twist in the genes that no amount of organic foods, aerobic exercise, healthy living, or faith could prevent. It just happened. And we could let it be our dreams' end or a beginning. What that beginning would become, I had no idea. But I knew I had no choice but to keep going. And keep going... Stronger now for the experiences I had with my love, David. And stronger because I had a front row seat to the most noble of fights.

Epilogue

We measure time not only by days, months, and years, but also by events. Those events mark time by the subtle and not-so-subtle starts and stops of life. For us, these events included our marriage, building our house, welcoming our sons into our family—all these happy changes pointing in a direction of more great things to come. We were living a life pregnant with promise. These events created divisions in time, invisible lines, neatly separating our before and after lives.

But no line was so great or deep as that which was created with David's diagnosis. As we crossed that line, little did we know how profound the impact would be on our young family. As we stepped over the line of happiness and into the world of leukemia, we would be forever changed. We could never go back to our lives full of innocence. We could never return to our blissful and fearless existence, our family life, one so full of hope and promise. We had hoped to survive leukemia and be better from it, to make the world a better place by learning from our unfortunate experience.

Each of us has moments like these in our lives, pivotal moments that determine the rest of our lives. I was determined throughout the ordeal to not be defined by the disease, but rather to be defined by our reaction to the disease. I felt that when David survived, we would use this experience for the better. Naively, I thought with God's help we could beat the odds. But the miracle would not be ours.

In the years since his passing, when people would talk to me about David's death, most assumed that he and I had the conversation about him not surviving his disease. Many felt that we were so brave in our handling of his illness, that "the conversation," although not easy, would be responsible and necessary. But neither he nor I could discuss the very real possibility of him *dying* from leukemia. For us, the conversation signified a sort of concession; death simply was not an option. More out of concern for David's psyche, innocence and fear, than irresponsible or pompous; I could not envision raising our three sons without their father, this incredible person. Losing him to leukemia was not only the end of our dreams, it was my worst nightmare.

My faith was my crutch. I would tell myself that this would be a test of our faith, and God, our God, would come through. Some might call it denial, others might call it ignorance, but our avoidance of the conversation and handling it in this way was hopeful and faithful coping.

Over the years when, out of sheer exhaustion, frustration and sadness, my faith has waned, I would question our experience in Room 5B. I'd ask myself, *"Did it really happen the way I seem to have thought it happened?"* I had times when I felt unsure and insecure in the experience. I would return to the evidence. I would return to what was documented in his medical record. I was reminded that it did not only happen to David and me, but to so many others who were in the room—the nurses, doctors, clinical, dietary, environmental services, information technology, pastoral care staff and many other departments at Hopkins. All witnessed what happened to David, so if I was deluding myself, then it was also a form of mass hysteria, because many others were, as well.

If you are feeling angry or spiritually bereft now that David did not survive, you are not alone. Some have said that they felt let down or something to the effect that God dropped the ball. During the course of David's illness, we were buoyed by the presence of God in his room. As He helped David through all of his critical-care challenges, we felt that we were carried by the grace of God as He worked his way through all of the many mini-miracles. We developed a shell of spiritual indestructibility and felt certain that since God has carried us through so many obstacles, then surely the grand prize of total healing was in the plan. We were blessed enough to have thousands of people praying for us all over the world. But we found our indestructibility was fallible.

I began to question what we had done, encouraging all of those loving hearts to become involved in our lives and pray so fervently for my husband. What did the prayers do? Was it simply an exercise in reverence? And if God did not listen to the thousands of people organized in prayer for a man as good as David, what hope could any of us have? But then I remembered my mother chastising me when David first got sick. And I remembered it was not my will, but His will. I realized that, as hard as I worked to organize all those prayers, manage his health care, and protect his environment, ultimately, I could not control the outcome. I could not make my will God's will, Steel Magnolia or not. But even though we may not have gotten our No. 1 prayer, in David's earthly healing, I couldn't ignore all the other good that came of it. There was no way that I could discount the other little miracles along the way.

And because so many of us are genuine romantics, so many wanted me to be rescued from my sadness by a knight in shining armor. Although no one was interested in having me forget David, many did not want to see me live the rest of my life alone. Many friends noted that raising three young sons alone is no simple task. Yes, that is true. So on the knight, I tried, but what I learned was that David Tiffin is simply irreplaceable. My dad always said there would never be another David Tiffin, and he was right. Besides, I did have a "happily ever after"; it just happened with David.

David's journey predated social networking. Facebook did not exist. Emailing from his room was our form of social networking. This was our David blog. Because of the experience, I was encouraged, after a short period following David's death, to write a book with the intention of sharing our experience to help others.

I remembered thinking that I had to write a book because no great person should leave this earth unnoted. His children, his parents, his entire family, and the community lost a fine man. And, more importantly, I felt that since the boys were so young, I would need to recreate their dad for them in a tangible and meaningful way.

Another reason was to show appreciation to a community. "It takes a village to raise a child or three sons"—to borrow from Hillary Clinton's 1996 book title. Our community, in the Central Susquehanna Valley, is the wonderful town of Lewisburg—whose Boys Scout leaders, teachers, coaches, church leaders, community leaders, and others filled in to assist with so many lessons for my sons, lessons I was unable to teach for one reason or another, and helped and continued to help serve in one way or another, as teachers/mentors/directors for my sons. Lewisburg, the quintessential safe, sweet, small town. A town where folks really do help their neighbors.

In a radio interview, Rosanne Cash, daughter of Johnny Cash, was talking about her hometown when she said, "The things you push away the hardest when you are young, you end up embracing when you get older."

I thought how appropriate. Isn't that the way we all feel about our hometowns? I thought mine was just too claustrophobic; I had to get away. Now, seeing the richness of our community, the beauty, the connectedness, it's amazing—it's been one of the greatest gifts of my life, besides my children. My parents really knew what they were doing when they landed our ship, that 1968 Dodge Polara, in this town, and I've been so grateful (if you just ignore those awkward teenage years).

One of my greatest regrets in having not completing this book earlier is that, in addition to finishing it for my boys, I also wanted to pay tribute to the people who were most instrumental in helping David Tiffin grow to be the amazing man he was—his parents, my in-laws James (Pa) and Margaret (Goo Goo) Tiffin. My sweet mother-in-law would often talk about my progress on the book when it was stalled and when I was moving at a good clip. They were both anxious to see it completed. And my parents, they, too, wanted me to see complete this story of love and faith in action. But all passed before I would complete this last chapter. For that, I have deep regrets. I am hopeful that both my parents and David's parents would be happy with the finished product.

Much has changed in the past fourteen years. But it has been important for me to fulfill the promises I made to David about raising our sons and what to make of this situation. In a way, I believe that we did survive leukemia. It did not destroy our loving family, as sometimes happens, nor did it compromise our values. My children have an awareness of others also struggling, and that's something they might have lacked if their dad had lived. As a family, we continue to try and improve the lives of others who have suffered a similar life-limiting illness, so we are living David's dream.

In my career, I left the world of technology, changed industries, and earned a master's degree. I started working for Geisinger Medical Center. A friend of the hospital heard about the international prayer chain that developed for my husband at Hopkins, and wanted to do the same thing for gravely ill patients. I created a program for the Geisinger Health System called PRAYERnet. Since its inception in January of 2006, this Web-based program has assisted more than 5,000 patients in their walk through illness. The praying supporters of the program come from all parts of the U.S. and eighty countries around the world. The goal was to offer comfort in much the same way that we were comforted.

Ironically, staying healthy and fit to live long, healthy lives were always top goals of ours. Toward that end, from the earliest days of our relationship and marriage, we exercised together. No matter how exhausting the workday and our schedules, David and I always enjoyed our running time together. We mostly ran at night. We found our night runs to be the perfect and peaceful way to catch up on happenings, run out the stress from each of our days and unwind. If we didn't have streets lights to light our way, we often ran by the light of the moon. The Swedish call that strip like reflection that lit our path a "mangata." The mangata led us, directed us out of the dark.

Several times in the story I referenced returning to running. I finally did, but as a single parent, I found that the only time I had to run was, once again, at night. And again, many nights, I ran by the mangata, but I felt I needed more. Without David there to run beside me, I also wanted to feel safer. I needed more light, and that was the inspiration for RunLites and my company Mangata. Could I have named it anything else?

This whole journey, life moving from one dream to the next, with one ending and another beginning is simply a journey from dark to light. From the unknown, to the slightly illuminated to the fully visible, which often happens ten or more years down the road. Today I have more clarity and more light illuminating from the darkness. And I realize to have light, we all must have darkness.

I also have come to realize that what we do while in that darkness can either keep us there or bring us and others to full illumination. I never wanted to dwell in the darkness of David's death and I certainly didn't think that a company would be born years after it. But in that tunnel, I did have faith that in addition to the goodness I received from others, there would be something more that would fill my heart with gratitude. I thought that would be my dream life *with* David the survivor. But who are we to think we know God's plan? Instead, I got a dream life *because* of David. And I am ever grateful for it.

My boys, our sons, continue to be one of my greatest gifts and loving reminders of a great love and life lost. I catch glimpses of their dad when we all least expect it. Whether they are playing basketball, telling a joke, combing their hair, or meeting a person, I see David in my sons. God really did know what he was doing by giving me three boys. We live happy and active lives in Lewisburg with our two dogs, and we look optimistically toward the future while treasuring our past. We once again live lives of great faith, hope, and promise.

Photo by **The Lewisburg Studio** www.lewisburgstudio.com

About the Author

Mary Tiffin was born and raised in New York City until she and her family picked up and moved to the small rural town of Lewisburg, Pennsylvania. There she lived until attending college in Virginia at Mary Baldwin College. Mary has had several successful careers, first in fashion where she worked directly for the President and CEO of the world's largest accessories company. Then in technology, then in healthcare for the Geisinger Health System. Mary's journey with her husband David who died of cancer in 2003, inspired her latest and most purpose-driven venture, Mangata, the company behind RunLites and other illuminated sports accessories. It was through her love for David, their joy of running in the evenings together and the need for illumination that Mangata, the Swedish word for moonbeam was born. Today, Mary leads an organization that lights the way for runners, cyclists and thousands of active people in America and abroad. She is also the founder of the Live the Light Foundation (LiveTheLightFoundation.org) a non-profit organization that brings people together to raise money and bring light to people who are in the midst of darkness, particularly those who are undergoing treatments for life-threatening illnesses.

"The moonlight lay everywhere

with the natural peace that is

granted to no other light."

~ Franz Kafka

In Loving Memory

Acknowledgments

Books are seldom the work of just one person, and although my name is on the cover, this book would not have been possible without the caring support of so many people. It has been more than fifteen years in the making; a labor I simply had to complete. I am so grateful for this privilege.

Thank you to my publishing partner, Kathy Heasley, for her wisdom, friendship, and direction. Thanks, too, to the rest of the team at HEASLEY&PARTNERS who helped bring our story to the world.

I am eternally grateful to my dear friends Lisa Perrone, Meenakshi Ponnuswami, Charmaine Welby and Nancy Marr for their reviews of my early and late manuscripts. Because of their guidance the final work is a more vivid reflection of the realities during a very challenging time.

Thank you to the Clinicians and staff of the Sidney Kimmel Cancer Center at Johns Hopkins Hospital for recognizing that we were a family with a disease, not merely a disease to be treated. You respected our needs and honored our traditions, your gifts of humanity made the impossible, possible.

A special thanks to the best advisors and mentors that a girl could ever dream of: Hank and Candy Stringer, Don and Mary Rosini, Dan and Karen Testa, Mary Jo Monusky, Gloria Gerrity, and Joan Kraspowicz. Your support and encouragement are gifts beyond measure.

To the town of Lewisburg, Pennsylvania, and our surrounding communities, thank you for being the sweetest small spot in America. There's no place like home. To the men and women of the United Parcel Service (UPS) Center in Northumberland, Pennsylvania, I thank you for still remembering David to my sons. Their hearts swell when you share stories about their dad.

And to the young men that give my life meaning, my sons: Christopher, Michael, and Stephen. There is no greater role in my life than being your mother. Thank you for allowing me to navigate these choppy waters with you. You are my greatest inspiration.

Please Write a Review!

Thank you for reading *At Dreams' End*.
If you enjoyed my book please share
your opinion with others on Amazon.com.
I would love to hear what you have to say
and greatly appreciate your support.

With gratitude,
Mary